changing
theories

changing theories

NEW DIRECTIONS IN SOCIOLOGY

Black Hawk Hancock &
Roberta Garner

University of Toronto Press

LIBRARY AND ARCHIVES CANADA CATALOGUING IN PUBLICATION

Hancock, Black Hawk, 1971-
        Changing theories : new directions in sociology / Black Hawk Hancock and Roberta Garner.

Includes bibliographical references and index.
ISBN 978-0-8020-9682-1

        1. Sociology—Textbooks. I. Garner, Roberta. II. Title.

HM586.H36 2009   301   C2009-901072-0

We welcome comments and suggestions regarding any aspect of our publications — please feel free to contact us at news@utphighereducation.com or visit our internet site at www.utphighereducation.com.

North America
5201 Dufferin Street
Toronto, Ontario, Canada, M3H 5T8

2250 Military Road
Tonawanda, New York, USA, 14150

UK, Ireland, and continental Europe
NBN International
Estover Road, Plymouth, PL6 7PY, UK
TEL: 44 (0) 1752 202301
FAX ORDER LINE: 44 (0) 1752 202333
enquiries@nbninternational.com

ORDERS PHONE: 1-800-565-9523
ORDERS FAX: 1-800-221-9985
ORDERS EMAIL: utpbooks@utpress.utoronto.ca

This book is printed on paper containing 100% post-consumer fibre.

The University of Toronto Press acknowledges the financial support for its publishing activities of the Government of Canada through the Book Publishing Industry Development Program (BPIDP).

Designed by Aldo Fierro

Printed in Canada

This book is dedicated to my friend, mentor,
and intellectual inspiration John Fiske.

Black Hawk Hancock

To my family.

Roberta Garner

Contents

Preface

The major aim of our project is to give our readers a comprehensive overview of contemporary sociological theories. Our project developed around four goals: 1) to identify major themes in contemporary theory, emphasizing their differences from earlier theoretical paradigms; 2) to chart the impact of recent social changes on theories; 3) to acquaint readers with the work of a sample of individual theorists—the 'transitional giants'—who shaped new theories; and 4) to trace how the great social theories of the past are being reinterpreted and incorporated into new theories. Our project is influenced by the work of Thomas Kuhn on paradigm shifts in the sciences, but we have modified his analysis in order to explain change in contemporary sociology and related fields of social inquiry.

This book was written with the support of many individuals: our colleagues at DePaul; Valerie Paulson; students in our theory classes; Monique Billings, Chris Carroll, Jessica Chiarella, Suzanne Hammond, Rachel Hanes, and Lydia Yip; our anonymous reviewers who made insightful suggestions; Karen Taylor, whose marvelous editing captured our intentions and improved their expression; and, above all, Anne Brackenbury at University of Toronto Press.

Introduction

WHAT IS THEORY, AND WHY DOES IT CHANGE?

In this book we will explore the invention and impact of new social theories.

We will look at two types of forces that influence theorizing: *internal forces*, processes within the field of sociology, and *external forces* that are part of the larger social context—which some call the 'real world.' A central theme of this book is the influence of the 'real world' on theory. We will explore how changes such as globalization, expanded markets, and the onset of the information age affected theories in recent decades.

An externalist view of change in theories does not mean reducing these changes to simple, automatic, and clearly identifiable effects of social forces. External forces are refracted in complicated ways into new ideas and concepts proposed by theorists.

Our writing is influenced by the work of Thomas Kuhn, a historian of science; in 1962, he published a book entitled *The Structure of Scientific Revolutions* in which he argued that, in the natural sciences, major changes in theory—paradigm shifts—take place when ways of doing science run into puzzles that cannot be solved within existing frameworks. These unsolved puzzles force scientists to think of new concepts for understanding the world and also influence them to revise their methods. We will apply Kuhn's ideas to changes in social theories, adapting and revising his argument as needed to understand the social sciences.

When Kuhn looked at the history of sciences such as astronomy, biology, chemistry, and physics, he found that the paradigms or big theoretical frameworks in each science formed a succession of approximations to an understanding of the natural world. Each successive paradigm improved or expanded our understanding but contained its own insoluble puzzles, precipitating further changes in theories. The unsolved puzzles can come to light for internal reasons, when scientists disagree about the interpretation of findings. They can emerge for external reasons; a major external force is change in technology that leads to improved instrumentation and so generates new information. For example, telescopes, microscopes, and, in the twentieth century, computers capable of sophisticated analysis precipitated changes in scientific paradigms. External forces include social upheavals that shape the way scientific questions are formulated. For example, in World War II, the race between Nazi Germany and the Allies to develop an atomic bomb shaped the way physicists approached subatomic processes and their choice of puzzles to prioritize.

Although Kuhn's discussion of unsolved puzzles and paradigm change can help us understand changes in the social sciences, the social sciences pose a different set of challenges than the natural sciences because, in most social-science fields, the subject matter is a moving target. Unlike molecules, atoms, DNA, or the structure of the universe, human affairs change perceptibly on a human timescale. *Human phenomena are historically situated.* Values, practices, and institutions such as political systems and economies are neither stable nor repetitive. Thus, it is not primarily flaws in concepts or methods that bring unsolved puzzles to the fore, nor internal discussions, nor external changes in the instruments of science, but changes in the objects of study themselves. In the social sciences, the unsolved puzzles that unsettle existing paradigms and precipitate paradigm shifts are usually historically situated events and trends—for example, expanded markets, globalization, social movements, the collapse of some states and the rise of others, contacts among previously isolated cultures, and turbulent labor markets. The external explanation of changes in social theorizing is not identical to externalist explanations of changes in natural-science paradigms. Paradigms in the social sciences are directly affected by changes in the subject matter itself. In the natural sciences, changes in instrumentation, information, and interpretation shift the paradigm while the objects of study change slowly or not at all. In the social sciences, the object of study—the social world—changes, and this change is a major force for paradigm change. Therefore, when we use the term externalist, we will be looking primarily at changes in society that lead theorists to believe new concepts and perspectives are required in order to grasp these changes.

Like most dichotomies, the external-internal distinction can be thought of as a spectrum with a number of in-between situations that contribute to change in theories in the social sciences.

At one end of the spectrum, we can place the *clearly external forces*, such as the global AIDS epidemic or the emergence of modern media and information technologies.

But many changes in theory originate from changes in *the intellectual climate* that are not so easily categorized as external. Changes in intellectual fashions may spark changes in scientific theories. The popularity of systems theory in the 1930s, of psychoanalysis after World War II, and of deconstruction in philosophy at the end of the twentieth century influenced the social sciences of their day.

Changes in *instrumentation and in technologies* available for scientific research may generate unsolved puzzles. The well-known historical example in the natural sciences is the refinement of telescopes, which made possible Galileo's discoveries in astronomy and helped to widen support for the solar-centered Copernican model of the heavens. In contemporary social science, the use of computers and sophisticated statistical software has impacted our views of theory and explanations of human behavior.

Trends in related fields may precipitate theoretical innovation and paradigm shifts. When these are policy-oriented fields, such as macroeconomics, public and population health, economic development policy, environmental studies, and criminal justice, the policies can impact the real world and generate new puzzles. For example, the shift to free-market policies in the 1980s was associated with structural adjustment policies of the World Bank and the IMF, and these, in turn, caused changes in many nations and societies. These policy effects are not so simply either *external* to the social sciences or *internal* to the interacting community of scientists and researchers engaged in the pursuit of knowledge.

In the social sciences, the external-internal distinction is complicated by the complex and relatively tight feedback loop from research to social policy to the study of the impact of such policies. These loops are not nearly so easy to observe or achieve in the natural sciences; the building of the atom bomb changed our thinking about nuclear energy, but it did not transform the behavior of atoms and subatomic particles.

At the same time that some researchers are feeding their findings directly into the making of public policies, theorists prefer a more abstract approach to their subject matter. Theorists write about social change more conceptually and less concretely than empirical researchers and policy analysts. Theorists step back from the detailed, concrete 'facts' and place them in a broader context. Paradigm shifts in theory often appear very distant from the 'real trends and events' that may have turned up an unsolved puzzle and precipitated the shift. But notice we use the word 'appear' because the theory may cut through to the heart of the real-world conditions in a way that a simpler and more empirical approach does not. An example is Bourdieu and Wacquant's recent work that links the decline of the regulatory and social-service functions of the state to the rapid increase in the rate of incarceration and the development of the penal state, which manages social insecurity, precarious employment, dissatisfaction, and unrest through policing and imprisonment. Making this connection requires a theoretical view of states and societies, not merely collection of data about current trends in incarceration and social-service delivery. The theoretical link helps us to make sense out of two bodies of data that might otherwise seem unrelated.

PERIODS OF SOCIAL THEORY

We have 'periodized' modern social theory, which is a fancy way of saying that we think it is useful to talk about distinct periods in the making of social theory rather than viewing it as an uninterrupted, smooth flow of ideas. In each period, theorists thought of new questions and found new ways to formulate answers to old questions. These new ideas were stimulated by changes in societies, in the intellectual climate, and in the tools available to researchers, as well as by interchanges among social scientists. The book will focus on the transition from the third to the fourth period.

CLASSICAL THEORY

The first period is usually called the period of classical theory. It started in the 1860s and ran until World War I (1914–18). Karl Marx and Friedrich Engels, Émile Durkheim, Max Weber, and Georg Simmel are often considered the giants of classical theory. All of them focused on the transition from traditional societies to modern society and considered capitalism and the money economy to be key elements of modern societies. They proposed these theories because they wanted to understand the momentous global changes in societies, economies, cultures, technologies, and patterns of geopolitical power that were taking place.

The classical phase of social theory began with the 'triumph of the bourgeoisie'—the global dominance of capitalist societies, the systematic application of technology to industrial production, and the formation of the liberal state, in the sense of a state dedicated to free markets and enlarging the space of civil society. Although modern industrial capitalism had begun with the industrial revolution in northern Europe in the late eighteenth century and the power of the bourgeoisie greatly expanded in the French Revolution, in most of the world, this victory was not fully discernible till the 1860s. The modern bourgeoisie, a capitalist class associated with industrial development and free markets, triumphed over feudal strata, the aristocracy, and landed interests. In the United States, the Civil War can be considered a conflict in which northern industrialists relying on free labor as a manufacturing workforce defeated plantation owners using slave labor to produce cotton for European textile firms. In Germany and Italy, the state was unified by political elites associated with industrial capitalist development. In Japan, the Meiji Restoration, which shifted power to the emperor at the expense of the shogun and the traditional samurai class, marked the defeat of feudalism and opened the way for modernization. In Mexico, Benito Juárez and La Reforma reduced the power of conservative landholders and the Catholic Church and transformed Indian communities into collections of free individuals. Even in Imperial Russia, the system of serfdom was ended. These political shifts were the culminating events of longer processes in which agrarian elites were displaced by or transformed themselves into classes committed to industrial capitalist development and free labor markets. Social theorists had differing perspectives on this transition into modern industrial capitalism, but they agreed that it was to be the central topic of social theory.

THE INTERWAR YEARS

The second period of social theory was fragmented and chaotic. World War I left 10 million dead in Europe and created a sense of despair. No longer could either socialists or bourgeois liberals discern systematic progress from the traditional into the modern, and social theorists abandoned their claims about understanding the direction in which history was moving. In the United States, social theorists turned from the macro themes of societal transformation to micro- and middle-range topics. The Chicago School observed immigration and assimilation, but the studies focused on neighborhoods and individuals rather than large-scale global change. Social psychology became more popular as an approach to understanding society. Meanwhile, in Europe, Marxist theorists were still at work, but they became increasingly interested in the study of culture, examining how images, perceptions, and media representations contributed to the rise of Nazi and Fascist movements and why working classes had not coalesced into victorious communist and socialist movements throughout the industrialized world. Some sought answers for the rise of right-wing extremism by analyzing irrational impulses such as fear, rage, and repressed sexual drives.

FROM STRUCTURAL-FUNCTIONALISM TO THE 'TRIAD'

In the third period, from the end of World War II (1945) to the 1970s, social theory regained coherence and momentum. The Cold War era was a golden age for the social sciences in the United States. Europe was still rebuilding after World War II, and exciting developments in the United States, such as the civil rights movement, gave renewed optimism and energy to the social sciences. For a few years, structural-functionalist theory was the dominant paradigm, but soon theorists proposed two new perspectives. By the 1960s, *structural-functionalist sociologists* were challenged by *conflict theorists* and *symbolic interactionists and other micro-theorists*. This clash between a structural-functionalist mainstream and its lively young opponents created a dynamic and exciting field of study. Social theory encompassed macro-analysis in the thought of structural functionalists and conflict theorists and microanalysis in the work of the symbolic interactionists and in Erving Goffman's dramaturgical model.

At least in the first half of this period, sociology and related social sciences were suffused with vigor and optimism. Many mainstream structural functionalists hailed social changes in the post-World War II era as evidence of a benign, positive pattern of modernization. They pointed to changes such as the end of Nazism and Fascism, decolonization, the civil rights movement in the United States and growing gender equality in the developed nations, and the growing prosperity of ordinary people in the developed 'First World' societies. Marxists and other conflict theorists, while less positive about the existing and emerging social arrangements, nevertheless could argue that these changes presaged further and more revolutionary change in both the developed capitalist world and the developing non-aligned nations.

Rapid advances were made in methods, especially in survey design and multivariate analysis. The growing use of computers made more sophisticated analysis possible, fulfilling Durkheim's vision of quantitative methods as a way of discerning social patterns. Many subfields of sociology emerged, such as the sociology of medicine, deviance, organizations, work and occupations, marriage and the family, religion, and social psychology. These subfields had their own middle-range theories, often loosely linked to the structural-functional paradigm and using a similar basic set of concepts, such as roles, institutions, and stratification.

THE EMERGENCE OF CONTEMPORARY THEORIES

Finally, the fourth period began in the 1970s as a period of fragmentation, confusion, and contradictory directions in society and social theory. By the mid-1970s, the floating of the dollar, the decline of the United States as an industrial giant, the upsurge of the European and Japanese economies, and the onset of the information age suggested that the post-war period of US hegemony was waning. Not only did structural-functionalist theory decline in popularity, but the 'triad' of structural functionalism, symbolic interactionism, and conflict theory fragmented further. Social theory seemed to lose its coherent organization, becoming fluid and formless. A decade later, the collapse of the Soviet Union marked new geopolitical directions, unpredictable patterns in the global distribution of power, and a crisis for Marxist sociology. Globalization, immigration, expanding markets, neoliberal policies, and global media transformed cultures. Movements in philosophy and theory, such as deconstruction, post-structuralism, postmodernism, and feminism challenged 'third period' ideas about social systems and structures, including the ideas of conflict theorists. New areas of agreement gradually emerged, but theories remained fluid. Some theorists like to lump these changes together as postmodernism, but we will take a more cautious approach, one more respectful of the multiplicity of new ideas, their apparently contradictory messages, and the complex sources of these ideas. We suggest the term 'conflict constructionism' for this set of ideas.

THE ORGANIZATION OF THE BOOK

What we propose to do in the pages of this book is to understand changes in sociological theories between period three and period four. In discussing this shift, we will look at three major processes that shaped these changes:

- *The impact of external influences on theories*: We will discuss how 'real world' events and trends have an impact on theory.
- *The recontextualizing of earlier theories*: We will show how theories from all four periods, and especially from the classical period, such as the contributions of Marx and Durkheim, are preserved but reworked and recontextualized into contemporary theories.
- *The contributions of 'transitional giants'*: We will identify the work of individuals who have contributed to the new directions.

PART I: CHANGES

In Part I, we will tell two intertwined stories: the story of social changes on a global scale in recent decades and the story of how social theories changed in the context of these social changes.

In Chapter 1, we will begin our story with a discussion of trends in the 'real world' after the 1960s. It is difficult to tell this story without using theories to select trends and events to feature in our story. The 'real world' is a phrase in quotation marks because we can make sense of it only by using theories and concepts, but in this chapter we will try to be somewhat down to earth, avoiding esoteric concepts and arcane interpretations.

In Chapter 2, we will tell a story that parallels the story of Chapter 1, but we will focus on how 'real world' events and trends were reflected into theory. Events and trends do not have a simple, automatic or one-to-one correspondence with theoretical concepts. Concepts and ideas are not simple reflections of events, trends, and experience. 'Real' events and trends have complicated effects on the thinking of theorists, and representations of such events and trends become fused with past and current theories to produce new conceptualizations.

PART II: TRANSITIONAL GIANTS

In Part II, we will look at how individual theorists helped to shape new theories. We identify 'transitional giants' who took the lead in inventing new ideas and concepts in the shift from the third to the fourth period: Erving Goffman, Michel Foucault, Pierre Bourdieu, and Stuart Hall. They seemed to invent new concepts out of thin air, yet they were influenced by older theories that they reworked or reformulated, by the ideas of their contemporaries, and by their own experiences of contemporary societies and social conditions.

CONCLUSION

In the conclusion, we note that the impact of contemporary theories on the field of sociology has been decidedly uneven, with some areas deeply transformed, other areas in contention, and yet others relatively little affected. We suggest reasons for this unevenness. In the last pages of the book, we return to the theme that, in sociology, paradigm shifts also involve reinterpreting the legacies of the great theoretical innovators. Theoretical innovation is the product of conversations among many theorists, including the ancestors.

REFLECTIONS ON THEORY

What is theory good for?

In his play *The Clouds*, the ancient Greek comedy writer Aristophanes made fun of Socrates the philosopher. The title implies that philosophy, theory, and abstraction are in the clouds, ethereal and detached from earthly realities. Theory takes what is happening in people's lives and transforms these events and experiences into abstract concepts and ideas, a phantasmagoria of images and leaps of the imagination. The benefit of this transformation is the ability to categorize, generalize, explain, and transcend immediate experience and develop lasting insights. The cost is detachment, loss of immediacy, indifference to relevance, and a disconnect from what most people experience as reality. Theory is often contrasted to practice. Practice is trying to make changes in the world as opposed to just thinking about it. Theory is also contrasted to experience. Universities offer experiential learning courses based on the premise that new ideas only sink into the brain when they are encountered in situations of intense immersion in the world of the senses. 'Boots on the ground' knowledge is different from 'head in the clouds' knowledge.

What is theory good for? Why bother to theorize? The answer to this question is that theory helps us to gain a big picture of what is happening to us. If we can think theoretically, we stop being mired in the details of our circumstances and can see them as part of a larger social condition or longer-term social trend. We stop thinking that some problem is ours alone, that we are alone in experiencing what we experience. We can see more clearly what is cause and effect in our lives. This realization may be the first step to gathering up the courage to change circumstances that we can change. A teenage girl is beaten by her boyfriend; a worker is laid off by a large car company; a farmer cannot get credit to buy farm machinery and seeds; a family loses its home in a mortgage default. Theory allows them and us to transcend these individual problems and understand them in a larger perspective. C. Wright Mills used the phrase 'the sociological imagination' to describe the ability to see personal troubles as public issues. Karl Marx said that the point is not to interpret the world but to change it.

On the other hand, there are limits to what can be changed. Max Weber believed that one of the tasks of science is to clarify whether an end can be realized and what means are necessary for its realization.

Science may show that an end is unattainable or attainable only at materially or ethically prohibitive costs. In other words, science—and here we would include social theory—shows that not everything is possible. Science often reveals 'inconvenient facts'—facts that make us realize that our values can't be realized. In this respect, theory may provide serenity, rather than enhance courage.

A few thought experiments may help us see the uses of theory. They will bring theories down from the clouds to the ground level of our everyday lives and experiences.

EXAMPLE 1: THINKING THEORETICALLY ABOUT
HIGH-SCHOOL EXPERIENCES

Think about your high-school (or secondary school) experience from the perspective of different theorists. What would each theorist see when he or she looks at your school?

For example, Marx and Engels would observe the class origins and the class destinies of the students. They would note how the school functioned to select and sort students for different occupations and social class locations. They might be interested in the various markers of class—cars, jewelry and clothes, vacation trips at spring break, or dilapidated homes—that set students apart from each other. They would be curious about whether students group together along class lines; whether there are informal labels that refer to class, such as 'burnouts' or 'trash'; and the extent to which students are taught differently on the basis of their class (both within the same school and among different schools). They would be intrigued by the problems teachers encounter in schools in which the students are uniformly poorer or richer than their educators.

Weber would also be interested in class and status. He might put more emphasis than Marx and Engels on the way class—economic position—intertwines with status, considering especially the power of racial and ethnic categories in the lives and experiences of the students. He would also look at the school as an organization with a bureaucratic structure governed by the logic of instrumental reason.

Durkheim might observe deviance and see it revealing the structure of the whole institution. Each school has its own forms of deviance, from an untucked blouse to gang violence, hard drugs, and guns. Deviance is defined and punished not only in the formal structure of the school but also by informal normative regulation among students. Some schools are highly anomic; others are rigidly regulated. Yet when a university class of forty students described the most varied forms of deviance in their high schools, every single student described a uniform set of punishments—detention and suspension. Two students who had attended private religious schools said there were also fines. Only one person had ever heard of corporal punishment, and that was in an elementary school in Houston, not in a high school. What produced this startling uniformity of punishment amid the enormous variety of schools and of deviant behaviors? What do you think?

EXAMPLE 2: THINKING THEORETICALLY ABOUT EATING HABITS
Here is a second example of how theories help us to look more deeply into issues and problems. There is increasing concern about unhealthy eating habits and the growing percentage of overweight and obese people in all but the poorest societies. Durkheim might use the concept of *anomie* to explain what is happening. Age-old traditions of eating and preparing food are breaking down. Traditional patterns are giving way to a situation of unlimited choices, many of them unhealthy. Norms governing when to eat, what to eat, and how much to eat are no longer operative, and the result is a condition in which people cannot restrain their own appetites even in a sphere—eating—where one might have thought that physiological limits would apply.

Marx and Engels, on the other hand, might use the concept of commodity and *commodification* to explore this social and medical problem. They would place less emphasis than Durkheim on the informal normative regulation of eating in families and peer groups and more on the way in which the capitalist food industry stimulates unhealthy wants for highly processed foods. They would be especially interested in the way giant food-processing corporations have induced schools to place soft-drink machines in prominent places, the role of advertising in shaping food habits, and the growing ratio of processed foods to healthier fresher foods. (Thanks to Britt Skaathun, one of our students, for this example!)

These examples should stimulate thought on the simple, direct ways that theories can help us think about our everyday experiences. Although theory is often written in abstract, 'cloudlike' language, it is not so difficult to bring it down to earth and use it to sharpen our thought about social problems and experiences. Often theories help us to formulate new, deeper questions and begin to answer them. For example, why is there so much variation among high schools in patterns of deviance? Why have so many schools in Canada and the United States turned to detentions and suspensions as punishment, while renouncing corporal punishment? Why is it so hard to keep people from eating junk food? And reflecting on Weber's remark about ends and means, we might ask whether government regulation of the food industry would be an effective way of halting increases in obesity.

EXAMPLE 3: DEBUNKING FOLK CONCEPTS AND CRITIQUING
CONVENTIONAL WISDOM

A third example will show another use of theory—debunking folk concepts that interfere with our ability to understand the world in which we live. As we construct theories and theoretical concepts, we are also *deconstructing* folk notions, which are usually simplistic, stereotypical, and based on limited experiences or mass media images. Various essentialist ideas about differences between men and women and among 'races' are examples of these folk ideas about the world: 'Men are rational, and women are emotional'; 'Mexicans are lazy,' or 'Mexicans are hard workers'; 'Asians are good at math ...' and so on and so forth. When sociologists develop theories about the construction of gender, the complexities of culture, the historical processes that shape identities and behaviors, and the great variation in behaviors within any of these socially constructed groups, we can see that the folk notions are superficial. Their use shows a lack of understanding of how categories are constructed, differences perpetuated, and behaviors shaped by historical conditions. The act of theorizing is a powerful way of dismantling misleading and inaccurate folk notions and stereotypes.

Sometimes myths and folk concepts creep into scholarly work. 'The underclass' and the 'disorganization' of neighborhoods with high crime rates are examples of folk concepts that were absorbed and repeated by criminologists and sociologists. Careful empirical studies (Venkatesh 2002; Pattillo 1999) cast doubt on these terms; high-crime neighborhoods turned out to be quite well organized—by gangs and their political allies. These empirical studies were linked to efforts to construct better concepts and theories for understanding social forces that operated in racially segregated de-industrializing areas of large US cities such as Detroit, Cleveland, and parts of Chicago's south side. Loïc Wacquant (2004, 2008b) linked crime within neighborhoods to historical changes in the racial formation of the United States, which he traced from slavery to legally sanctioned segregation to urban ghettoization and finally to present-day racial disparities. He showed how the term 'underclass' masked the effect of unemployment on the condition of the most disadvantaged parts of the working class; and he emphasized the power of the state to encourage or refuse to encourage a full employment economy, to substitute welfare for full employment, or to decide to cut social services while tolerating high levels of joblessness.

In other words, theoretically guided empirical work removes folk notions and myths from the field and forces scholars (and the public as well, if scholars are able to assert themselves as public intellectuals addressing a larger audience) to think about social processes with more historical insight and analytical depth. So the first punches of theoretical endeavor may aim at critiquing and debunking the conventional wisdom.

The expanding community of theorists

Until quite recently, theorists were men of European ancestry and middle-class backgrounds. Most lived and worked in western Europe and North America. We are now on the threshold of a major shift in the composition of the field, a rapid opening to many new kinds of people. The point is not to turn away from theory because most theorists are 'dead white males' (as one of our students said disgustedly) but to recognize the possibility of a much more inclusive conversation.

Certainly the great classical theorists and most theorists of the early twentieth century were men of European origin. Many of the leading classical and early twentieth-century theorists were of Jewish background (Marx, Durkheim, Simmel, and Benjamin, for example, though not Engels, Weber, or Gramsci), reflecting the situation of Jews in pre-Nazi western Europe—often economically comfortable or even wealthy, well educated, and yet politically and culturally marginalized, a condition that bestowed a critical gaze and the refusal to take social arrangements for granted. Other ethnic minorities in Europe and North America, with limited access to formal education and few resources, faced barriers to entering intellectual life. W.E.B. Du Bois, E. Franklin Frazier, and Chicago School writers St. Clair Drake and Horace Cayton were among the relatively small number of African Americans engaged in theory in the first part of the twentieth century. Women of all ethno-racial and class backgrounds were excluded and often seen as inherently incapable of theoretical thinking. For example, Jane Addams was not recognized as a theorist by her male colleagues who expected her and other educated women to be engaged as social workers, teachers, and social reformers. All people of working-class background faced enormous difficulties in becoming scholars and intellectuals before World War II; universities were for all practical purposes inaccessible to them, and the few that were able to attend often felt pressure from family, mentors, and their own values to enter professional and practical fields such as engineering, law, medicine, and social work rather than soar into the clouds of theory.

After World War II, universities in North America opened markedly across class and gender lines, thanks to growing affluence throughout US and Canadian society, as well as the GI Bill in the United States and the Veterans Rehabilitation Act in Canada, both of which supported higher education for veterans. Yet during the period of structural functionalism, most theorists were still white men, and so were many conflict theorists and micro-theorists of the 1960s. The intellectuals whose writing took theories into the contemporary era were predominantly North American or European men. Women began to do theory, but initially they were often confined to feminist theories, while people of color worked on theories of racial and ethnic relations. As recently as the early 1990s, a popular theory textbook graciously opened its pages to women and African American scholars, but it segregated these theorists into 'chapters of their own' as if they had little to say about theory in general. But we are finally moving away from this type of confinement.

Fortunately, these ascriptive barriers to the world of theory began to disintegrate at the end of the twentieth century, and today men and women of diverse ethnic and national origins are writing many different kinds of theory throughout the subfields of sociology and related areas of inquiry. In a time of immigration and globalization, many people find themselves in the condition of diaspora that previously had given Jewish intellectuals a critical view of the social order, an outsider perspective also shared by sexual minorities. Yet while celebrating the expanding tent of theory, we need to remember that, like most social barriers, obstacles to the opportunity to become theorists are not disappearing as fast as one might wish. The barriers to education, theoretical work, and intellectual professions for working-class and rural people in less economically developed nations remain formidable.

KEY TERMS

- paradigm shifts
- external and internal influences on theories
- periodization and periods of theory
- creating new theories versus reinterpreting existing theories

WORKS CONSULTED

The introduction and the first two chapters are broad interpretive essays drawing on the ideas of theorists and historians; therefore, instead of providing numerous in-text citations, we provide references for further reading in a 'works consulted' section. See the section 'References and Suggestions for Further Reading' for complete bibliographic details.

Best and Kellner 1991

Feyerabend 1975

Hobsbawm 1987, 1994

Jay 1996

Kuhn 1962

Ritzer 1996a, 1996b

PART I: CHANGES

Chapter 1

1968–2009: WHAT HAPPENED?

We will begin this book with a direct account of what has happened on a global scale in the last forty years. By 'direct' we mean we won't do a lot of interpreting and theorizing here but just identify major trends. But a warning is in effect. Not everyone would agree that these were the main trends, and, even if they agreed to the list of trends, they might disagree with our descriptions. There is a real world out there, a world that exists objectively to be viewed and completely grasped, perhaps, by a disinterested and non-human extraterrestrial, but human observers will necessarily see the world incompletely and have different perspectives on it. Even relatively untheorized descriptions of trends, events, and conditions contain an interpretive point of view.

WHY 1968?

The year 1968 is not an arbitrary starting choice. It marks the first signs of a transformation in capitalism and the global system that became much more visible by the early 1970s. The entire period from 1968 to 1980 was marked by instability in capitalist economies and worldwide political ferment. Scholars and political observers call 1968 'the year of the barricades' because of its numerous incidents of campus rebellion, worker strikes and factory seizures, and violent confrontations in the streets (Caute 1990). These upheavals were diverse and included student dissatisfaction with university bureaucracies in many countries, worker demands for better wages and working conditions, protests against the war in Vietnam, violent responses to police mistreatment in African American neighborhoods of US cities, the crushing of Czechoslovakia's attempted disengagement from the Soviet bloc, the assassinations of Martin Luther King, Jr., and Bobby Kennedy in the United States, a government massacre of hundreds of demonstrators at Tlatelolco in Mexico City, and the elite-manipulated Cultural Revolution in China. The Tet Offensive, a major thrust by the North Vietnamese army into territory held by the US military, showed the weaknesses of US strategy in Southeast Asia. All in all, these violent and tumultuous events heralded a period of instability in the economy and disruptions in a relatively stationary Cold War stand-off between the United States and the Communist bloc. A few years later, in 1971, as a result of inflation triggered by the costs of the war in Vietnam, President Nixon had to 'float the dollar,' decoupling it from gold. By 1973, soaring petroleum prices rocked the developed industrialized world in the aftermath of the Yom Kippur War between Israel and neighboring Arab nations. These economic disruptions ushered in a period of stagflation—inflation combined with high unemployment—in many developed nations. In 1973, the investigation of the break-in at the Watergate complex in Washington, DC, revealed the plans of the Nixon administration to use illegal means to defeat the Democrats, and, two years later, the helicopters taking off from the roof of the US embassy in Saigon showed the world a defeated and vulnerable superpower. In retrospect, 1968 was not the beginning of a global revolutionary period (as young leftists hoped and conservatives feared), but it did signal problems in the form of capitalism that had been so successful from the mid-1940s to the mid-1960s, a long boom based on relative cooperation between capital and labor, a thriving welfare state, and optimistic plans for government-led development in newly independent nations.

As on earth, so in the clouds of theory. After the 1960s, the neat triad of structural functionalism, conflict theory, and symbolic interactionism became contested, fragmented, and blurry. After 1968, dramatic cutbacks in federal funding for research created uncertainty for US sociologists and graduate programs, and the mood of hopefulness among intellectuals and the public about increasing prosperity and racial integration turned into anger and disillusionment.

This global political and economic crisis was eventually resolved. Capitalism did not collapse. On the contrary, it was renewed and transformed, and it was its twentieth-century rival, state socialism (or communism), that collapsed. This rebuilding of capitalism, in a new form with a greatly expanded market structure and reduced social and economic intervention by the state, is often referred to as *neoliberalism*, and it provided the foundation for changes in the intellectual climate and in social theory. We will begin our discussion with a look at globalization, one of the most obvious aspects of the neoliberal transformation, and then dig deeper into the origins of neoliberalism.

A NEW GLOBAL ORDER: GLOBALIZATION, NEOLIBERALISM AND MARKET EXPANSION, AND HYPER-INDUSTRIALIZATION

GLOBALIZATION

Everywhere we look, we can see evidence of globalization. The labels on our clothes tell the story of textile and apparel industries moving from western Europe and North America to Asia and Central America. Sweaters may be assembled in Mongolia of fibers produced in China. Cars that were once made in Detroit, Turin, or Bavaria, and later in Japan, are now made in Brazil or Mexico. And people as well as products are crossing borders. You (or your parents) may well not be living in your country of birth. Filipinas work as domestics in Taiwan and Dubai; Indian computer experts immigrate to Canada; Nigerian and Russian women are forced into sex work along Italian roads. In 'all walks of life,' people are on the move across national boundaries. Yet it may be useful to keep in mind that, in recent years (2002, to be specific), only 2.6 million people migrated from poor to rich nations—less than 1/20 of 1 per cent of the 5 billion people who live in poor countries (Milanovic 2007).

Products and people form the obvious, visible transnational flows. But more intangible flows of capital and ideas—of information—are also surging across borders.

This is not the first time that the planet has been 'globalized'—characterized by rapid transnational flows. The end of the nineteenth century was also highly global in terms of the circulation of people, raw materials, and finished goods. For example, a larger percentage of US residents in 1900 were born abroad than is the case now. But today's globalization involves areas that previously were rural, remote, and traditional. New means of communication and transportation speed up the flow of people, products, ideas, and capital across boundaries.

The causes of globalization are complicated and have to do with a changing transnational economy, population pressures, heightened economic expectations, capital flows, and new technologies. We will examine the causes later; here we will briefly identify a few consequences.

Cultures are now in multiple contact with other cultures, creating new hybrid forms and patterns of transculturation far beyond the one-way forces of assimilation and colonialism of the past, when powerful bearers of Western culture compelled others to adapt themselves to it.

Friction and conflict can arise from cultures 'rubbing up against each other,' from fears of the natives that newcomers might threaten their values, ways of life, or economic standing—whether the newcomers are Muslims in Europe, Nicaraguans in Costa Rica, Zimbabweans in South Africa, or Mexicans in the United States, to name a few examples.

New communication technologies of television and the Internet carry new ideas and new versions of old ideas that disrupt existing patterns of belief. Evangelical Protestant churches compete with the Catholic Church throughout Latin America. Sectarian forms of Islam gain new followers. Faith in the market and free trade convert elites in newly industrializing nations, and they renounce socialist and nationalist development models. Billions of people are enchanted by the images of consumption that they see on television. They turn away from frugal, fatalistic, and traditional ideals of the 'limited good' and wish they had more of everything, from possessions to opportunities.

Flows of capital, and the accompanying shifts in production, disrupt local economies and leave a swathe of disinvestment and unemployment. Examples include the shift of manufacturing jobs from western Europe and North America to newly industrializing Asian nations, the shift of software engineering from Silicon Valley to India and China, and the flood of Chinese-made goods, such as toys and apparel, into previously protected light-industry markets in Mexico. Whether new types of production and employment can arise in areas 'left behind' by shifts in industry is still an open question. This phenomenon was already noted by Karl Marx and Friedrich Engels in the nineteenth century when they described how Indian handicrafts production was swept away by the flood of British cotton goods made by low-wage English factory workers processing cotton produced by slaves in the American South. No wonder that a century later Mahatma Gandhi, India's great nationalist leader, wore handwoven cotton clothing and carried a spinning-wheel in protest against the global flow of cheap textiles.

Globalization affects financial markets as well as manufacturing. In the autumn of 2008, the world saw the rapidly cascading and globalizing impact of instability in financial markets. Defaults on sub-prime mortgages and the bursting of the speculative bubble in residential real estate in the United States quickly spread a credit crisis and bank failures across the globe because the mortgages had been bundled into mortgage-backed securities and derivatives held by investors in many countries.

NEOLIBERALISM (AKA FREE MARKETS AND FREE TRADE)

Globalization is intimately associated with marketization. Goods and services are produced and distributed by private firms, for profit, through the market mechanism. Today, the global flows of products, capital, and ideas are able to take place because national governments at the end of the twentieth century became less willing and able to hold back these surges, although they continue to restrict the movement of people. A person born around the middle of the twentieth century can remember unpleasant moments at border crossings: customs officials pawed through luggage, currency was carefully controlled, books and certain types of clothing caused delays. These little personal encounters were part of a much larger pattern of governments trying to control and organize the flow of products, ideas, and capital across borders, ostensibly—and sometimes really—for the benefit of their citizens; and these policies were, in turn, part of the larger program of activist states intervening in transnational markets in order to shape distinct national economies and societies.

In the first part of the twentieth century, governing elites self-consciously defined themselves as active, as agents of national development, as keepers of national dreams. These active states included the fascist states that formed the Axis of Nazi Germany, fascist Italy, and Japan (defeated by the Allies in World War II), as well as the Communist states, the liberal-democratic states in western Europe, and the New Deal reconfiguration of US government functions and agencies that was introduced during the presidency of Franklin D. Roosevelt. Although there were major differences in ideology and respect for civil liberties among these states, they shared a vision of the state as a positive force for developing a national economy and promoting a definite view of the good society.

After the war, in western Europe and North America, an activist view of the state persisted in the liberal democracies. The model of the activist state in capitalist democracies came to be called 'embedded liberalism.' It was liberal in contrast to socialist. In this context, 'liberal' means that the state has given 'liberty' to a large sphere of private enterprise and civil society. The government did not run most economic enterprises directly, though, in many countries, electricity, phone systems, railroads, airlines, and energy resources were public. Most social services, such as health care, schools, and mass transit, were provided by governments and funded primarily by tax revenues. This model was 'embedded' in the sense that private enterprises remained connected to the nation and the national government. Markets had not been entirely liberated from regulation by government. Firms were believed to have a responsibility to contribute to the economic growth of the country, to employment, and to general well-being; and it was considered appropriate for governments to regulate them accordingly. In many European countries, strong parties on the left such as the socialists and communists, as well as unions, supported these policies of embedded liberalism.

By the 1970s, this model of the active, positive state faced challenges. The fascist versions had been dismantled at the end of World War II (with the exception of a few holdouts like Franco's Spain and Salazar's Portugal). Despite high growth rates, the Communist states (the Soviet Union and its eastern European 'bloc,' as well as China and North Korea) had difficulty in shrinking the gap in economic productivity and living standards between themselves and the capitalist democracies. But the capitalist democracies themselves—the 'First World'—experienced difficulties too: falling rates of profit, rising labor costs, and, in the case of the United States, Vietnam-era inflation. As income inequality reached historical lows, the proportion of income that went to the wealthiest strata was reduced, causing disappointment and unrest at the top (Piketty and Saez 2003; Harvey 2005; Kerr 2001). Capitalist elites increasingly defined 'the welfare state model' (the commonly used term for embedded liberalism) as a failure, a historical fluke started in the liberal democracies during the emergency of the Great Depression and then consolidated during World War II, when class cooperation was required to win.

By time Margaret Thatcher and Ronald Reagan took office (as Prime Minister of the United Kingdom in 1979 and as President of the United States after the 1980 election, respectively), the will and the power were present among business and governing elites to shrink the welfare state and challenge embedded liberalism as the leading model of capitalist development. These two administrations took the lead and set the pace for other developed economies. The new packages of economic policies are often referred to as 'neoliberal policies.' 'Liberal' here refers to the original meaning of the term, a state policy of little or no intervention in the workings of the market. The state 'liberates' markets from government control, intervention, and planning. International trade is 'liberalized.' Neoliberalism contrasts with embedded liberalism, the post-war model in which governments were involved in providing public services, regulating industries, and stabilizing the economy.

Firms in the sector of public infrastructure (railroads, state broadcasting systems, telephone systems, energy resources, and so on) were privatized. Regulated industries like airlines, trucking, telecom, and, above all, banking and financial markets were completely or extensively deregulated. The safety net of social services was lowered, and government took a much harder line in confronting public-sector unions, setting a precedent for decreased union membership and influence in the private sector (Milkman 2008).

Because the welfare state was quite weak in the United States compared to western Europe, it was more easily dismantled there. The UK became an intermediate case, retaining popular programs such as the National Health

Service, but many other western European countries, such as France and Norway, maintained more institutions of the welfare state. One can emphasize the general neoliberal shift or, alternatively, highlight the strong variation among economically advanced nations in the extent to which their governments went along with this shift. Countries varied in the degree to which they aligned themselves with the neoliberal model. The widespread resistance and refusal by voters and governments in western Europe to implement all policies of the neoliberal program of 'advanced insecurity' are also parts of the story (Sennett 1998; Wacquant 2008b).

At the global level, policies of reducing the public sector were institutionalized in international agencies, especially in the World Bank and the IMF. Developing nations, which had relied on large public sectors to boost social services and create a middle class of state employees, were forced to cut back this sector in order to be approved for credit. These cutbacks were called 'structural adjustment policies.' After the collapse of the Soviet Union, international credit agencies insisted on the application of these policies not only in developing nations but also throughout the former Soviet bloc.

Along with structural adjustment policies came pressure to reduce protectionist policies such as tariff barriers and import quotas, to open trade to global markets in imports, and to produce for the export market rather than for domestic markets. Policies of 'import substitution' (in which countries manufacture products domestically, even at the cost of less efficiency) gave way to 'export promotion.' Formation of regional free trade zones, such as the one created by the North American Free Trade Agreement, accelerated and supported these economic shifts. So did the World Trade Organization, an international organization committed to free trade and the elimination of protectionist barriers to trade.

One of the most important areas of transnational deregulation was the global financial marketplace. Capital flowed freely across national borders, with a large pool of money streaming into what appeared to be profitable investments. In 2008, the cascading global effect of problems in US sub-prime mortgage lending became an example of the risks inherent in this policy of financial deregulation.

The most extreme form of the difficulties of the model of state involvement in the society and the economy came with the collapse of the Soviet Union and its associated Communist parties in eastern Europe. The model was beset with a host of problems including shortfalls in consumer goods, corruption and mismanagement, political repression, and a failure of the imagination in creating an attractive alternative to capitalism. Were these defects inherent in the Communist model, or were they products of its lower initial level of productivity, the brunt of World War II, and the debilitating effects of the escalating arms race? This question may be debated, but what is inescapable is that the Soviet system could not sustain itself in competition with advanced capitalist nations and collapsed in 1989.

These new neoliberal economic policies had social consequences. The old model of embedded liberalism relied on relatively high wages to pump up domestic demand, local production of goods that kept employment high, and a large state and social-services sector. The downsides of the old model were inflation, inefficiency, regulatory constraints on entrepreneurship and innovation, and an uneven quality of public services. But the new model also had major downsides—unemployment, lower wages, the collapse of national industries, growing income inequality (Piketty and Saez 2003), cutbacks in social services including health care and education, and the potential for rapidly propagating and cascading problems in global financial markets.

The consequences of the neoliberal model that took shape after the 1970s can be debated. Some areas, especially in eastern Asia, had a marked economic take-off into industrial development and rising standards of living. Yet a careful look at these regions—especially South Korea, Taiwan, Vietnam, and, more recently, China—suggests that they continue to have a substantial amount of state involvement in the economy.

In western Europe and North America, routine manufacturing suffered major declines, in part offset by new technological development, high-tech specialty products, intellectual production, information management, and entertainment industries in fields ranging from medicine to pop culture. Employment became considerably less stable, however, and an hourglass or (more accurately) bowling-pin economy and society took shape in the United States and in many world cities, with a small top that enjoyed very high and rising incomes, a stagnant or even shrinking middle class, and a rapidly growing bottom formed by a 'precariat' of low-wage workers with insecure jobs. (The term 'precariat'—combining 'precarious' and 'proletariat'—is suggested by Loïc Wacquant [2008a].)

In yet other regions, such as Africa and parts of Latin America, structural adjustment policies and freer trade had devastating effects on local industries and agriculture, hobbled states' efforts to provide health care and education to the poor, and shrank the middle class.

We end this section with a few cautionary notes.

- In many places, such as western Europe and North America, the neoliberal model was not a new phenomenon at all but a partial return to nineteenth-century models of a laissez-faire economy and a 'nightwatchman state.' In this view, the earlier model had been only temporarily displaced by the welfare states, largely as a result of working-class pressure during and immediately after World War II (Kerr 2001). After several decades, working-class gains were successfully contained by business interests, and the system returned to the original trend line of capitalist development with only limited state intervention.

- The apparent 'shrinkage of the state' was itself a deliberate state policy, not a force of nature. Markets are no more or less natural than political systems; and both markets and state-run economies are social constructs. Somebody—political elites with interests in market economies—made decisions to expand the market and shrink the role of the state.
- The United States, one of the world's largest and most powerful nations, actually expanded state surveillance and regulation of behavior, especially drug possession, which resulted in huge increases in the numbers of incarcerated people at the same time that economic regulation and social programs were cut back. So the state did not become uniformly more 'liberal,' but primarily liberal in its treatment of private enterprise.
- Although many states withdrew from economic regulation, they did so unevenly, and, in some of the most dynamic economies, such as that of Japan in the 1980s and later South Korea, Vietnam, and China, the state continued to have an active economic role.
- Because many of the interventionist states of the mid-twentieth century—especially in the Soviet Union and the 'third world'—had been plagued by corruption, mismanagement, absurd infrastructural and industrial mega-projects, and repression of individual freedom, neoliberal policy and ideology often found a strong base of popular support. It was an 'easy sell' for pro-market elites to persuade large sectors of the population that everyone would be better off with neoliberal cutbacks in government functions.

The neoliberal turn had powerful consequences for political ideology, government action, and public, intellectual debate. The ideology of neoliberalism is expressed in the terms 'freedom' and 'democracy.' Freedom implies less government intervention in and regulation of the economy or civil society or both. Democracy is used to mean regular, orderly elections with the possibility of the peaceful alternation of parties that hold office. It becomes easier to sustain these values when the state renounces the functions of economic regulation, the provision of public services, and—most destabilizing of all—the project of reducing disparities. When these goals are no longer at stake in the political system, government or 'the state apparatus' is less of a prize for contending forces, so democracy is less threatening and more limited in its possible consequences. The limited role of the state makes it easier to establish and sustain a democracy in a market system than in a state-managed or command type of state and society.

HYPER-INDUSTRIALIZATION AND NEW TECHNOLOGIES

Our readers may be surprised to see the term 'hyper-industrialization'—extreme industrialization. Don't we live in a post-industrial era?

Hyper-industrial is a better term than post-industrial for what we are experiencing. From the point of view of people living in countries with a long history of manufacturing—Japan and nations in North America and Europe—it may look like a post-industrial era. The percentage of the labor force in manufacturing is declining, factory jobs are disappearing, and rust-belt plants stand empty, while jobs in financial services, software design, entertainment, education, and health care are growing.

But we argue that these changes only appear to signal a post-industrial shift. Actually two interrelated processes of hyper-industrialization are taking place. One is the rapid growth of industrialization in regions that were previously non-industrial or had only light industry, especially in eastern Asia and India. The other process is the penetration of new technologies into many areas of human life that had not been previously industrial, such as information processing, management, communication, media and entertainment, education, and health care, as well as agriculture and the production of raw materials themselves.

Of course, the extension of technology, machinery, and industrial processes into areas of human life beyond manufacturing is not a new phenomenon. For example, photography, film, radio, the recording industry, and all forms of the 'mechanical reproduction of a work of art' began in the nineteenth century and advanced rapidly during the first decades of the twentieth century. Steamships, trains, telegraph lines, cars, telephones, and planes shrank the globe well before our lifetimes. But, by the end of the twentieth century, electronic media, computers, the emergence of a global network society, and very sophisticated telecommunications systems amounted to a great leap forward. New information technologies changed the way we interact with others, how we perceive the world, and how we experience space and time. They have contributed to globalization because production processes can be 'disintegrated' physically and organizationally and distributed among many countries (Reich 1991). Places that seemed very far away are now very close, and information can be conveyed instantaneously. Knowledge transfer and data access across national borders collapse space and proximity and seem to speed up time. A digital divide is opening up between information haves and have-nots, between individuals and also between organizations and nations that have easy access to information technologies and those on the wrong side of the digital divide, who do not.

The new media, layered on top of existing media such as television, film, radio, and the audio-recording industry have created a dense global 'mediasphere,' which some observers believe forms a 'total symbolic environment' on an unprecedented scale, with effects on perception, cognition, and collective action that we do not yet understand very well. Some theorists (notably Castells 1996) suggest that 'informationalism' is a new mode of development, one linked to capitalism as a mode of production but with its own distinct technologies and social relationships.

Expansion of technology and the new hyper-industrialization have had many consequences. Peasants and farm laborers lost their meager livelihood when the 'green revolution' based on modern farm machinery, high-yield hybrids, fertilizers, and large energy inputs made agriculture in Asia much more capital intensive and much less labor intensive. Decades of agricultural mechanization precipitated massive migration to cities and industrial zones. Factories in the newly industrializing nations absorbed some of the 'excess' labor, generally drawing displaced rural populations into low-wage jobs with long hours and bad working conditions. Women and children faced especially exploitive conditions, and they often found work in sweatshops producing goods for export. Large transnational corporations tried to distance themselves from these sweatshop conditions by contracting production to local subcontractors.

In some economically developed countries, new technologies have hastened trends toward an hourglass or bowling-pin economy. Well-paying blue-collar jobs in manufacturing were exported to lower-wage economies, shrinking the middle of the class structure, but there was growth at the bottom, in low-wage service jobs, and at the top, in professional and managerial positions in high tech, information, research and development, education, entertainment, health care, and 'advanced corporate services.' New computerized communication and transportation technologies, such as the containerization of shipping, made possible the geographical redistribution of jobs in the last decades of the twentieth century. Lay-offs became common in many industries, in white-collar as well as blue-collar work.

In addition to making possible labor force shifts and changes in job structure, new technologies affect investment. There is a speed-up in the application of technology to production, with shorter life spans for fixed capital (machinery). Nations and companies experience greater pressure to keep up technologically with their competitors. Products contain higher levels of industrial inputs. Synthetic fibers, processed and fast foods, lique-fied natural gas—to name only a few products—are more processed and technologically transformed than their past counterparts and require more capital and energy inputs for production and distribution.

Humanity now finds itself at the brink of a new area of industrialization—biotechnology—with the promise (or threat?) of engineered and industrially produced living tissues and organisms: cloned organisms, new organs grown from stem cells, genetically modified plant and animal forms, and so on. Of course, biotechnology is not a totally new phenomenon—it was already incipient in Jenner's use of cowpox as a vaccine against smallpox in the late eighteenth century, in plant and animal breeding experiments in the early twentieth century, and in the development of antibiotics during the 1930s and 1940s. But, as in telecommunications and information technology during the past two decades, we now seem on the brink of qualitative leaps in biotech and face the possibility of a brave new world of cyborgs and bioengineered life-forms.

To conclude our section on hyper-industrialization, we offer the prescient comments of an observer with whom we concur: 'Late capitalism, far from rep-resenting a post-industrial society, thus appears as the period when all branches of the economy are fully industrialized for the first time' (Mandel 1975: 191).

ISSUES WITHOUT BORDERS: POPULATION GROWTH, URBANIZATION, HEALTH AND ENVIRONMENTAL PROBLEMS, AND REGIONAL CONFLICTS

DEMOGRAPHIC CHANGES: POPULATION GROWTH AND URBANIZATION

Between 1950 and 2005, the world's population more than doubled, rising from 2.6 billion to 6.45 billion. Between 1975 and 2005, it went from 4 billion to 6.45 billion. These increases took place largely in the developing world—nations and regions outside of Europe, North America, Australia-New Zealand, and Japan. The developed nations and regions had already undergone a demographic transition in the late nineteenth and early twentieth century from high population growth to slow or no growth. The increases in population in the less developed regions of the globe in the second half of the twentieth century had enormous consequences.

Governments have experienced difficulty in providing basic public services to an expanding and youthful population. In the 1960s, the nations in this grouping (some of them actually new nations formed from former colonies and others newly developing nations) already faced problems of poorly developed infrastructure, rural-urban disparities, and low levels of education and health care. They had not undergone industrialization, and many of them had been 'underdeveloped' by colonial and neocolonial policies that turned them into suppliers of cheap raw materials: copper from Zambia, diamonds and gold from South Africa, rubber from Congo and Southeast Asia, and so on. Already behind the industrial nations in the development of infrastructure and social services, they found that catching up under these difficult circumstances became impossible as their populations soared.

Absolute poverty increased markedly, and a larger percentage of the world's population now lives in conditions of famine, malnutrition, and inadequate housing than in 1960. Of the world's more than 6 billion people, over a billion live on less than $1 US a day. Whole countries (at the time of this writing, for example, Niger and Malawi) face famine.

Pushed out of the countryside by growing poverty and falling demand for agricultural labor, millions of people crowd into cities where there are neither employment opportunities nor sufficient housing. With over half of the world's population now urban, the globe is becoming a 'planet of slums'—vast shantytowns as well as decaying inner-city cores (Davis 2004).

Population growth has heightened the potential for conflict. For example, it is probably not coincidental that the genocidal Hutu-Tutsi conflict took place in Rwanda and Burundi, one of the most densely populated regions on the planet, where population pressures and claims on scarce resources are extreme.

Vulnerability to natural disaster is also growing. Population pressures are destroying forest cover in delicate zones, as people farm hillsides and build homes and communities in precarious locations. For example, in Latin America, mudslides that destroy whole villages now accompany tropical storms, and there is enormous loss of life in floods in Bangladesh that devastate densely populated coastal regions. More people than ever before are living on hurricane-lashed coasts, earthquake fault lines, and volcanic slopes.

Faced with growing poverty in the countryside and growing urban slums, governments have responded by withdrawing further from the historic goals of development and the reduction of disparities in income and opportunity. This economic, social, and organizational vacuum created by the absence of employment, social services, and a satisfying, predictable social order is being filled by criminal organizations, 'mafias,' and 'drug cartels,' as well as by smaller local gangs. Transnational traffic in drugs, illegal immigration, prostitution, and contraband are global manifestations of increases in criminal activity. High rates of petty crime in many large cities, police corruption, banditry and piracy, and the emergence of neighborhoods that police refuse to enter attest to growing insecurity and the inability of governments to control the entire national territory.

At a higher level of abstraction, one can conclude that rapid population growth and urbanization have produced a crisis of 'governability.' The movement, activities, and basic health and safety of hundreds of millions of people, especially in poorer countries, are no longer fully under the control of a central government. Historically, people in 'remote areas' like Appalachia or Amazonia were often left to fend for themselves, but the phenomenon of unmanaged—perhaps unmanageable—urban populations is new in the modern era. (It existed in pre-modern cities but was greatly reduced by the nineteenth century, with the establishment of Scotland Yard marking a turning point.) In some countries, the government can no longer make good on its claim to have a monopoly on the use of force within its entire national territory (a key feature of the modern nation state, according to classical theorist Max Weber). Political scientists even identify an extreme end of the spectrum of governability, for which they use the term 'failed states'—whole nation-states in which a central government exists only nominally and has no effective control of the national territory, which is the object of contention among clan organizations, warlords, sectarian militias, or criminal bands.

ENVIRONMENTAL PROBLEMS

Both population pressure and rapid development contribute to environmental destruction. Fragile environments are degraded and destroyed when mining and industrial processes produce toxic wastes, when desperate pastoralists allow their flocks to overgraze in the Sahel (a dry plains area south of the Sahara desert), and when wealthy tourists' feces are dumped from cruise ships along the Alaskan coast. Well-intentioned and internationally funded infrastructural projects, such as dams in India and the trans-Amazon highway, devastate the homes of indigenous peoples, and so does petroleum extraction in the Amazon region and the Niger Delta. Gold mining poisons river systems. Endangered animal species, such as rhinoceros and sea cucumbers, are killed to meet demand for their supposedly aphrodisiacal body parts, and other species succumb to habitat destruction in the expansion of farming and logging. Huge chemical spills in the Tisza in southeastern Europe and in the Amur River system along the China-Russia border threaten water supplies and kill animal species. The examples could go on and on. Most governments do little to stop these problems and even encourage environmental overuse and mismanagement in the name of 'development.'

One of the most serious effects of development and fossil fuel use may be global warming. There is no doubt that the earth's mean temperature is rising, and the effects are quite noticeable, from the melting of glaciers and the polar icecaps to the increase in Atlantic and Caribbean water temperature, a factor in the increased force of hurricanes. Increasing numbers of scientists believe that the evidence suggests that this rise in temperature is not just a natural cyclical phenomenon but a product of 'greenhouse gases'—carbon dioxide emissions originating from the burning of fossil fuels, which creates a gas layer that traps heat. The largest producer of CO_2 emissions, the United States, is responsible for about 24 per cent of their production, but the US government has been reluctant to set any mandatory limits (with the excuse that India and China have not signed on to limits either) and, under the Bush administration, denied that the problem of global warming is serious, imminent, and caused by human activity.

HIV/AIDS AND OTHER EPIDEMICS

By the early 1980s, the AIDS epidemic was taking shape. Its first victims were located in eastern Congo, and, shortly thereafter, illness and deaths were reported among gay men in the United States and Europe. The disease then rapidly spread among heterosexual populations, especially in Africa. What made it different from earlier epidemics, such as cholera in the nineteenth century and the 'Spanish flu' after World War I, was its long latency period and pattern of sexual transmission. Its transmission by sexual contact and injection drug use (as well as by blood transfusions and perinatal infection) made it a taboo subject in many cultures. Religious elites and government authorities were reluctant to discuss the means necessary to halt or at least slow down transmission—use of condoms, testing, needle exchange, and the open discussion of sexual behaviors. In an imaginary world, abstinence and fidelity would have contained the epidemic. These were not behaviors to be realistically expected, however, and so the epidemic spread through sexual networks where unprotected sex took place, and it quickly moved along trans-national transportation routes. Practices associated with gender inequality, such as sexual assault, the demand for unprotected sex with prostitutes, female genital cutting, the double standard of marital fidelity, and the levirate and sororate (marriage of a surviving spouse to an in-law) contributed to the spread of the disease and heightened women's vulnerability. (Women in heterosexual relations were already more vulnerable than their male partners because of the physiology of transmission.) Many countries now have a large number of people infected with HIV/AIDS—over 30 per cent of the population of some countries in southern Africa, such as Malawi and Botswana. Large amounts of antiretroviral drugs (ARVs) are needed to keep their young adults alive. Both globally and nationally, resources that could have gone into general health improvements, education, and infrastructure have to be used for ARVs. Many individuals, especially in poor countries, cannot afford these expensive drugs and die at a very high rate, with devastating effects on their families, communities, and local economies.

Meanwhile other epidemics—kala-azar, malaria, multidrug-resistant tuberculosis, and various types of flu—as well as the effects of nutritional deficiencies on children—are also on the rise and contribute to a poor outlook for humanity's health in much of the world.

REGIONAL CONFLICT AND LOW-INTENSITY WARFARE

Conflicts continue across the face of the globe, though, at the moment, they are not 'world wars' fought by alliances of large nations with large armies over vast territories.

Contemporary conflicts take many forms, which in recent decades have included

- Ethnic conflicts accompanied by expulsions ('ethnic cleansing') and genocidal attacks (in Yugoslavia in the 1990s, Rwanda, and Sudan's Darfur region, for example).
- Struggles over territory and state power among armed bands and warlord-led militias (which may have an ethnic base), as in Liberia, Sierra Leone, and parts of Uganda and Afghanistan.
- Conflicts between central governments and criminal organizations that control large territories, as in Colombia.

- Conflicts between states and insurgent paramilitary forces that control territory, as in the case of Colombia and the FARC, Russia and Chechen rebels, and Sri Lanka and the LTTE, in which both territorial claims and ideology may be at stake.
- Terrorist acts committed by small numbers of combatants within what is otherwise undisputed national territory, such as 9/11, IRA bombings in England, and Chechen rebels' terrorist acts in Russia.
- Occupations in which a national government uses its military or other national security forces to support an influx of settlers or enterprises into annexed territory, as in the case of Jewish settlements in occupied Palestinian territories, the integration of Tibet into China, and Indonesian annexation and economic exploitation of Irian Jaya (Western New Guinea).

Although the numbers of dead in these conflicts are lower than the tens of millions killed in World War I and World War II, fatalities are often, nevertheless, large in absolute terms—probably more than half a million in Iraq and perhaps as many as 5 million in Congo; and the wide dispersion and persistence of these conflicts make them a source of ongoing insecurity. They destroy communities and create terrible losses and hardship. The global feeling of insecurity is heightened by the possibility that terrorists could use weapons of mass destruction (many of them left over from the cold war) such as 'suitcase bombs' and biological agents.

Accounts of all these conflicts are highly subject to spin by political forces and their media allies. One person's 'terrorist' is another's 'patriot and freedom fighter.' Many nations look like 'rogue states.' 'Peaceful settlers' are also 'invaders.'

THE EMERGING DISTRIBUTION OF ECONOMIC INEQUALITY

A key aspect of the emerging global condition is a high level of economic inequality; this feature is not new in human history, but we now have data collection and analysis techniques to understand it more clearly and identify emerging forms of inequality.

The analysis is complicated because there are many relevant ways of measuring and explaining inequalities. In quantitative analysis, inequality is measured as dispersion or variability in the distribution of income (or wealth). We can try to identify predictors of individual incomes; and, in current versions of this model, between-nation variability accounts for about three-quarters of the total variation in the incomes of individuals on the planet and within-nation (class) disparities for another 15 per cent of the variation. (Where do you, personally, fall in the global distribution of income—and is it easy to predict your position?) We can also examine the rank order of nations in terms of their mean (per-capita) national incomes. (What is the per-capita income of your country, and how does it compare to the per-capita incomes of other countries?) We can look at the amount of disparity within nations—countries can have the same mean income but very great differences in how income is distributed among residents. (Where do you fall in the distribution of income within your country?) We can look at the distributions of wealth as well as income, and the wealth distributions are far more concentrated. And we can ask whether these various types of inequalities are increasing or decreasing over time.

INEQUALITIES AMONG NATIONS

An indisputable fact about the global condition is the presence of enormous economic differences among nations. If we created a chart showing where all the individuals in the world fall according to their household income in terms of a standardized measure of purchasing power ('purchasing power parity' or PPP), we would see a shape like the cross section of a pyramid with a wide base of all the people at the low values of the PPP and a small bulge of people at the top at the high values of the PPP. The top is formed by the populations of a small number of fairly large countries (Germany, Japan, France, the United Kingdom, and the United States) and a larger number of small countries (such as Denmark, Canada, Luxembourg, and Sweden), as well as by very small numbers of very rich people in poor countries. At the bottom, the very wide base of the distribution is composed primarily of huge populations in India, Indonesia, most African nations, and rural China. In between are populations in places such as Russia and Mexico or, in more general terms, in Latin America, some of the former Soviet bloc, and the rapidly developing nations in Southeast Asia. Poor individuals in rich nations are generally located in the upper third of the global distribution—in other words, poor people in countries such as Canada, the United States, Australia, and the United Kingdom enjoy higher purchasing power than about two-thirds of individuals in the global distribution of individual purchasing power. This fact is not inconsistent with the reality that the poor in wealthy nations feel disadvantaged or that they are overworked and underpaid within their own societies.

Milanovic (2005, 2007) argues that between 60 and 90 per cent of *variation* in individual incomes can be explained (or predicted) from the nation in which the person lives and that 75 per cent is a good guess for this percentage.

The Gini ratio for world income inequality is about .65, which is larger than that of any single country, even the two with the most inequality (Brazil and South Africa). (The *Gini ratio* or *coefficient* is a number between 0 and 1, with 0 meaning a completely equal distribution of income, or whatever goods are being measured, and 1 meaning maximum inequality.) To put it brutally: forget all your hard work, entrepreneurial spirit, or expensive education—what really matters in determining your economic situation as an individual on a global scale is whether you were born in a poor or a wealthy country.

It is difficult to determine the effects of neoliberal policies on between-nation inequalities. There has actually been relatively little movement up or down in the rank order of nations by per-capita income, even though there have been changes within nations, often in the direction of a growing middle class but also toward greater poverty in the lower tier (Warner 2006). The nations of the European periphery, such as Italy, Greece, Ireland, and Spain moved up after World War II; so did a number of east Asian nations in the later part of the twentieth century. A number of Latin American nations moved down in terms of per-capita income. But few of these moves were by a lot of rank orders, and movement slowed down after the 1980s (Warner 2006). Although the rank-order listing has not shifted dramatically, there appear to be growing gaps in per-capita income among nations, with the ratio between the incomes of the top countries and the bottom ones increasing over the past 50 years.

These data do not support neoliberal hopes about the salutary effects of markets in leveling national incomes upward and diffusing well-being among nations. Let's clarify this comment: in recent decades there has been expansion of the middle class in some countries and mass pauperization in some countries—and sometimes both trends in the same country. These changes in within-country income distributions may be associated with neoliberal policies; but when we examine the rank order of countries in terms of national income, rather than disparities within countries or the fate of individuals, we see that the rank order of nations has not undergone any seismic shift. The global capitalist system is characterized by immense inequalities among nations and regions, and they seem to be a very long-term, stable feature of the system. The theoretical implication is probably a thumbs up for world systems analysis (a form of Marxist theory), which argues that the uneven structure was formed in the early centuries of the modern period with European conquest, settlement, and colonization and the formation of core capitalist countries, a semi-periphery, and peripheral poor nations and regions (Wallerstein 1974). The mechanisms of reproducing these inequalities have changed over the centuries—from conquest and pillage, to colonialism, to dependency and neo-colonial trade polices, indebtedness, and structural adjustment policies.

WITHIN-NATION INEQUALITIES

We need to look at income dispersion within countries and not only the mean (per-capita) income of each nation. Countries that have higher mean incomes tend to have less inequality in their income distributions. The wealthiest countries in the world in terms of per-capita income, such as Denmark, Sweden, France, Finland, Canada, Norway, and Japan, also are the most egalitarian in the distribution of income. Countries of the former Soviet bloc such as Hungary and Slovakia have somewhat lower inequality than other countries at their level of per-capita income; but the Gini coefficient of inequality rose in Russia after the 1980s, increasing from a level comparable to that of Norway to one similar to the level of the United States by the late 1990s (Hunter 2004: 418–19).

The United States is rather anomalous, although some evidence of wage dispersion has also appeared in Australia, the UK, Canada, and Japan (Australia Department of the Parliamentary Library 1995). For a country with a relatively high per-capita income, the United States has a rather high and growing level of inequality in recent decades, almost returning to pre-World War II levels of inequality (Piketty and Saez 2003; Bernstein and Mishel 2007). The United States also has a higher proportion of people—especially children—in poverty and a high number of the medically uninsured compared to other countries with high per-capita incomes, such as France, Sweden, Denmark, and Finland. The configuration of economic stratification in the States is marked by rapid growth in jobs in the lower tier of the US income distribution, with stagnation or even decline in the proportion of well-paying jobs at the middle levels, and soaring incomes at the very top (Bernstein and Mishel 2007; Massey and Hirst 1998; Piketty and Saez 2003; Sassen 2000). There are growing gaps in earned income not only among occupations but also within them, for example, between the highest paid earners and the middle and lower ranks of the same occupation (Kim and Sakamoto 2008).

How is growing inequality in the United States to be understood? On the one hand, this distribution may be the shape of things to come in all economies under the impact of globalization and neoliberal policies; or, alternatively, it might be another example of US exceptionalism because other economically developed countries have political institutions in place that protect these societies from growing inequality.

RACE-ETHNICITY, GENDER, AND CLASS

In many societies, there is a strong racialization of economic or class inequality. Locations in the class structure are occupied by distinct ethno-racial groups, and we need to ask ourselves how these differences came about. These overlaps of racial and class stratification are certainly not a new phenomenon, and they have characterized 'New World' societies from the start, as these were formed through the conquest and enslavement of Indians and Africans.

Globalization and transnational immigration have meant flows of immigrants from post-colonial societies into the former colonial powers and from poor nations into wealthier nations. Furthermore, historically, ethnic minorities with educational and entrepreneurial skills were at risk of violence from indigenous populations who lacked these traditions, as in the case of Chinese in Southeast Asia, South Asians in Uganda, and Jews in eastern Europe (Chua 2002). Because of complex, historical, and cumulative processes, more or less favorable occupational positions are closely related to national origins and ethnic identities. States have a major role in creating these complex stratification systems by the formulation of immigration laws and policies concerning citizenship rights (Cheng 2006; Chua 2002).

Concurrently with the racialization of the class structure, one can observe class differentiation within ethno-racial categories that had previously been clustered around one location on the class-income distribution. For example, in South Africa, a black middle class is emerging after the fall of the apartheid regime, which for decades had relegated all blacks to the lower tiers of the class structure in terms of occupations and incomes. In the United States, income and occupational dispersion of African Americans is discernible with a growing middle class. Dispersion in the class location of ethno-racial categories has political implications for identity and collective action (Pattillo 2008; Soja 1996).

Gender hierarchies were transformed in the last decades of the twentieth century with the massive entry of women into the paid labor force in practically all economically developed nations and many developing ones. This economic transformation was accompanied by new ideologies of gender—generally ones that promoted greater equality between the sexes—and by more participation of women in politics. Feminist movements emerged from and supported the participation of women in all spheres of society. Gender hierarchies and gender arrangements that had been taken for granted—often considered 'natural'—broke down. Yet there remained areas of resistance to gender equality, for example, in many occupations, in higher management and the CEO selection process, and in political office (Khurana 2002). A backlash to the equality and full participation of women emerged, both promoted by and fuelling fundamentalist and neo-traditional religious movements that drew their energy from a revitalized and media-borne ideology of patriarchy (Riesebrodt [1993] 1998).

Meanwhile, women were increasingly drawn into the stream of transnational migration, often performing traditional 'women's work' as wage laborers, for example, as caregivers for children and the elderly, lower-tier health-care workers, housekeepers in private households and the hotel industry, and sex workers (Cheng 2006). A feminization of poverty took place because of the precarious and poorly paid character of these jobs as well as the lack of social support for single mothers in a very large range of countries. In short, women increasingly had a class position of their own, distinct from that of fathers and husbands.

THE WEAKNESS OF EXPLICITLY CLASS-BASED COLLECTIVE ACTION

The profound between-nation inequalities and the noticeable within-nation inequalities have generated remarkably few explicitly class-based movements in the neoliberal period. Although resentment is expressed at the actions of the United States and international organizations such as the World Bank and the International Monetary Fund in many poorer countries, these feelings are only occasionally linked to systematic collective action and organization. Furthermore, elites and dominant classes in poorer countries are able to steer oppositional consciousness away from themselves, often encouraging nationalist and religious identities to form while discouraging class-based activism. A considerable slippage between objective conditions and subjective understandings and framings of these conditions seems to exist, and, indeed, there is no relationship between the percentage of people in a country who believe that differences in income in their country are too large and the actual level of inequality in the country (Lübker 2004). Theorists and empirical observers have offered micro-level analysis of this slippage; for example, Burawoy and his students (1991) provide ethnographic documentation of class conflict, linkages to other types of collective action, and the prospects and limits of these actions based on micro-level observations in bakeries, schools, unions, and ethnic enclaves in the United States. Sennett probes the cognitive maps that workers and small-business owners have of the new landscape of flexible capitalism and neoliberalism and confirms that 'class consciousness' is not a major signpost in this terrain (Sennett 1998).

CULTURAL CONSEQUENCES: POSTMODERN CULTURE AND IRONIC HOPELESSNESS

Many of the changes we identified in the preceding pages are tangible and down to earth: population growth and urbanization, expanding industrial development and new technologies, global flows of migrants, capital, and products, HIV/AIDS, regional conflicts, persistent economic inequalities on a global scale, and government policies that favored markets over state planning.

Cultural change is more nebulous. One term that became popular in the last decades of the twentieth century was *postmodern*. It refers to a mood or feeling that pervades cultural production rather than to a definite set of values, norms, or types of artistic expression. It is most explicitly expressed by intellectuals, but a less self-conscious version of it may be widely diffused across the globe and is associated with the impact of TV and other new media. The postmodern mood is one of a loss of hope and faith in progress. This loss of faith in progress is portrayed and experienced as irony and detachment, rather than despair, especially in the economically developed nations. In other regions, there may still be a buoyant but cynical desire for economic growth, increasingly measured by individual financial success rather than collective well-being. Others turn to modern versions of traditional religious answers to cope with feelings of discontinuity and anomie; these neo-traditional responses may be expressed within social movements and supported by regimes that rely on the latest technology and media to convey fundamentalist faiths.

Much of the modern period from the Industrial Revolution on was marked by optimism, a faith in material progress and science, as well as hope for more equitable and affluent material conditions so everyone could dream of being 'middle class.' Among Marxists, there was hope for a coming socialist revolution. The horrendous experiences of World War I (about 10 million dead, mostly young European soldiers) dampened this faith, but strangely, after World War II (about 50 million dead, civilians as well as combatants, in

Asia as well as Europe) the mood was surprisingly optimistic again. The victory of the Allies meant the suppression of ideologies of fascism, racism, and white or 'Aryan' supremacy. New nations cast off colonial rule. In the United States, the leading power after the war, formal, *de jure* equality between the races was finally established, as the civil rights movement gained elite support under pressure from Cold War global ideological competition. Killer diseases like malaria, smallpox, and polio were reduced or eliminated, and antibiotics extended lives that once would have been cut short by infections. Income distribution in the developed countries was becoming more equal. In both the West and the Soviet bloc, there was rapid upward social mobility, as the children of hardscrabble workers and farmers were able to complete secondary school and go to universities. Elites and masses in both the West and the socialist nations thought they were well on the way to making their own model of state, economy, and society work—to win an intense but nevertheless largely peaceful competition with each other. 'We will bury you!' boasted Soviet leader Nikita Khrushchev, and the American public didn't buy it, but the tone of the altercation signaled optimism on both sides.

Postmodernism, on the other hand, is a loss of faith in modernity as progress. The human species no longer seems to be progressing toward better living standards, democracy, socialism (for those who believed in it), peace, affluence, good health, equality or equality of opportunity, the end of racism, or most of the other good things people wished for in the 1950s and 1960s. Now, none of these goals seems imminent for the majority of the world's population. The privileged populations in the West and the affluent strata in the developing world—people who enjoy some of these goods—are often worried about being able to hold on to them.

The mood is therefore one of skepticism about all the 'big stories' of human progress, the 'meta-narratives' that claimed we can discern evolution, revolutionary potential, or at least forward motion in human societies over the past centuries. Instead, life now looks like a bleak struggle for survival for billions of people in poor countries and regions. In the developed countries, even the privileged cannot escape the rat race of competition and economic risk, which a few love and many find stressful (Schor 1998; Sennett 1998). There is a sense of insecurity in the face of terrorism, crime, poverty, financial instability, and ethnic and religious conflict. Racism, ethnic and racial marginalization, and coded ideologies of white supremacy have reappeared in many countries. Science and technology do not seem to make us wiser, happier, or more humane.

These unpleasant thoughts are reflected into cultural forms, in music, art, film, literature, electronic media, and journalism. The reflection is not always direct, nor is it explicitly despairing or gloomy. It takes the form of escapism, an expression of disillusionment or fragmentation, a fascination with celebrity and spectacle without meaning and with fast-paced action and 'surface intensities' without deeper feeling (Jameson 1991). The media project a world with its own virtual reality (Castells 1996), which everyone follows avidly while knowing that it is not true or meaningful. Spectator sports, soaps (the telenovela as world literature), infotainment, the flim-flam of speculative bubbles, and a barrage of commercials contribute to the mood of irony, cynicism, disbelief, and pessimistic playfulness. The only large groups that still appear to share a faith and sustain a collective vision are religious fundamentalists who reject modern values and scientific knowledge.

With a loss of faith in the future comes a loss of interest in the past. Time is compressed, and memory fades to retro, a celebration of style and fashion, of the surface look of things in the past. Combined with the shrinkage or virtual annihilation of space through contemporary telecommunications, this compressed sense of time squeezes us into the *here* and *now*. In the chapter on the work of Erving Goffman, we will explore how views of the self began to shift toward the self as a performed persona instead of a fixed personality, perhaps in response to the increasing compression of time and space and the emergence of pervasive mass media.

HOW AND WHY DID ALL THESE CHANGES HAPPEN?

The answer is complex. Any simple answer is not satisfactory. There are at least three distinct but intertwined processes at work.

CHOICE AND AGENCY

One cause lies in the choices made by billions of human beings. Human beings feel they have a will and purpose in their lives and actions. They experience 'agency.' They take action. Their choices reflect their understanding of their interests. They may take into account survival, material well-being, and values they hold important. They may act in their own individual interest, but more often on behalf of their family and community or even some wider ideal such as a nation, humanity, all life on the planet, and so on. It is presumptuous to label some of these choices as 'rational' (often the materially or economically motivated ones) and others as 'irrational' (often those associated with spiritual values, personal relationships, or hedonistic desires). All choices emerge from life conditions and the totality of circumstances.

A paradox associated with human agency is that any given individual feels free to make choices, yet often these choices turn out to be highly constrained and the results are large, statistically predictable patterns of human behavior, as quantitative researchers like to point out.

CONSTRAINT AND STRUCTURE

The constraints on choices are the second force that explains changes. These constraints include natural phenomena (climate, physical geography, and natural disasters), the humanly created landscape and infrastructure (including the way 'nature' can be transformed into 'resources'), and the laws, regulations, institutions, norms, values, and organizations created in the past. All the humanly produced constraints can be lumped together as 'structure,' and the perspective that emphasizes them is called 'the structuralist perspective.' The constraints appear to have become solid and real, constructed 'things' that limit and shape action. The predictability of patterns of action among large numbers of people arises from these constraints. Social change is not simply the net outcome of many individual choices. The effects of these choices and the choices available are shaped and limited by existing conditions.

ELITE DECISIONS AND COLLECTIVE ACTION

Finally, a third force is formed by collective actors, by groups of people acting together with a shared purpose. Among these collective actors are very powerful groups—governments and the parties that control them; corporations and investment banks; international organizations, such as the IMF, the World Bank, and the WTO; and organized movements, religious organizations, and interest groups. These collective actors are able to quickly create new structural constraints and thus channel individual choices—to enact laws, declare war, market new products, create new financial instruments, and exercise coercive force. The newly created constraints guide the choices of large numbers of people. One of the reasons that we can predict patterns of behavior statistically, even though each individual appears to have free choice, is that collective actors are able to create constraints on the choices. Emphasis on collective actions and decisions is often termed the 'instrumental perspective,' because it emphasizes actors' deliberate use of the instruments or tools of power as means for achieving their goals.

When we look at the new trends we listed in this chapter, we can see that some appear to be the product of individual agency, the net result of the choices of hundreds of millions of people. Urbanization is one of these; in recent decades, hundreds of millions of people left the countryside and moved to cities. Yet many of them moved because rural life had become too harsh and the demand for their labor dropped when landowners turned to capital-intensive farming, buying new farm machinery manufactured by transnational corporations. The population explosion of the later twentieth century is in part the product of couples having large numbers of children; it is also caused by steps that collective actors took to reduce death rates, such as vaccination campaigns, spraying malarial swamps, improving water systems and sanitary infrastructure, and making available antibiotics, and by steps they didn't take, such as providing inexpensive, effective contraceptives. The growing problem of obesity in affluent nations is the result of individual food choices, which are constrained by collective elite choices about product development, marketing, and supermarket product placement. The AIDS epidemic was spread by human agency—choices about sexual behavior that, in retrospect, were ill advised; but these choices were made within existing structures of norms about sex, family and gender hierarchies, religious and cultural norms, and discourses about silence and sin. Collective actors—the Centers for Disease Control and Prevention in the United States and the World Health Organization, governments, churches, the Gates Foundation, research institutions, pharmaceutical companies, and so on—have also intervened in ways that may slow down or spread the epidemic.

On the other hand, the policies that produced the neoliberal shift and supported free trade and market expansion were more one-sidedly the result of decisions made by key elites: the Reagan and Thatcher administrations, decision makers in financial markets, corporate executives, the IMF and the World Bank, and so on. Nevertheless, these collective actors were not totally free—they too were responding to existing structures such as the welfare state and regulatory policies, as well as to other collective actors, such as unions and parties of the left.

Hyper-industrialization and rapid technological innovation are also propelled both by powerful collective actors and by individual choices, but agency is channeled and constrained by structure, by histories of technological change, and by the existing distribution of resources, know-how, and wage rates.

We could go down the whole list of trends, and, in each instance, we would see outcomes shaped by the mix of aggregate individual actions, the decisions of key collective actors, and the 'force of circumstances.' By the 'force of circumstances,' we mean the constraining structures inherited from the past, formed by human agency, that have since become frozen into all-too-solid limits on what is possible in the present. The mix of structure and individual and collective agency may be quite different for each trend. Contemporary sociologists talk about the dialectic of agency and structure. Marx said that human beings make history, but not in circumstances of their own choosing. And we are familiar with the prayer that asks for the courage to change what can be changed, the serenity to accept what cannot be changed, and the wisdom to know the difference.

MYTHS

We have to be careful to reject the myths that are associated with each of these social forces. The myth of agency is that every individual can control circumstances and realize his or her will. This is the myth of personal responsibility: 'go for the gold,' and 'where there is a will there is a way.' The limits of this myth are quite clear in the statistical probabilities of outcomes. It is not impossible, but highly unlikely, that a starving and illiterate maize farmer in Malawi will become CEO of Fox News. The myth of agency has powerful ideological functions because it makes people feel completely responsible for their own problems and unrealistically proud of their successes. For example, many middle-class white people in the United States believe that, after World War II, they rose from working-class origins entirely by their own hard work, ignoring the role of social policies such as Pell Grants (grants to college students) and generous federal spending in the military-industrial sector that boosted employment and wage levels throughout the economy. The myth of the market is another illusion associated with agency. 'Free choices' in the market are actually highly constrained, in part for structural reasons and in part because powerful collective actors have made decisions that shape market options. Public transportation vs. private cars or affordable housing vs. million-dollar mansions—the way these options present themselves to us in the market is not simply the result of millions of individual choices but has to do with government transportation and housing policies.

Elite dominance is the myth associated with the force of collective actors. Some people attribute everything that happens to powerful elites who are cohesive, cunning, and capable—veritable 'masterminds' able to control every detail of society. They believe that all trends and events were set in motion by an elite and that all changes redound to its benefit. The extreme version of this myth is 'conspiracy theory.' These myths neglect the facts: many policies have unintended and unanticipated consequences, some areas of behavior are not amenable to elite planning, there are many elites with competing goals, and elites are constrained by existing structures like everybody else.

Finally, there is the ideology of structural determinism, an overemphasis on constraint. Taken to the extreme, it becomes not only the view that 'what is real is rational' but also that it could never be otherwise. It rules out not only human agency but also 'contingency,' the role of random or unpredictable factors in human affairs. This kind of helplessness in the face of existing conditions has an ideological function, discouraging individual and collective action for social change. It suggests that human beings are helpless against market forces, elite power, and the weight of the past.

While every myth contains a grain of truth, each focuses on only part of the whole, and each, taken to the extreme, leads to a profoundly distorted view of the world, which blocks rather than enhances realistic action.

CONCLUSION

At this point, the reader is hopefully ready for a deepening of the argument. How are we to think about the momentous changes of the last forty years?

Maybe you have already considered several different interpretations.

MORE MODERNITY?

One perspective is that all of these changes are only the further extension of trends that were already apparent with the Industrial Revolution and the onset of 'the modern' in the late eighteenth and early nineteenth centuries. Globalization, market economies, rapid technological innovation, environmental destruction, and so on have been part of the human experience for centuries.

ADVANCED CAPITALISM?

Many Marxists support a focused version of the 'more modernity' view by asserting that all these trends are not just modern but specifically capitalist. Marx and Engels had already spotted all these trends in 1848 when they wrote the *Communist Manifesto,* in which they list technological change ('constant revolutionizing of production'), globalization ('exploitation of the world market'), population growth and urbanization ('enormous cities ... populations conjured out of the ground'), free trade, 'immensely facilitated means of communication,' and the destruction of old established national industries and cultures as key characteristics of capitalism, of the new world the bourgeoisie was creating. A close look at the first pages of Part I of the *Communist Manifesto,* in which Marx and Engels outline the revolutionary impact of capitalism on human societies, will reveal a rather accurate prophecy about conditions that actually exist 160 years later, minus the emergence of proletarian consciousness and socialism. In this view, the transformation of the past forty years is a shift within capitalism toward an advanced or late stage that extends and amplifies features that have always been its essential elements, such as the market, private ownership of the means of production, technological innovation, global reach, and large numbers of dependent workers divided among themselves by nation, ethnicity, culture, and gender.

POSTMODERNITY?

Postmodernists argue that the changes of recent decades are too momentous to be interpreted as 'extensions of the modern' or 'late or advanced capitalism' and that, instead, these changes constitute a qualitative leap within capitalism, a new phase in human history and a form of capitalism that is distinctly different from the past. This new phase requires new theoretical concepts and a new label, the postmodern. To use existing theories of capitalism and modernity would be like making the mistake of generals who are always using strategies from the last war to plan the current one. But where will we find new concepts and theories? Can we modify existing ones, or do we have to come up with new ones from our observations of new realities?

SUMMARY

We described changes that took place in the social context of theory, in the external circumstances of the period 1968–2009. These changes included globalization, neoliberalism, the expansion of media and information technologies, hyper-industrialization, urbanization, population growth, emerging inequalities among and within nations, and a host of trans-border issues including terrorism, regional conflicts, and epidemics. These changes in the 'real world' became the topics of theorizing and transformed the intellectual context of social inquiry.

KEY TERMS

- ◎ '1968'
- ◎ 'advanced capitalism' versus 'postmodern' as the best label for the contemporary condition
- ◎ economic inequalities: ways of measuring inequality, within-nation and between-nation (or among-nation) inequalities
- ◎ embedded liberalism and neoliberalism
- ◎ explanations of social forces: agency, structure, elite decisions, and collective action
- ◎ global trends and issues: urbanization, population growth, population health, environmental problems, regional conflict
- ◎ globalization
- ◎ hyper-industrialization
- ◎ markets

WORKS CONSULTED

See the bibliography for complete citations.

Appadurai 1993
Bell 1973
Best and Kellner 1991
Castells 1996
Caute 1990
Collins 1994
Davis 2004
Delaney 2005
Feyerabend 1975
Harvey 1990, 2005
Hobsbawm 1987, 1994

Jameson 1991
Jay 1996
Kerr 2001
Kuhn 1962
Mandel 1975, 1978
Marx and Engels [1848] 2002
Reich 1991
Ritzer 1996
Sassen 2001
Schor 1998
Sennett 1998

Chapter 2

CHANGES IN THEORY

INTRODUCTION: MAKING THEORIES

In this chapter, we will trace how theories changed after the 1960s and identify the main characteristics of the new theories that emerged. Theorists
invented new concepts for understanding the trends and upheavals of the
end of the twentieth century, and they modified and reinterpreted existing
theories.

We could offer a very simple explanation of new theories by linking them
directly to real-world trends. Changes in social reality—in the world that
forms an external context to sociology and theorizing—had a direct impact
on theories. Theorists had to accommodate these new conditions in their
theories. Expanded markets and neoliberal policies stimulated interest in
exchange and rational choice models of behavior. Conditions now appeared
to ebb and flow depending on the direction and volume of individual and
micro-level actions. These market processes also stimulated a resurgence
of Marxist-inspired theories focused on capitalism; some of these theories
avoided the label 'Marxist' (out of fashion after the collapse of the Soviet
Union) but nonetheless were influenced by Marxists' critical approaches
to the social consequences of the market. The growing power of the media
and information systems stimulated theories of images and representation.
The entry of large numbers of women into the paid labor force encouraged the
diffusion of feminist theories. The general uncertainty and insecurity of
the age of globalization contributed to postmodern perspectivism and a loss
of faith in both Marxist and liberal views of social progress. Indeed, in broad
outline, these straightforward matches between 'realities' and 'theories' are
discernible. But this analysis would be *reductionist*, reducing the complicated

51

creation of theories to a simple reflection of clearly identifiable real-world trends, events, and conditions. The correspondences are often more nuanced and complicated. When theorists address changes in society, they highlight key images, refocus concepts, and shift emphases. Theories are not direct reflections of social change into ideas.

In this chapter, we will discuss how new theories were formed not only as direct explanations of events and trends but as more complicated and processed sets of ideas. Theories are rarely proposed simply as explanations of or abstractions from the chronicle of events and circumstances. The process of making theories always involves many influences—from the community of theorists, the general intellectual climate, and changes in the social environment. New theories generally incorporate parts of older theories or offer new readings of existing theoretical work. The net outcome of these influences means that theories are highly processed products, not simple reflections of events and trends.

ESTABLISHING NEW THEORIES: UP FROM THE UNDERGROUND

Theories change by several intertwined processes. Internal changes emerge from processes within the community of theorists—a vaguely defined community, to be sure. They evolve from criticism, discussion, and dissemination of ideas. These internal changes are the product of conversations and the exchange of ideas with other social theorists. Changes in theories are also stimulated by changes in the larger intellectual climate, by fashions and trends in social thought. For example, Freudian psychoanalysis was popular in the decade after World War II and affected research and theories in the social sciences, including sociology, anthropology, and political science. At the end of the twentieth century, deconstruction as a theme in philosophy became an intellectual trend and affected sociology and related fields.

The second major type of change is externally generated; theorists change their ideas as a result of observing and thinking about changes in the social environment. The internal and the external changes are not completely distinct because theorists tend to see changes in society through the lens of their theories and concepts and in images derived from the prevailing intellectual climate, which, in turn, are influenced by changes in society.

We can think of theorizing as a manufacturing process in which a raw material is transformed into a finished product. The raw material is society itself. It is already considerably transformed by the time it is delivered to the theory factory, much as iron ore might be delivered to a steel mill in the form of pellets and not as it occurs in the ground. Raw human experience is processed into pellets, such as events, data, and narratives about experiences, and these pellets are the materials on which theorists work. Empirical research articles published in scholarly research journals are also pellets to be molded by theorists. Once the internal organization of the theory factory gets to work on the raw material of society, the products can be very varied and unpredictable. Iron ore can end up in a car body, a ploughshare, or a weapon of mass destruction, and, in our metaphor, theorists can transform the pellets of experience into different types of theories. To continue our manufacturing metaphor, we must also emphasize that a lot of theory is made out of recycled old theories, broken up and melted down to provide new raw materials.

Once theories are dreamed up and the pellets of experience and data are molded into the design, they will survive only if they are disseminated and accepted among a larger community of scholars. The first step in building a new theory is often to attack an existing theory. New theories are unveiled in the form of attacks on current and past theories, critiques of widely used theoretical concepts, or critiques of empirical work linked to the theory that is the actual target of criticism.

The process of establishing new theories is usually communal. The new theoretical guru attracts disciples, often graduate students, and they take part in disseminating the teacher's works, attacking and discrediting old theories and spreading the new ideas. From a small cell of the faithful who follow their dreamer, the band of disciples may grow to a new school of thought and set a national and transnational intellectual fashion. As the paradigm shift gathers power, more theorists want to jump on the bandwagon. They start using the new terms and concepts. They frame their research questions in the new theoretical language. Instructors assign as class readings the works of the guru and the disciples. Young faculty label older faculty as out of date if they fail to switch to the new paradigms. Intellectuals are as susceptible as young teens to the lures of following the alphas, the trend-setters. So the new theory moves from small but aggressive beginnings to establishment as a leading paradigm, eventually to be attacked and superseded in its turn.

Of course, not all new theories survive. They can survive only if they *partially align with existing frames*, in both research and broader intellectual endeavors. For instance, overlaps in the work of symbolic interactionists, feminists, Erving Goffman, and French philosopher Michel Foucault (whom we will meet in the next part of the book) boosted the acceptance of Foucault's ideas and transformed them from weird delvings in the history of sex and madness into a major paradigm of contemporary theory. His ideas on discourses of normality and deviance aligned with labeling theory, the symbolic interactionist framework, Goffman's observations of mental hospitals, and feminists' interests in micro-power relationships and the construction of gender.

HOW AND WHY HAVE SOCIOLOGICAL THEORIES CHANGED IN THE PAST FORTY YEARS?

This chapter focuses on changes in theory that have taken place in the past four decades. These changes reflect shifts that have occurred in society since the 1960s, but not in any simple way. Reality is never charted into theory in a one-to-one mapping. Like a funhouse mirror, theory turns reality into something fantastical and unsettling. The entire 'blooming buzzing confusion' of reality cannot be captured, so some things must be left out while others get magnified and enhanced. Theory is not like a 'paper of record'—like *The New York Times*—claiming to compile dutifully all the news that's fit to print.

Furthermore, theorizing is always influenced by previous theory and not only by the 'external world' or current intellectual fashions, so the theories of any historical moment are a blend of concepts inherited from past theories and new theory designed to capture new features of society. Theory is always a response to the external world and an internal conversation (or ghostly boxing match) with theoretical ancestors. We will remind readers of this theme in the conclusion, where we sketch the ways that classical and early twentieth century theories have been reread, reinterpreted, and incorporated into contemporary theories.

As Kuhn noted in *The Structure of Scientific Revolutions*, theory grows by criticism of existing theories. The enterprise of theory is extensively one of criticizing concepts, arguing that these concepts do not encompass the nature of social reality, either because they were initially poorly designed or because they no longer fit what is happening on the ground. In some cases, concepts are dropped from theoretical discourse. For example, 'race' was a favorite concept of late nineteenth-century social theorists, a leading paradigm for explaining variation among societies, and a term applied to differences that we would today refer to as 'ethnicity' or 'nation.' For modern readers, it is startling to see how the British press heralded the Robert Scott-Roald Amundsen competition to reach the South Pole in 1911 as a contest in which a British victory would demonstrate the vigor and vitality of the British *race*. (The Norwegians won, thanks to Inuit-inspired fur parkas and dog sleds, while the British died insisting on the superiority of European wool coats, pony sleds, and military hierarchy.) The concept of race turned out to be fundamentally flawed because genetically inherited traits do not cluster consistently and stably into 'races,' and there is no evidence that genetically inherited physical traits are linked to cultures or ways of thought. Before modern population biology, an early warning sign that race was not a useful concept in sociological inquiry came in the form of studies that showed that people of the same alleged race did not behave in uniform ways. 'Race' was a poor predictor of behavioral outcomes, as Émile Durkheim showed when he examined the relationship between 'race' and suicide rates (Durkheim [1897] 1951). In this case, further research led to discarding the concept.

In other cases, an existing concept or theory remains perfectly valid in the abstract but encompasses a shrinking set of empirical situations. For example, the construct 'feudal society'—meaning an agrarian society of fixed status differences—remains an excellent concept for analyzing historical societies in Europe and Japan, but, in an age of global capitalism, it may be of only limited value for analyzing contemporary events, conditions, and social structures.

THE RELATIONSHIP BETWEEN THEORIES AND REALITY IN HISTORICAL PERSPECTIVE

Let's briefly review theories of earlier periods in order to think about the ways in which classical and mid-twentieth-century theories were preserved as well as superseded in contemporary theories. As reality moves on, theories that at one point had addressed it directly become increasingly detached from the contemporary scene, but not therefore worthless. The best theories—those of the great inventors of theory such as Marx and Engels, Durkheim, Simmel, and Weber—retain their value, even if they are now no longer a direct commentary on or explanation of contemporary events. These old theories 'stand the test of time.' The ideas remain valuable, outliving any specific events or empirical data. For example, Durkheim's concept of anomie is valuable even though the specific data on suicide rates and business cycles in nineteenth-century Europe are no longer relevant. Similarly, Marx and Engels' concept of capitalism is still of interest, even though conditions in English factories are not the same as they were in the mid-nineteenth century.

How did the theories of the immediate post-World War II period emerge from their predecessors: classical theories and theories formulated during the interwar period marked by fascism, the Great Depression, and the outbreak of World War II? How were the theories of the 1950s and 1960s transformed into the theories that prevail today? What ideas of classical, interwar, and post-war theories are still important and recognizable today, which ones were dropped, and which ones gradually mutated into something new? Our history of theory will be clearer and more coherent in the earlier part of the story because classical theories have stood the test of time, while it is hard to judge which mid-twentieth century and contemporary theories will survive.

Classical Theory

Classical theory was born during the age of empire, from the middle of the nineteenth century to the beginning of World War I (1914). Its major focus was the emergence of capitalist modernity. Karl Marx and Friedrich Engels, Émile Durkheim, Max Weber, and Georg Simmel are the classical theorists whose work continues to be read and debated today.

Classical theory reflected European global dominance as well as capitalism (Hobsbawm 1987). In so far as capitalism was challenged, it was challenged by socialist movements emerging from European cultures and societies. There was, as yet, little challenge to capitalism and colonialism on a global scale. Of course, there were local insurgencies and acts of resistance, as well as growing nationalist movements (Anderson 1983), but these movements were only beginning to be theorized systematically and in global terms by anti-colonial intellectuals such as José Marti, the Cuban writer who opposed both Spanish colonialism and US imperial domination at the end of the nineteenth century.

After the classical period, the project of theory became more difficult, and more difficult to write about. Theorists no longer had the easy task of charting the traditional-modern divide but the more difficult one of identifying and explaining variation within the modern, including both changes over time and differences among modern societies. Part of what we mean by 'postmodern' is the discovery that there are many different ways for a culture or society to be modern.

The Interwar Period

In the years between World War I and World War II, sociological theorists were thinking about new media (film and radio), the emergence of fascism, and economic upheavals, especially the stock market crash of 1929 and the Great Depression. Marxists were disappointed by the failure of socialist revolution to spread beyond Russia and the dominance of capitalist culture even in a period when capitalist economies seemed shaky or failing. Many Marxist and critical theorists in this period were concerned with the convergence of technology, politics, and economics. They believed that society was becoming increasingly controlled in new ways by capitalist ruling classes and their allies in anti-democratic mass movements such as Nazism and Fascism. These new forms of control relied on 'the culture industry,' media that diffused commercial popular culture to create passivity, foster false needs, and appeal to irrational unconscious impulses of fear, rage, repressed sexuality, and the desire to surrender to 'strong leaders' (Adorno 2001; Benjamin 1968; Buck-Morss 1989; Gramsci 1971; Jay 1996; Lowenthal 1984).

It is noteworthy that two leading theorists of the period, Antonio Gramsci and Walter Benjamin, died as the result of Fascist repression and Nazi genocide (Gramsci after prolonged incarceration in Fascist Italy, Benjamin by his own hand when he was detained during flight from the Nazis). Neither the classical theorists that preceded them nor the post-war theorists faced these conditions.

In the United States in the interwar years, the Chicago School turned toward a kind of miniaturism, focusing its gaze on the neighborhood and individual level. Chicago School sociologists certainly responded to global and national processes, such as immigration, the acculturation of immigrants, urbanization, city growth, and the expansion of organized crime, but they observed these macro-processes at a micro-level of neighborhoods and individual life narratives of immigrants and petty criminals. Many of them were strongly influenced by the work of Georg Simmel ([1950] 1978), but they tended to read Simmel as a micro-sociologist who contributed to the study of group processes and interactions rather than as a macro-theorist interested in the money economy. This pattern is typical in the history of theories; the legacy of great theorists of the past is redefined to emphasize the portion of their work that resonates with contemporary intellectual fashions and themes. Other parts of the legacy are left out of the conversation.

After World War II: From Structural-Functional Dominance to the Triad of Theories

In the post-World War II period, after the turmoil of two world wars and the Great Depression, the global situation was very different from that of the age of empire. The world was bipolar, and 'real socialism'—actually existing Communist states as opposed to ideal socialism—competed with capitalism for the allegiance of the third world and the non-aligned nations newly formed from colonial empires. Racism appeared to be defeated forever, with the unconditional surrender of Nazi Germany and, within a generation, the victories of the civil-rights movement in the United States. Forged in the class alliance that underpinned Allied victory in World War II, embedded liberalism (popularly referred to as the welfare state) was a successful route into a long economic boom. New media, progressing from radio and film to television and gigantic early computers, reshaped society's representations of itself. New nations emerged from the colonial empires, some in a peaceful process and some in the turmoil of insurgency and guerrilla war. Either way, colonialism seemed to be a structure of the past.

These changes were reflected in sociological theory, in a hopeful spirit following the defeat of Fascism and Nazism. The 1950s were characterized by structural-functionalism—Kingsley Davis (1959), a prominent sociologist, even argued that all sociologists are functionalists. In retrospect, it is remark-able—even bizarre—that following the deaths of tens of millions of people in two world wars, theorists constructed views of society that emphasized shared values and stable, coherent institutions.

Talcott Parsons ([1937] 1961, [1951] 1968) was one of the leading structural-functionalist theorists and was influenced not only by the work of Émile Durkheim but also by Weber's concept of action and by systems theory, a popular theme in the fields of biology and engineering of the period. He looked at society as a system (the social system), one of three systems govern-ing human life, the other two being the personality system (the individual) and the cultural system. The cultural system is a structure of values, norms, and ideas, with no will or direction of its own—a social force without actors, agency, or a subject. The social system and the self, on the other hand, are systems capable of action, of purposive, meaningful behavior, although, of course, action does not always result in the intended outcomes. Within the social system, only some elements are actually capable of action, notably the state, which directs and leads the whole society. At mid-range and micro-levels, organizations, social movements, administrative agencies, and management or executive offices are capable of action.

Note that Parsons' view of society was not identical to Durkheim's, although other functionalists claimed to be influenced directly by Durkheim's perspec-tive on society. Durkheim did not believe that action was a useful concept in sociology, and Parsons' use of the term is based on Weber's view that action is meaningful and worth studying. Durkheim believed that it is the task of sociologists to study the social patterns that are the outcomes of human behaviors shaped by social forces, patterns that emerge regardless of the will, consciousness, motivations, and purpose of individuals. Parsons and the structural-functionalists stressed Durkheim's *functionalism* and argued that

Durkheim had looked at society as a coherent system. We will see later in the book that Goffman and many contemporary theorists use Durkheim's ideas about *normative regulation* but do not read Durkheim from the functionalist perspective of the 1950s and consequently have little to say directly about institutions, functions, or society as a structure. Durkheim in 2009 is different from Durkheim in 1958.

The search for social patterns led theory to close linkages with new methods of multivariate analysis. Functionalism was connected to positivist, quantitative methods in the search for persistent patterns, reaffirming the link Durkheim had forged at the beginning of the twentieth century between sociological perspectives and statistical methods in his masterpiece, *Suicide.*

In the post-war period, structural-functional theories were not only paired with the growing area of multivariate statistics but also with psychoanalytic theories. Psychoanalysis became the psychological paradigm that explained behavior at the level of the individual (Parsons' self system), focusing on how individuals were socialized to assume social roles and how different cultures produced different characteristic types of personalities. The work of Sigmund Freud was popularized in the United States and modified to fit with functionalist views of the self, the family, and the socialization process. Dr. Freud would have been shocked at the taming and domestication of his controversial view of humanity! His work emphasized the pain and loss caused by the renunciation and repression of instinctual drives, and he was certainly not a fan of adjustment (Jacoby 1986).

By the 1960s, structural-functionalism had been reduced to one of three contending paradigms, competing with a revival of conflict theories (mostly derived from Marx and Weber) and symbolic interactionist theory (influenced by Simmel, the Chicago School, and the social-behaviorist work of Cooley and Mead). These developments reflected and signaled impending changes in society. By the later 1950s, North American culture was loosening up. The Korean War and McCarthyite witch-hunts against Communists were over, reading Marxist theory was no longer subversive, the civil-rights movement was gaining legitimacy and struggling for reforms, educators and journalists felt freer to voice critical views of American institutions, and rock and roll and the Beat Generation transformed North American culture. Graduate students poured into universities with new ideas about sex and sociological theory. They avidly read C. Wright Mills ([1954] 1963, [1959] 2000) as a conflict theorist and then retrieved Marxist thought from dusty library shelves and boxes in the attic. Inspired by themes in Beat Generation writing and jazz, they celebrated rebellion against conformity and explored the subcultures of drug users, musicians, hipsters, and juvenile delinquents (Becker 1963; Goodman 1962).

Symbolic interactionist theorists questioned the labeling of deviants (Lindesmith and Strauss 1956; Strauss 1959) and explored the worlds of 'outsiders'—the title of Howard Becker's influential book about jazz musicians and marijuana users (1963). For a few years, it seemed possible to identify a stable triad of sociological theories—persisting structural-functional approaches, conflict theory, and symbolic interactionism.

Both external and internal forces were at work in the shift from structural-functional dominance to an identifiable triad of theories. The community of sociologists was influenced by external events and trends such as the civil-rights movement of the 1960s, the growth of a rebellious youth culture, and the emergence of new nations carved out peacefully or in guerrilla insurgencies throughout the former colonial empires in what were later termed the 'post-colonial' areas of the globe. Of these movements, the independence movement in Vietnam met the most resistance from the colonial power (France) and eventually precipitated the long and extremely bloody engagement of the United States that left over three million dead. As the movement against the war grew in the United States during the later 1960s, so did a more critical perspective on US institutions such as the media, the military-industrial complex, and universities as bureaucracies that supported war-related research.

Internally, large numbers of young scholars and graduate students questioned the premises and uses of structural-functionalism. In theory, structural-functional analysis could encompass institutional dysfunctions and even the collapse of systems that are completely dysfunctional and unstable. In actual use, however, it appeared to offer little beyond apologetics for the American way of life and gave insufficient attention to racial inequalities, gender hierarchy, heterosexism, and conformity in cultural and political spheres. Davis and Moore's market-based functionalist explanation of economic class inequalities (1945) seemed typical of the complacency engendered by functionalist theory; it explained differences in income and wealth in terms of the 'functional importance' of roles and individual willingness to improve one's own human capital.

The more politically radical students and young faculty devoted their attention to a revival of conflict theories, as they termed the legacy of Marxism and certain elements of Weberian theory. They connected struggles against US racism with opposition to the war in Vietnam, and many of them linked both of these issues to underlying capitalist domination. Throughout North America and western Europe a critical conflict perspective began to be applied to the analysis of media (Debord [1967] 1995).

Sociologists who focused on cultural issues as well as on the marginalization and labeling of subcultures and those termed 'deviants,' gravitated toward the expansion of symbolic interactionism into a radical critique of the normative order, institutional labeling, and the manufacture of deviance by powerful cultural, political, economic, professional, and organizational interests.

After the Sixties: The Transition From the Triad of Theories to Contemporary Theory

But even this moment of three contending paradigms was short lived and unstable. From a clear contrast between a structural-functional mainstream and countercurrents of conflict theory and symbolic interactionism, the flow of concepts swirled into ever more confusing eddies and whirlpools.

Turbulent external circumstances challenged theoretical paradigms. Socialist insurgencies gained ground in the third world, and new types of social movements, such as anti-racist movements, environmental movements, the women's movement, and the gay-rights movement appeared within the developed societies. The hope sparked by the formation of new nations was dimmed by the emergence of new forms of global inequality and by an economic imperialism without colonial occupation, as well as by the failures of nationalist movements to create flourishing economies and democratic states once they were in power.

DISSENSION AMONG CONFLICT THEORISTS

Conflict theory of the later 1960s had relied heavily on a rereading of Marxist and Weberian social theory. These perspectives continued to inform theoretical work on the media (Bagdikian 1983; Debord [1967] 1995; Ewen and Ewen 1982; Gitlin 1983, 2003; Hertsgaard 1989), urban development (Davis 1992; Mollenkopf 1983), global cultural processes (Taussig 1985; Wolf 1999), criminology (Quinney 1974), and many other areas of sociology. But in the arena of political action, the role of Marxist and Marxist-influenced intellectuals in radical movements in the United States was increasingly challenged by other movement activists who gave priority to women's liberation from gender inequality or to the struggles of people of color for equality. Paralleling this challenge within radical movements, in the academy and intellectual circles, feminist and anti-racist theorists challenged not only the status quo ante of functionalist dominance but also the way conflict theory rested on Marxist and Weberian analyses of class and power. As long as gender and racial-ethnic stratification were given a low priority in the analysis of social conflict (or left out altogether), conflict theory was not only incomplete but actually complicit in the reproduction of inequality in society. Under the impact of these challenges, conflict theory split into at least three strands—Marxist theories, feminist theories, and theories of racial dominance and white supremacy. Everyone acknowledged that these bases of dominance are intertwined, but theorists in each strand assigned different priorities in the analysis, with different implications for collective action. As an observer of this contention noted, Marxism and feminism did not have a happy marriage (Hartmann 1979); and the three main divisions of conflict theory did not form a happy *ménage à trois*. Furthermore, even within each of the three main groupings of conflict theory (Marxism, feminism, and anti-racist theories), additional splits took place. For example, feminist theories split into liberal feminism, radical feminism, and multi-racial feminism.

The rise of the 'new social movements' (as both theorists and activists called them) led to further fragmentation in the increasingly divided community of theorists. The new social movements formed a plethora of groups and networks, single-issue campaigns, scattered mobilizations, and instances of collective action; they addressed a wide variety of issues such as gay rights, anti-nuclear weapons activism, environmental problems, and the need for affordable housing. They were particularly active in Europe where they seemed to presage a new era of intense and progressive mobilization. Both in North America and Europe, these movements appeared to be increasingly detached from any fixed demographic base. Although—or perhaps precisely because—many of their supporters were young, educated, white, and of middle-class background, the movements made no claims to represent any specific social category or to be a vanguard for an identifiable historical subject, as Marxist movements had claimed to represent the proletariat or as feminist and anti-racist movements were associated with women and people of color as their prime constituencies. Although sociological theories that focused on the new social movements were defined as conflict theories, they were far more diffuse and fluid in their conceptualizations of society than previous conflict theories.

The theoretical analysis of movement activity was further complicated by the fact that, in the United States, movements on the left were balanced and even outweighed in political impact by countermovements on the right, which formed to oppose the liberalization of abortion and to take conservative stands on other social issues. In Europe, anti-immigrant political movements and parties emerged. Conflict perspectives in theory had to take into account the rightward tilt of conflict in practice, a direction that was generally not congenial to theorists. This situation forced them to move away from schemas that defined conflict in terms of a (bad) establishment or power structure versus (good) opposition movements. They moved toward more complicated conceptualizations of conflicts as ongoing, open-ended, shifting contention that takes place in political and cultural fields of multiple collective actors, including the state. These new theories were most powerfully and clearly formulated by Pierre Bourdieu, as we will see in Part II.

CHANGE IN THE INTELLECTUAL CLIMATE

Change in the intellectual climate also transformed sociological theory. European social thought was moving in new directions that eventually impacted sociological theory. French philosophy underwent a rupture, a break with Marxist thought. A new generation of theorists coming of age in the later 1960s and 1970s tried to throw off the powerful influence of Jean-Paul Sartre and his fusion of existentialism with Marxism. They remained attracted to his commitment to the marginalized and oppressed, but they sought to distance themselves even further than had Sartre from the Communist Party of France and the socialist states of the Soviet bloc. A few claimed to be Maoists but eventually found that the model of the Chinese revolution, which occurred in an agrarian and partially feudal society, was difficult to transfer to France.

The drift away from orthodox Marxism and Sartre's Marxist existentialism was associated at first with the rise of structuralism, a discourse that permeated anthropology and new Marxist theories in the later 1960s and 1970s (Althusser 1971a, 1971b). These theories emphasized highly rigid structures in discourse, in kinship systems, in the ideological and coercive apparatuses of the dominant bourgeois state, and in almost every other area of human activity. These structures, according to structuralists, existed regardless of individual purpose or agency; they formed rigid patterns, similar to the grammars of languages. Structuralist theories were grandchildren of that part of Durkheim's legacy that emphasized social patterns without purposive individual actors, as well as of twentieth-century linguistic analysis. Eventually, many French intellectuals broke with structural theories and began to explore new critical perspectives on discourse and thought.

This rupture was most strongly associated with two thinkers, Michel Foucault and Jacques Derrida. We will examine the work of Foucault in more detail in the next part of the book, so here we will just briefly mention the way in which Derrida's work was received by social theorists. Derrida encouraged his readers and audiences to consider how texts are constructed and thereby to question underlying assumptions about the bedrock of Western thought. Questioning had to center, above all, on the initial act that makes possible logical thought and mental and verbal creation—the establishment of *difference*. How do we think about difference, and which differences make a difference? A second bedrock assumption he questioned was *presence* and, more concretely, the ways in which certain discourses are favored or privileged over others. He believed that, despite the association of elites with writing and literacy, Western thought consistently favored speech and dialogue because they are validated by the presence of the speaker while writing remains dead and defenseless. This argument of Derrida's was a conversation with the ghost of Socrates, who had favored dialogue over writing.

Derrida's writing was difficult, heavily larded with French puns, and densely linked to the writing of Plato, Nietzsche, Freud, Marx, and other philosophers. Derrida's challenges to bedrock assumptions of Western philosophy became popularized (among intellectual fashion setters) as *deconstruction*. Derrida exposed how difference is established in language and is then taken for granted and perpetuated and how certain types of texts and language acts are privileged over others.

As they incorporated deconstruction into their thought, sociologists began to examine critically how societal inequalities are replicated, reproduced, and perhaps even initially established in discourses or texts, such as laws and media representations. Interest in Derrida's deconstruction of texts converged with more down-to-earth ideas in symbolic interactionism, such as labeling theory. Labeling theorists had argued that authority figures constantly create narratives that usually are also preserved as written texts in files and dossiers in which those with power label and stigmatize those they wish to define as deviants. The new current of deconstruction tilted social theory in the direction of theories of culture focused on *texts and representations* rather than on the observation of *behavior* or the analysis of *structures* of power and exchange.

The impact of deconstruction in North America reveals the dialectic of change in theory. On the one hand, deconstruction became a new dominant intellectual paradigm that made existing theories such as structural Marxism and structural-functionalism seem tired, outdated, and rigid. Graduate students and young scholars showed their enthusiasm for the new ideas and their disdain for the old ones. Yet deconstruction caught on, in part, not because it was a radical break with existing perspectives but because it aligned well with several of them—with labeling theory, micro-conflict theories, feminist thought, and themes in the popular and accessible work of Erving Goffman.

The 1960s theoretical triad turned out to be unstable, and, although it was enshrined in many textbooks, by the 1980s it had become a poor guide to theory as an ongoing activity. The three neat little boxes became interconnected sacs, with ideas sloshing around in several of them at once and spilling out from a lot of leaks.

TOWARD CONTEMPORARY THEORIES

The last two decades of the twentieth century saw a new round of dramatic changes in the global political economy and in forms of representation, discourse, media, knowledge, and data. At the level of the global political economy, neoliberal policies meant accelerated movement of capital among countries, deregulation of markets, privatization of social services, and increased transnational migration. These changes were often linked to or even summarized by the term 'globalization.'

Populations burgeoned and urbanized. More than half the planet's population is urban. Many people live in new mega-cities, and often in slums. The Internet, computers, and telecommunications created a new spatial fabric for the planet, and not only at an elite level. Media reached almost everyone on the planet and represented social reality as a 'society of the spectacle,' to borrow Guy Debord's phrase. New large-scale problems emerged, such as the HIV/AIDS epidemic and the imbalance of aging populations in the developed world and growing, young populations in the developing world who face increasing poverty. With these demographic and economic changes came extreme pressures on the natural environment and planetary resources, arising from both overpopulation and overconsumption. At the same time, global warming began to transform entire regions and threatened to set in motion desperate migrations.

Geopolitically, the globe lost its bipolar power structure with the collapse of the Soviet Union and the market transition of the Chinese economy. The United States was the hegemonic military power, though losing ground in economic dominance. As it lost manufacturing strength, the debt burden of its government, businesses, and individuals soared. This situation, coupled with the impact of neoliberal economics, placed social movements in a more complicated position than before. They had lost the bargaining power they enjoyed in the bipolar system, and Soviet-style socialism no longer represented a viable alternative to capitalism. Identity politics, ethnic movements, and religious fundamentalism and integralism (the ideology that state, society, and religious faith must be an integrated whole) competed with alternative-globalization movements as challengers to the market system. Shifts in the global system were connected to an increasing number of cross-border issues including epidemics, terrorism, illegal immigration, and organized crime.

As we look at the emergence of new types of theory in the last decades of the twentieth century, we will see several large clusters of concepts forming to encompass new social phenomena. In North America, in the internal dynamics of changing theories, these new clusters grew out of a fusion of conflict theories and symbolic interactionism (and other micro-theories), resulting in an emphasis on the social construction and mobilization of difference.

A key topic theorists investigated was contention over representation and the framing of issues. For example, theorists were intrigued by the way media contributed to the identification of drugs as a major social, moral, medical, and legal problem; put this problem on the agenda for public discussion; and chose specific images to portray users and sellers of drugs (often images of ethnic minorities in numbers disproportionate to their actual involvement). The new social constructionist perspectives produced a rash of quotation marks around words and phrases such as 'drug problem' to show that these problems were the products of discourses and framing practices and did not necessarily exist in reality (or in 'reality'—because, in postmodern discourse, reality itself was seen as a construct). Increasing numbers of social-problem textbooks no longer discussed *problems* but rather *the construction* of social problems by states, media, and organizations that have a vested interest in drawing attention to the situation in question.

The work of Durkheim, which had been a foundation for structural-functional theories, was reread and reinterpreted (primarily by Erving Goffman) to emphasize normative regulation through frames (or discourses) and interactions. A new generation of theorists came to see normative regulation as an interactive, ongoing, ever-changing, language-based micro-process. Normative regulation remained the core Durkheimian concept, but it was now understood quite differently than in the period of structural-functionalism.

In North America, the fusion of conflict theories with symbolic interactionist and micro-theories in sociology and, in Europe, the converging growth of new theories of discourse, difference, and deconstruction were forces internal to theoretical communities that contributed to new themes in sociological theory. This internal evolution (change taking place within the communities of theorists) was also influenced by external forces, the changes in the larger social environment that we listed above, such as new types of social movements, the development of post-colonial societies, the emergence of neoliberalism, and transnational flows of people, capital, and ideas.

Our discussion has four sections. We begin with a brief survey of trends in the intellectual climate linked to changes in sociology as a field of inquiry. Many of these trends in social thought are linked to external social changes as well as changes in intellectual fashions and themes. In the second section, we identify five major new directions in sociological theory. In the third section, we argue that these five major directions could be interpreted as forming one overarching paradigm. We call it 'conflict constructionism' and suggest that it overlaps the five major directions and may be a useful way of thinking about all of them at the same time. Conflict constructionism can trace its ancestry to symbolic interactionism, Erving Goffman's dramaturgical model and other micro-theories, conflict theories, Marxism, feminism, anti-racist and post-colonial theories, sociological perspectives on the state and politics, and Durkheim's radical sociological premises. Foucault's work made major contributions to it, and it is incorporated into many aspects of the writing of Bourdieu and Hall. It is a vigorous and fertile hybrid.

But we have to be very careful not to overestimate the unity and dominance of these trends. The field remains without a stable, clearly identifiable 'dominant paradigm' (to use Kuhn's terminology). Ideas swirl together but do not cohere into a stable framework. A major division can be discerned between postmodernist and Marxist-influenced theories, although both use ideas of conflict constructionism. This postmodernist versus Marxist division is based on disagreements about the act of theorizing, and we will discuss it toward the end of the chapter.

We will conclude the chapter with a brief discussion of the uneven impact of contemporary theories on sociology (a topic to which we return in the conclusion). There are forces at work in the field that impede or soften the impact: older paradigms persist and are being elaborated and revitalized; in some subfields of sociology, theories are altogether resisted, often because they interfere with partnerships between researchers in the discipline and policy makers in related areas such as public health and criminal justice; and, for some sociologists, the sophistication of quantitative analysis substitutes for the construction of theory as a way of understanding the world.

THE CHANGING INTELLECTUAL CLIMATE

We begin our discussion with an overview of trends in social thought and the organization of sociology as a field of inquiry. These trends accompanied, signaled, and perhaps even caused the growth of contemporary theories. Shifts in the intellectual climate and the community of social theorists provided a context for new types of theories. Many of these changes were, in turn, linked to changes in external circumstances (neoliberalism, new functions for states, globalization, proliferation of movements, and so on), conditions that shaped the thinking of communities of scholars, educators, and intellectuals.

In the next section, we will suggest that these changes led to five major new directions in sociological theories.

The Blurring of Theoretical Boundaries

The 1960s triad of sociological theory proved unstable. The impact of social change throughout the world in the last three decades of the twentieth century crushed the three little theory boxes into sloppy, leaky, plastic bags. Much of the contents of the bags sloshed together, forming theories of social construction within conflict frameworks. For those who don't like this metaphor, perhaps the Japanese imagery of wood and water is more attractive: theories stopped being wood (fixed, solid, structured, and distinct from each other) and slipped into the fluid, floating world of water. Few scholars any longer explicitly defined themselves as affiliated with any one of the triad. It became harder for instructors to write multiple-choice exams with mutually exclusive answers.

Fragmentation and Proliferation of Conflict Theories

Conflict theories proliferated. Some of them were explicitly Marxist; others included many variants of feminism and theories of racial dominance, soon to be joined by queer theory and, eventually, by generic conflict theories not linked to any single demographic or cultural base of contestation but simply affirming that conflict is a given in all social contexts. Many of them drew a basic framework from Marxism, namely the premise that there is no such thing as society, no entity with a coherent value system and institutions that function in general. There are only contending groups with fundamentally different interests, uneasily held together by institutions that function better for some than for others. This theoretical proliferation reflected external changes: first, challenges from feminist and ethnic movements to the dominance of Marxist-inspired movements and statements; then, conflicts within and among these challenging movements as well; next, the emergence of new social movements with multiple bases of contention, as well as countermovements on the right end of the political spectrum; and, finally, the presence of a proliferating number of contentious movements

and bases of identity, as varied as Al-Qaeda and global gay-rights mobilizations (Meyer, Whittier, and Robnett 2002).

New and Revived Themes in Marxist Thought

The revival and revisiting of Marxist theory focused on the analysis of culture
and drew on the work of Antonio Gramsci (1971), especially his concept of
hegemony, and that of Walter Benjamin (1968) and other Frankfurt School
theorists. Accompanying their attention to culture, Marxists re-examined
the state. They leaned increasingly to the analysis of *fields* of power and
political action in place of the metaphor of a state *apparatus* as a rigid structure of ideology and coercion. Marxism had to encompass the collapse of
the Soviet-style socialist systems, the rise of neoliberalism, the shrinkage of
the state in the areas of economic regulation and social services, and the
proliferation and growth of the media.

Deconstruction and Social Construction

French deconstructive philosophy and the work of Michel Foucault added a
new twist, shifting the focus from what had traditionally been termed 'material
conditions' and 'observable behaviors' to discourses and practices of control and
marginalization. Discourses express the axioms or rules of thought of particular historical periods. The discourses appear to be composed of 'just words,'
but they are linked to intensely physical and material practices in regimes of
punishment, incarceration, surveillance, and social control exercised over the
body. Ultimately, these practices are just as material as the organization of a factory or the contents of a stock portfolio (the material referents of many Marxist
theories). The material worlds of the Marxists and Foucault are indeed more
closely related than appears to be the case at a superficial level. For example,
class inequality can be understood in terms of the question of whose *bodies*
are forced to be *compliant* to whose orders. We will examine these ideas in our
discussion of Foucault in Part II. These perspectives were 'recombined' with
the fragments of Marxism left in most conflict theories and bits of symbolic
interactionism and other micro-theories to create the new types of social constructionist theories that became the leading paradigms in the fields of gender/
sexuality and critical race theory. The work of feminist scholars, and especially
black feminists (Collins 2000; Davis [1984] 1990; hooks 1990; King 1988) fused
with theories proposed by Foucault (Butler 1990, 1993, 2004).

Theorizing Representation, Images, and the New Media

Social constructionist theory was also propelled by the media explosion. Representation became a major part of reality itself. The analysis of representations—images, discourses, symbolic violence, encoding and decoding—formed a growing part of sociological theory, as we will discuss in chapters on Erving Goffman, Pierre Bourdieu, and Stuart Hall in Part II.

Multiculturalism and Globalization in Theory

Increasing attention in sociology was given to cultural conflict, not so much as a melodramatic clash of civilizations between Islam and the West, but in the many forms of tension within multicultural societies formed by the carving up of colonial empires, immigration, domestic migration, and cultural or religious identity movements that sharpen divisions. Theories of culture were revised, adjusted to global flows, and associated with social constructionist theory and theories of representation. A first step in this process was the debunking of Eurocentric and evolutionary models of culture. A major influence from beyond the discipline of sociology was Edward Said's work *Orientalism*, which deconstructed the European representation of the Middle East as exotic and mysterious, an ideology associated with political domination and colonial rule. Increasing attention was given to transculturation (flow from colonized and indigenous culture into the apparently dominant European-based culture), hybridity, creole cultures, and trans-border processes (Appadurai 1993; Garcia-Canclini 2003; Gilroy 1993; Hannerz 1992). We will return to these topics in the chapter on Stuart Hall in Part II.

Agency, Markets, Probability, and Statistical Reasoning

Neoliberal economics accompanied the growth of rational choice theories that focused on individual behaviors under market conditions. Other sociological theorists disagreed with rational choice theorists but were influenced by them as well. They became more open to the concept of 'agency'—purposive human action—and moved away from some of the deterministic assumptions built into structural theories (both structural-functionalism and structuralist Marxism). However, most sociological theorists criticized two assumptions in rational choice theories. One criticism of rational choice theory was that 'rational' was too often used to mean 'economically driven' or 'profit maximizing.'

The other criticism focused on the conflation of rational choice with personal responsibility, increasingly a code word in neoliberal discourse for eliminating state-provided social services and support systems.

Although agency and the focus on market choices appeared to be a challenge to structural determinism, the use of these concepts unintentionally welcomed in a different form of deterministic reasoning—statistical determinism. Realizing that market choices and the illusion of agency have to be understood in probabilistic terms took sociological theory back to a profound insight of Durkheim's that had been neglected during the decades when Durkheim was read as a structuralist. This insight was that social patterns—social facts as Durkheim called them—are statistical and probabilistic rather than fully determined phenomena. For example, in *Suicide* Durkheim states that the higher suicide rate of Protestants compared to Catholics and Jews is a social fact, yet suicide is a rare occurrence for all social groups. The sociologist must focus on these statistically defined social facts and the associated probabilistic patterns while remaining indifferent to individual-level motivations and the individual's illusion of free choice and agency. As in casino gambling, individuals make choices and any single event is unpredictable, but, overall, the pattern is predictable (the house wins). Durkheim's statistical model of social processes was formulated at the same time as Freud's argument that human action is not freely chosen but shaped by unconscious forces; and these perspectives can be seen as converging views that human life has a non-rational but scientifically comprehensible basis. Durkheim's pioneering use of statistical reasoning is an alternative to both agency and structure and, at the same time, a way of grasping the outcome of their dialectical relationship. Durkheim's statistical analysis also coincided with the development and application of statistical techniques in biology and with the origins of quantum physics, the probabilistic model of subatomic phenomena initiated by the discovery in 1899 that the decay of radioactive atoms follows a law of probability (Ford 2005).

Changing Boundaries of the Discipline

Sociological theorists have become more relaxed about disciplinary boundaries and feel free to use ideas and whole theoretical frameworks from areas such as cultural studies, anthropology, philosophy, cultural geography, and so on. Departments of women's studies, gender studies, transnational studies, and ethnic studies emerged, somewhat in competition with sociology for students and university resources, and became venues for teaching the new types of theory. Meanwhile, sociologists have also increasingly partnered with colleagues in practical, applied fields and policy-oriented areas, such as public health and criminal justice, and these partnerships have tended to dampen or even eliminate the presence of critical perspectives. Pressures from outside academia, for example, the need to cope with problems such as the AIDS epidemic, the growth in gang activity, and the transnational organization of crime precipitate practical partnerships while reducing interest in theorizing. The involvement of sociology and other social and behavioral science disciplines in states' social control and penal functions also diminishes commitment to critical theories (Wacquant 2008a).

Attention to the Postmodern

A recurrent theme in contemporary social thought is the concept of the postmodern (Best and Kellner 1991; Jameson 1991). Are we experiencing extreme capitalism or postmodernism? The global social transformation of the late twentieth century can be interpreted as an extension of potentials that were present in modernity from the very start. It can be seen as an extreme development of the trends spotted by classical theorists: accelerating pace of change, technological innovation, rationalistic calculation, commodification, globalization, and a collapse of all fixed, ascribed, and stable identities. On the other hand, this transformation can also be interpreted as a radically new departure—what some theorists choose to call 'postmodern.' Although terms such as postmodernism and postmodernity are often used interchangeably, a brief clarification should be given. Postmodernity refers to a historical break from modernity ushering in new social and cultural changes. Use of this term suggests that society, social relationships, technology, and culture are different now than they were in most of the twentieth century. It refers to a definite era or period with characteristic types of societies. Postmodernism refers to new modes of thinking and expression that emphasize the breaks in knowledge and culture between modernism and what came after. Postmodernism requires a definition of modernism. Modernism includes the forms of knowledge, art, and culture that were characteristic of the period of the late nineteenth century to the 1970s, in Europe, North America, and, a bit less clearly, in Latin America. Modernism refers to ways of thinking, perceiving, feeling, and representing these feelings and perceptions; the term includes changes in philosophy, the social sciences, the arts, media, and culture generally. Modernism often implies an explicitly critical and innovative stand toward the prevailing culture, whereas postmodernism seems more ironic, as if its critical perspective could best be expressed by an exaggerated and playful embrace of the dominant forms. For example, in the visual arts, cubism and abstract expressionism (Jackson Pollock's paint squiggles) are usually said to be modernist, while conceptual art or Ed Paschke's TV-like, brilliantly colored, hyper-real images of people and faces are considered postmodern. James Joyce's and Marcel Proust's experiments with language and the treatment of time in writing ushered in modernism. Postmodernist writing blurs the line between fiction and non-fiction, literature and pop culture, the book and the blog. Post-structuralism is a theme in the larger postmodernist movement and refers to a mode of theorizing about society and culture. This term specifically draws attention to a shift from the emphasis on a fixed patterning of social relationships or cultural symbols (the focus of structuralist theorists) to new, more fluid ways of thinking about relationships among people, groups, and symbols. (See Best and Kellner 1991, for further discussion of these terms.)

FIVE NEW DIRECTIONS IN THEORIES

These trends in the intellectual climate form the basis of five major new directions in sociological theory. These changes involve not only new ideas and perspectives but also a critique and partial incorporation of older theories. Remember our statement that now theories are not firm, solid things sealed into distinct wooden boxes but more like liquids kept in plastic bags? By the later part of the twentieth century, a lot of these fluids started to slosh around, spill out of the sacs into which they had been placed, and dribble into other sacs. All that spilling and sloshing led to strands of theories being recombined with each other to form new theories—recombinant monsters that disrupted any apparent stability in theorizing.

One change is the ongoing *transformation of Marxism* in response to the collapse of the Soviet bloc, the difficulties encountered by left-wing movements, and the challenge of neoliberalism. This transformation made Marxism more open to social constructionism and concepts shared with micro-theories and symbolic interactionist thought, but it also embroiled Marxists in vigorous debates with postmodernists about the very foundations of social thought. The second shift is the new theorizing of *difference and identity, especially as these are related to dominance.* The third is a perspective on *deviance and social control* that is apparently new but in fact has deep ties to Durkheim's pioneering work on crime, punishment, and normative regulation. The fourth is the effort to encompass *the growing role of the media* and new forms of representation, enormously accelerated by new technologies of communication. The fifth is a *re-examination of the state* as a major force in constructing difference and shaping social processes; sociologists have always been interested in the state, but contemporary theory has linked new perspectives on social construction with the actions and policies of states in the neoliberal era.

1. Goodbye Lenin? Marxist Mutations

In the next pages, we will devote a considerable amount of space to the transformation of Marxist theory. Students in our classes often vote for Marxism as their favorite type of theory, so we need to consider carefully the paradoxes of Marxism at the start of the twenty-first century. On the one hand, the global economy is capitalist and dominated by the market, so Engels and Marx's analysis of capitalism seems astoundingly fresh and relevant. Yet their predictions about socialist revolution seem completely unfulfilled. Given the popularity of Marxist theory among sociology students, we need to explore what happened in and to this perspective and why the left appears so intellectually attractive but politically futile and irrelevant—offering a towering critique of capitalism but with no praxis of change to match.

Mutations in Marxist theory sprung up in the last decades of the twentieth century. These changes emerged for several reasons. Marxists had to contend with the failure of the Soviet system and the lagging energy of Marxist parties and social movements within the capitalist world. They also had to explain why, in a capitalist world, so little of the opposition to the status quo was Marxist, socialist, or based on the proletariat. Some Marxists turned to the analysis of culture, updating theories about culture, media, and consumer capitalism that had begun in the work of Antonio Gramsci, Walter Benjamin, and the Frankfurt School. Others sought to find the Marxist project of liberation in movements and struggles far removed from historical Marxist parties, Communist states, and even Marxist theories. In the boxed insert, we provide more detail on the political changes that Marxist theorists had to confront as they sought to refresh Marxism.

POLITICAL JOLTS TO MARXIST THEORY

The problems of 'real socialism'

In recent decades, Marxists have had to contend with unpleasant facts about the socialist states led by Communist parties—the countries of 'really existing socialism'—most notably the Soviet Union, but also China, Cuba, North Korea, and states in eastern Europe. For a host of reasons, these states did not turn out to be viable models of an alternative to capitalism. Marxists have to deal with the fact that many of them were highly politically repressive, that the economies had many flaws, and that, after several decades of stagnation, the Soviet Union collapsed along with the states in its eastern European bloc while China became a sort of state capitalist society, with an authoritarian political system led by a Communist party that fosters and presides over an increasingly inegalitarian capitalist economy. The combination of repression, stagnation, collapse, and shift to capitalist development has made it more difficult for Marxists to argue that socialism represents an advance over capitalism.

In addition to this fairly concrete issue, the problems of existing socialist states underlined that Marxism as theory probably focused too much on the power of a dominant economic class, which became a ruling class through its control of the state. The trajectory of these socialist states showed that, even when the bourgeoisie was removed from both state power and economic dominance, unequal power relations persisted throughout the society. Following socialist revolutions, educational opportunities and medical services became available to large populations who were previously excluded. Millions of people enjoyed intergenerational mobility primarily through free education that enabled children of poor farmers and manual laborers to enter professions and managerial positions. Living standards improved dramatically for poor people. Yet many lines of difference continued to be lines of dominance, disparity, and marginalization—among them were gender, ethnicity, sexual orientation, hierarchy in the workplace, residence in rural or remote regions, and the kinds of ideas people voiced. Inequality, power, and also resistance to power were diffused throughout society, and this condition was as prevalent in socialist societies as capitalist societies. Socialism did not solve the problem of inequalities.

The problems of Marxist parties and movements

Furthermore, theorists were highly dissatisfied with the ideologies proffered by Marxist-inspired parties and social movements. They believed that the parties of the left not only were making profound strategic mistakes but were out of touch with the many new currents and identities in society. Both in the East, where they ruled, and in western Europe, where they contended for a role in government, the

large parties were hierarchical, patriarchal and paternalistic, and culturally retrograde, in the view of radical young theorists of the latter part of
the twentieth century. When parties of the left did succeed in forming
governments in democratic Western states, they were forced to compro-
mise with political forces that remained committed to capitalism; or like
Salvador Allende and the Chilean socialists they ended up displaced,
tortured, and murdered when a fragile democracy fell to a military coup
on September 11, 1973 ('the other 9/11'). Meanwhile smaller parties and
groups of the left seemed to be deteriorating into sectarian irrelevance.
Many of the smaller, self-styled vanguard parties were internally rigid
and hierarchical and out of touch with exciting new cultural currents, so
they were becoming increasing unattractive to young people across the
globe in the last decades of the twentieth century.

In the 1970s and 1980s, the exciting action was increasingly in
the new social movements, movements of women, gays, ethnic minorities, environmentalists, and peace activists. These movements
seemed far more lively, innovative, egalitarian, anti-hierarchical, and
culturally creative than the parties of the old and new left. Perhaps
these movements were also less threatening on the issue of economic
redistribution than the old and new left were; and the issues they
articulated had more resonance for the affluent citizens of the West.

A consequence of the problems of 'real socialist' states and smaller
Marxist movements and parties was the decoupling of the thought of
Marx and Engels (transformed into Marxism as theory) from Lenin's
ideas about revolution and the vanguard party. It appeared that the
former had a future as a critique of global capitalism, but the question
of practice was put on a backburner and, at least for the time being, not
answered in Leninist terms.

All of these failures of the left—failures to adapt Marxist paradigms to the
emerging situation—turned theorists away from traditional Marxist formulations. It seemed more promising to look at cultural struggles, local conflicts, and
ways in which left-wing ideas were put into action in anti-racist mobilizations,
local activism, alternative globalization movements, and a galaxy of ongoing,
open-ended, heterogeneous cultural contentions—instead of continuing to
theorize the final victory of a firmly structured proletarian party that claimed
to represent a universal subject.

One response to this crisis of states, parties, and movements was to return
Marxist theory to a focus on culture. To understand the contemporary shifts
in Marxist theory toward theories of culture—the emergence of a whole field

called cultural studies—let's go back to an earlier historical moment when Marxist theory had to change to encompass political changes. In the period between World War I and World War II, Marxists were disappointed to find that most of the economic conditions for a socialist revolution existed but that this revolution did not happen in a form strong enough to topple any bourgeois states except the retrograde Russian tsarist one. In hindsight, one could argue that they were mistaken about the economic preconditions for revolution, but, at the time, and in the minds of many Marxist theorists even today, the problem was that consciousness did not match the economic conditions—in short, proletarians and petty bourgeois should have had a revolutionary consciousness but did not. Marxists concluded that cultural processes—rooted in the media and the production of ideas—interfered with socialist consciousness, that bourgeois culture blocked out socialist consciousness and colonized people's minds. This line of analysis produced very sophisticated perspectives on the bourgeois production of culture, especially in the theories of Antonio Gramsci, Walter Benjamin, and the Frankfurt Institute.

The puzzle has resurfaced: Why is it that the planet is dominated by advanced forms of neoliberal capitalism but people's consciousness is formed by individualism and consumerism, religious faiths, racial-ethnic loyalties, and just about everything except a commitment to socialism? To a Marxist, the situation seems absurd. Just about every major trouble, from the closing of automobile plants in the United States and Canada to the weather itself, can be traced to capitalism and the political forces associated with it. So why can't the masses see that, or if they do see it, why are they so quiet about it? Marxist theorists have once again been forced to look at the production of culture and especially the role of the media to explain this paradox.

Theorists who explicitly call themselves Marxists are joined by others who eschew this label but hold similar views of the media, globalization, neoliberalism, markets, and new forms of social inequality. Marxist theory suffered setbacks in recent decades, yet many of its ideas and themes are now widely shared among social theorists. It has 'seeped out of its container,' and its ideas and concepts are widely diffused in the analysis of social inequalities, globalization, media, restructuring of health-care systems, and many other areas, even if they are not always cleared labeled 'Marxist.'

2. Theorizing Difference and Identity

Another force for change in theory was attention to a cluster of emerging concepts focused on difference and identity and their association with

power, dominance, and inequality. Post-colonial cultures, massive immigration, and new social movements of many types helped to problematize
identity. It went from being a fairly stable, taken-for-granted characteristic
of individuals to an aspect of selves and groups that was highly contentious and unstable. In the fifties, theorists assumed that identities based on
race, class, gender, religion, sexual orientation, national origin, and so on
were ascribed—fixed characteristics of the self. By the end of the century,
it seemed as if all these categories, and often the terms themselves, were
contentious and fluid.

Difference (and hence identities based on differences) is constantly
constructed, deconstructed, and reconstructed in new ways. Even in an
institution as stodgy and official as the US census, 'race' is, on the one
hand, affirmed decade upon decade as a meaningful category of thought
and an identity worth recording, yet the specific categories for coding race
are redefined from one census to the next and intertwined in ever-changing
ways with ethnicity (Yanow 2003). In contrast, the French census is not
even permitted to ask these questions. Many theorists are now particularly
focused on these processes of definition and categorization of differences,
construction of identities, labeling and self-labeling, and the role of the
state in creating and perpetuating difference.

THE FOUNDATIONAL ROLE OF SYMBOLIC INTERACTIONIST THEORY AND THE DRAMATURGICAL MODEL

The groundwork for new theories of difference was laid in symbolic
interactionist theory, which included a strong component of questioning
prevailing categories and debunking the presumed biological basis of
human society and behavior. Closely aligned with symbolic interactionism was Erving Goffman's dramaturgical model and the conceptualization
of the self and its social roles as performances. These theoretical perspectives that emerged in the 1950s and the 1960s already destabilized the
concepts of a self that was relatively fixed and connected to crystallized
statuses (wife, husband, man, principal, steelworker, black, Catholic,
white, Democrat, and so on). The performed self was much more fluid
than the self based on ascribed statuses and stable roles. Furthermore, in
the view of the symbolic interactionists, other fixed positions such as 'drug
addict' and 'mental patient' turned out to be categorizations with only a
flimsy physiological base (Lindesmith and Strauss 1956). These identities
were created by labeling and constructed by ongoing expectations about
role performance.

DECONSTRUCTION AND THE INTEREST IN DIFFERENCE

In addition, new trends in philosophy and feminist theory also were internal forces, forces operating within the community of theory and social thought, that promoted attention to difference and supported more critical ways of thinking about the categories into which human beings put themselves and others. Derrida and deconstructionist philosophy made social theorists sensitive to the ways in which difference is established. Differences are not simple natural phenomena that we can take for granted; they are established in human thought and speech. Deconstruction became essential to sociology because it provided a way to understand cultural systems of meaning based on a never-ending play of differences, which are always relational and in flux. The philosophical attention to the establishment of difference is, in turn, connected to the sociological and social-psychological observation that individuals can present or highlight different identities in different situations as well as attempt to force others to assume a specific identity. These matters are always in contention, never settled or firm. It is essential for theorists to turn the analysis of construction and the creation of difference onto their own categories of thought, to be reflexive; otherwise, sociological concepts will inevitably merge with the notions of conventional thought portrayed in the media and found in official policy. Social theorists must be wary and critical of the categories of their research subjects as well as those of the conventional wisdom: All unexamined folk categories are potentially misleading (Wacquant 2002, [2004] 2008, 2008b).

NEW IDENTITIES: GLOBALIZATION, NEW TECHNOLOGIES, AND NEW SOCIAL MOVEMENTS

In addition to the forces within theory—symbolic interactionist thought, the role of Erving Goffman, feminist theory and especially the influence of Judith Butler (1990), and deconstruction—experiences in the global system promoted new ways of thinking about difference. One important force was post-colonial experience, transnational migration, and the rapid creation of new hybrid identities. The scattering of ethnic communities across many nations destabilized static identities (Appadurai 1993). For example, a Canadian citizen whose national origin is Sri Lankan, whose ethnic identity is Tamil, and whose languages are English and Tamil might construct her identity in multiple ways—and her Canadian and Tamil identities might not be as important to her as gender, sexual orientation, or property ownership! Weber, in his discussion of class, status and 'party' had already argued that there is neither an automatic nor a 'correct' transformation of class and status categories into the basis of collective action (Weber [1946] 1958: 194–95).

A second force was new technologies and, in particular, the role of the Internet in creating new, fluid, fragmented, deterritorialized, and even outright deceptive new identities. New social movements challenged the idea that identities exist a priori and form relatively stable bases for social attitudes, action, and mobilization. New movement activists worked to bring out identities that would impel people to join their cause. These campaigns could even be seen as constructing identities rather than heightening the salience of an existing latent identity (Mansbridge and Morris 2001; Meyer, Whittier, and Robnett 2002).

For example, feminists found that women did not automatically join women's movements. Factory workers can organize along ethnic lines, and ethnic communities can split along class lines. Identities are made, not born or ascribed; they are constantly constructed and negotiated. In the analysis of social movements, theorists had once assumed that movements would try to rally people who shared an identity (proletarians, women, minorities, etc.), but now it seemed as though social-movement activists created and defined these identities in the first place and then demanded that individuals recognize themselves as sharing the identity the activists had created. Many movement activities such as demonstrations do not function to change the behavior of elites but primarily to create and disseminate an identity for potential movement followers. These activities are designed to polarize the potential base into those who embrace the identity and those who remain hostile or indifferent to it.

The destabilization of identity was linked to new technologies, which became vehicles for new identities, for the diffusion and confusion of identities. Print had helped to form the 'imagined community' of the nation in the nineteenth and early twentieth centuries. People across a large territory who could read the same language were able to picture themselves as part of a single community—the nation. Literacy linked large numbers of people in ways that oral communication had not. Some theorists believe that literacy and print were a major precondition for revolutions and independence movements from the late eighteenth to mid-twentieth century (Anderson 1983; Tarrow 1998). The Internet allowed a vastly expanded construction of imagined communities. In the information age, people can use the new technologies to establish identities, call on others to share identities, create false identities, and participate in multiple identity-communities without being seen by old neighbors or new friends (Castells 1996; Turkle 1997).

HYBRIDITY AND TRANSCULTURATION IN THE CONTEXT OF GLOBALIZATION AND POST-COLONIAL CULTURE

The dissolution of the stable, fixed self locked into unchanging ascribed roles was accelerated by decolonization. Simmel had already commented on the emergence of these fluid self-defining identities at the beginning of the twentieth century: In villages, everyone knew everyone else's business and identity, but, in the metropolis, it became easy to define the self in more fluid, calculating, negotiable, secretive, and deceptive ways (Simmel [1950] 1978). The Internet has created not a global village but a global metropolis. There are villages located within it, but most people live in more than one village, many are indifferent to the frowns of neighbors, and many play with multiple identities. In the villages, no one can be trusted, all products are fakes, and nothing is as it seems.

This destabilization, denaturalization, and problematizing of identity took place both in theory and in reality. In many societies, increasing numbers of people rejected historical labels or rejected one set of labels and insisted on another set. 'Proletarians' fragmented along ethnic and religious lines, for example.

FEMINISM AND RACIAL DOMINANCE THEORIES: DEBUNKING FIXED CATEGORIES IN THE SOCIAL SCIENCES

As on earth, so in the clouds of theory. Theories focused on deconstructing historical labels and ascribed identities, showing how purportedly scientific discourse had perpetuated popular fallacies of racial and gender essentialism. The emergence of critical, deconstructionist theory questioned the use of ascribed categories such as race and sex. These categories were no longer seen as firmly rooted in biology but as pseudo-biological constructs. Of course, biologists and social scientists had already debunked race as a category by the beginning of the twentieth century. Even during the peak period of 'scientific racism' in the early 1900s, Émile Durkheim had shown its uselessness in explaining social phenomena. Anthropologists such as Franz Boas thoroughly dismissed the notion of race and the pseudo-scientific mumbo jumbo that had popularized it among Europeans in the later nineteenth century. But, although their value as a concept in biology was over, racial categories had been used carelessly and uncritically in social scientific research.

Critical race theory and whiteness studies began to focus on how race is used both in ordinary discourse and in the social sciences and on the process of defining racial categories and placing individuals into them (Allen 1997; Bay 2000; Gilroy 1994; Hartigan 1999). For example, researchers looked at how 'the Irish became white'—in other words, how people of diverse European national and ethnic backgrounds came to be defined as members of a single privileged 'white' category in North America (Ignatiev 1996; Omi and Winant 1994; Roediger 1999). Comparative studies showed that racial categories and racial politics were quite different in Brazil and the Caribbean. Many of these studies revealed intertwinings between the creation of racial discourses and actual contention for power and resources—for example, how landowning, slave-holding children of Chickasaw and Choctaw mothers and white settler fathers in Mississippi were defined as Indians and pressured to sell their land to whites and accept removal to Oklahoma (Frank 2005; Perdue 2003).

A major focus of feminism and critical race theory was the criticism of how social scientists had used terms like 'sex' and 'race' as if they were simple, stable biological traits of individuals rather than historically and collectively constructed categories of discourse and meaning, often associated with role performances as well as dominance and power differences (Butler 1990, 1993, 2004).

But the critical theorists ran into a fundamental dilemma when theory pointed toward policy. These terms had been misused in essentialist thinking for so long that the erroneous, reified categories had developed a considerable historical and social force of their own. 'Race' is a case in point. In terms of biological science, 'race' is a complete non-starter, a term with no material or genetic basis. 'Race' was an ideology cooked up by Europeans to justify practices of slavery and colonialism. Yet race is a social reality in many countries; people have different opportunities and life conditions on the basis of their racial classification and have developed racial identities. They are seen by others and see themselves in terms of race. Communities are created along racial lines in everyday experience and eventually imagined and celebrated. Cultures emerge that are associated with these identities. There is a long history, with enormous everyday consequences, of people being treated differently—including being discriminated against by the state—on the basis of racial categorization. This situation creates the dilemma of how to undo this mistaken category—whether by ignoring it (as the French state does in its prohibition on using ethno-racial categories in official reports) or by recognizing it and attempting to undo its deleterious effects by affirmative action or similar policies. This dilemma applies not only to government policies but to data collection and analysis as well. For example, should racial categories be used in biomedical research because their social consequences have made them meaningful for understanding disparities, or does their use serve to perpetuate racism? (See the articles by Stolley, Krieger, or LaVeist in Navarro and Muntaner 2004.)

DISCRIMINATION IN THE POST-CIVIL RIGHTS ERA: DOMINANCE, INTERACTION, AND THE MICRO-POLITICS OF POWER

The 1960s and 1970s were a period when social movements helped to sweep away *de jure* barriers to equality in most of the Western democracies. Up to that time, racial segregation had been legal and pervasive in the United States, and powerful effects of historical racial dominance persisted in much of the western hemisphere and settler states in other regions. In almost all developed nations, women were discriminated against well into the post-World War II period. For example, job postings were almost always divided by sex, women lost rights to their own property when they married, and many educational and political institutions simply excluded women. After the civil-rights movement in the United States and the women's rights movements throughout the developed democracies, most of these legal forms of discrimination disappeared. Their after-effects were slower to dissipate, as can be seen from the great economic disadvantages of African Americans (and other people of color) in the United States, the marked disparities in many societies in the Americas and elsewhere between people of European descent and others (indigenous populations, descendents of slaves and other unfree laborers, and immigrants of color), the high incarceration rates of many ethno-racial minorities, the lower earnings of women, and the meager presence of women in political office in practically all of these countries. These persistent inequalities led some to call for affirmative action, policies to overcome the effect of centuries of outright discrimination. Many observers argue that apparently race-neutral policies have the effect of perpetuating racial disparities (Schlesinger 2009). The impact on theory was an imperative to examine the more subtle forms of discrimination, now perpetuated in interaction and informal practices since discrimination could no longer be embodied in laws and overt codes. Feminists and race theorists began to look more closely at the interpersonal and institutional practices of creating difference and perpetuating inequalities that are lodged in ways of talking, joking, child-raising practices, school expectations, marginalization, the creation of hostile climates or glass ceilings in organizations, and informal exclusion. To understand these processes, an edgy and conflict-oriented form of interactionist theory seemed more useful than structuralism.

Interest in the micro-politics of power was closely related to the new attention to the body. Sociology of earlier decades had been curiously disembodied. Structural-functionalists and conflict theorists seemed to write as if people did not exist as bodies but as roles, statuses, classes, groups, identities, and so on. The body began to make a reappearance in Goffman's work (in his attention to gestures, visible stigma, the mortification of the bodies of inmates in total institutions, and the positioning of the female body in gender advertising), and it moved to center stage in the work of Foucault and the feminists. It is precisely because the characteristics of the body are no longer taken for granted in a naturalizing perspective—no longer seen as the natural foundations of race and gender—that bodies have become the focus of analysis in the creation of categories, a site where power and dominance are enacted and expressed, and the venue for performance of race, gender, and other socially constructed categories. The phrase 'inscribed on the body' became important for understanding power, categories, identities, and action. In Part II, we will see how Pierre Bourdieu developed the concept of habitus to incorporate the body with social dispositions.

3. From Deviance to Difference, Diversity, and Social Control

A third theoretical shift was a new view of deviance, which was now defined by concepts of difference, punishment, and control. Structural-functionalists in the 1950s had used the term deviance in a relatively unselfconscious way. They assumed that there was a structure of norms and laws and that deviance meant breaking these rules. Deviants were people who broke the rules or, in a slightly different view, those who had been caught breaking the rules. Structural-functionalists were agnostic on whether specific rules were good or bad, but they generally assumed that some set of rules was necessary in every society. The symbolic interactionists, on the other hand, were more questioning about rules and tended to voice more sympathy for the deviants. They were more inclined to write from the deviants' perspective and to observe the ways in which some people who broke rules became labeled as deviants, while other, more powerful people could 'get away with murder.'

The work of Michel Foucault in the 1960s, 1970s, and early 1980s dramatically pulled the sociological gaze from the deviants to the process of social control. It may be surprising to remember that Durkheim had already insisted that deviance is a process in society and not something individuals do, let alone a relatively fixed characteristic of the norm breaker. Thus Foucault's dramatic recentering of the analysis of transgression and deviance from the transgressor to the process of social control was a revisiting of the original Durkheimian position.

Foucault returned to the Durkheimian position that deviance is an intrinsic part of every normative order, not an individual characteristic or behavior, although his formulation seemed so fresh in French theoretical circles that its similarity to Durkheim's work was not readily acknowledged. It might be helpful to remember that Foucault was seen as a rebel against Marxism, Sartre's existentialism, and structuralist theory, so everything he proposed seemed radical and startling. Foucault became interested in discourses that define certain acts or even entire persons as deviant—mad or bad. These discourses have changed historically, though Foucault provides little insight into why changes take place. In the most recent major shift, the onset of the modern, definitions of deviance, transgression, and normality are increasingly the domain of the human disciplines—medical practice, social work, education, psychology, sociology, and so on. Once again there was an interplay between developments in theory and intellectual circles (for example, the influence of Foucault's work in sociology) and on-the-ground changes in activism and attitudes. People whose behaviors and identities had been labeled deviant and marginalized now insisted on inclusion and civil rights. The gay-rights movement (which surfaced dramatically in the 1969 Stonewall riot in New York) made major contributions to this rethinking of deviance and normality.

The new attention to difference and identity was closely linked to these changes in conceptualizing deviance. A lot of what had previously been considered deviance was reconceptualized as difference. Difference and social control eventually were hooked up to critical views of the neoliberal state as well as to analyses of racial and social class inequalities. Foucault emphasized the creation of difference and deviance in discourse associated with discursive formations that persist for centuries, but, more recently, French theorist Loïc Wacquant (a student of Pierre Bourdieu) connected the analysis of punishment to the rise of the neoliberal state, the downsizing of social services, the new role of the penal state, zero-tolerance policies, surveillance, and mass incarceration. Punishment and the establishment of a penal state tightly overlap class and racial stratification and enable the state to manage the new 'precariat' of underemployed and low-wage workers at the bottom of the structure (Wacquant [2004] 2008, 2008a, 2008b).

4. Media, Knowledge, Framing Practices, and New Technologies of Representation

Theory changed in response to the increasing role of the media in society. Marxists writing during the period between World War I and World War II had already been interested in the culture industry, pop novels, radio and film, and, more abstractly, the 'work of art in an age of mechanical reproduction' as Walter Benjamin (1968) termed it. They were interested in the media as a type of capitalist industry, producing cultural commodities, as well as in the ideological effects of media consumption, the dulling of class consciousness in more or less subtle ways. These theorists used the concept of consciousness extensively, a term that faded in recent years.

The early efforts at analysis were buoyed by the new surge of media in the second half of the twentieth century, beginning with television and later including the Internet. Compared to movies, print, and radio, these new media grabbed much larger chunks of the public's time. They seemed to affect profoundly how people experienced the flow of time and how they saw all of the world beyond their own immediate experiences. Individuals' worldviews and even basic categories of thought were shaped directly by media rather than by circles of family, friends, and local opinion leaders as had been observed in the 1950s.

Media framing became a key concept, with Erving Goffman taking the lead in introducing the term. The media represented their subject matter, whatever it might be, through framing practices. These practices tended to fit events and experiences into relatively standardized categories and made the information highly subject to ideological manipulation. The analysis of framing practices in the media linked to and enlarged theoretical attention to discourses. Marxists and other structural theorists had historically been opposed to explaining social phenomena in terms of ideas; they insisted that social being shapes consciousness—that social structural position and interactions shape how we think about things, not vice versa. But the modern media had become such a powerful and undisputedly material force that theorists began to treat them as a determining element.

Convergence among Marxists, feminists, symbolic interactionists, and micro-conflict theorists became evident in the analysis of the media. Theorists who previously had been in distinct camps developed similar perspectives on media framing practices, the total symbolic environment created by the media, the encoding and decoding of messages, and the concept of hegemonic discourses. Marxists looking at neoliberal ideology, feminists examining gender construction, race theorists observing stereotypes, and many others saw similar patterns and began to use each other's concepts and methods of discourse analysis. Particularly in modern capitalist democracies with their relatively unrepressive states, texts and representations are powerful methods of social control, velvet blinders in place of iron fists. Interest in the media and representation converged with new theories of social control and analysis of discourses that create difference, insecurity, fear of deviance, and moral panics, which in turn can be manipulated to tighten social control.

In addition to analyzing the framing or representation of specific issues and types of people, theorists began to look at how the media as a whole produced a 'society of the spectacle' (Debord [1967] 1995). Marshall McLuhan (1964), a literary critic at the University of Toronto, had already startled public opinion with his writing on the media, especially television, and a host of phrases he invented slipped into popular discourse: icon, cool and hot media, the global village, and the medium is the message/massage. McLuhan argued that we are entering a new age of perception and cognition, as strikingly different from the consciousness associated with print ('the Gutenberg galaxy') as the age of print was from medieval worldviews. McLuhan wrote with professorial detachment and amusement, but French activist Guy Debord took a decidedly more critical view of this shift when he published *The Society of the Spectacle* in 1967, as campuses and factories throughout Europe were heating up. For Debord, the media are among the tools that dominant classes use to create a pseudo-world, the society of the spectacle, that completely distorts our perception and annihilates our capacity for critical thought. Ancient and traditional elites had, of course, also used spectacle, religious ritual, and pageantry to befuddle the masses, but modern media and markets greatly enhanced the capacity to create fantasy worlds to promote social control and compliance. Debord was influenced not only by Marxist theory but also by anarchism, surrealism, and Dada, which sensitized him to the encompassing, enchanting, and enthralling character of the pseudo-world as a phantasmagoria of images and desires. In the years since Debord's pioneering work, the media are increasingly analyzed as a 'total symbolic environment,' an all-encompassing system of meanings and images that profoundly shapes the cognitive maps we have in our brains (Castells 1996; Gerbner 2002; Jameson 1991).

Media were not the only cultural industry that dominated people's understanding of the world. The university as an institution; the fields of scientific inquiry; the human sciences and their applications in medicine, social work, education, criminal justice, and public policy; and the organization of knowledge itself were subjected to scrutiny. Theorists examined the relationship between knowledge and power, between knowledge and the academic disciplines, and between knowledge and the state. This analysis became increasingly important as power processes were reconfigured to involve the private sector and civil society in some areas while expanding the role of the state in others. In some matters, such as health and education, the state ceded control to private providers, while in others, such as criminal justice, security, and counterterrorism, the state actually expanded its role and power.

5. Bringing the State (Back?) In—Neoliberal Policies, Political Fields, and 'Governmentality'

The fifth direction is revived interest in the state. The state is not a new concept in sociology. Weberians and Marxists have a long record of examining the state as a social institution, and even Parsonian functionalists viewed it as the guiding mechanism of a society. Interactionist studies of labeling already targeted the state as the main institutional site of this process because of its role in the involuntary commitment of the mentally disordered, the compilation of records on juvenile offenders, the incarceration of drug addicts, and so on. Conflict theorists in the 1970s certainly included the state in their analysis, and Marxists, in particular, saw it as a powerful structure of coercive and ideological apparatuses. Contemporary theory builds on these approaches but expands them with constructionist concepts. What is new is not the idea that the state is a major societal institution and power center but the strong emphasis on the state's role in constructing difference, defining deviance, and formulating and implementing social policies. The state is a key transmission belt between the micro- and the macro-level. The circumstances of everyday life and interactions—the micro-level—are highly constrained by decisions and choices made by actors in the state at the macro-level. State policies are implemented and enforced at meso- and micro-levels throughout society, in government agencies, businesses, prisons, hospitals, schools, and many other venues at the 'capillary level,' to use Foucault's term.

The state in all modern societies has a key role in establishing categories of individuals, for example, citizens and non-citizens, legal residents and illegal immigrants, those entitled to government services and those not entitled to them, and so on (Cheng 2006; Yanow 2003). This categorization of individuals does not simply or even primarily reflect underlying demographic cleavages; it creates them in the first place. For example, the US census defines categories of race and ethnicity (a practice that is not permitted for the French census). Even the category of 'resident alien' can be broken down further; for example, in Taiwan and many other countries, middle-class professionals and managers who are resident aliens with passports from economically advanced nations have rights that are denied to domestic workers from developing nations (Cheng 2006).

One of the main categories defined by the state is that of deviance. In all states, certain acts are defined as deviant, but these definitions are by no means uniform across all societies. States vary enormously in definitions of deviance and criminality; religion, culture, and historical period are factors that explain some of the variation. For example, heresy is no longer a crime (or even seen as deviant) in Western societies, although it had been punishable by death in medieval times.

The function of defining and punishing deviance has existed as long as there have been states, but the work of Foucault and social constructionists has drawn new attention to it. One of the most striking cases is the soaring rate of incarceration in the United States as a large number of drug-related behaviors are treated as major criminal offenses with long mandatory sentences as well as 'enhancements' (related to the circumstances of the criminal act) that lengthen sentences. These policies appear to be race neutral but are contributing to higher incarceration rates of African Americans (Schlesinger forthcoming). Wacquant interprets them as measures that are not only racist but also designed as forms of control of the 'precariat'—the growing stratum of people forced into insecure low-wage work punctuated by frequent unemployment (Wacquant [2004] 2008, 2008a, 2008b). As the incarcerated population of the United States tops the two million mark, the role of the state in producing deviance has become very noticeable. Another area of deviance production by the state is the growing function of surveillance.

Beyond establishing difference and generating deviance, the state has drawn theoretical attention for its role in the shift from embedded liberalism to neoliberalism (Harvey 2005). The neoliberal shift actually began with a deliberate self-shrinkage, a self-imposed downsizing of state functions, as governments in the United Kingdom and the United States withdrew from many of their regulatory activities and from the management of public services. In the United Kingdom, the state had managed public infrastructure such as railways, and these services were privatized. The state also shrank its functions of income maintenance and protection of labor rights, especially in the United States (Milkman 2008). This withdrawal of the state can be seen as an active choice, as was discussed in the preceding chapter (Harvey 2005). Researchers such as Klinenberg (2002) have shown how this withdrawal of the state and the reconfiguration of social services as options that have to be researched, selected, and sought out by 'smart consumers' can have devastating consequences for vulnerable populations, such as isolated, elderly people during the 1995 Chicago heat wave.

Some observers argue that the withdrawal of the state from social services was intimately linked to its expanded police and penal functions. The atrophied social state is necessarily accompanied by a super-sized and hyperactive penal state (Wacquant 2008a, 2008b) to take up the slack in managing and controlling so-called problem populations in the lower tier of the class structure.

Although the state withdrew from many of its social-service functions in the later decades of the twentieth century and the first decade of the twenty-first, it continues to have a role in formulating policies with social impacts, for example family policy, urban policy, public health, and income distribution and maintenance policies.

Finally, new attention to the role of the state focuses on variation among states in their mix of policies. As noted in Chapter 1, although a neoliberal shift took place across the globe, some states went much further than others in shrinking regulatory, distributional, and social-service functions. While the viewer might find filmmaker Michael Moore's view of public health in Canada,

Britain, France, and Cuba a bit utopian, his point is valid: not all societies have leaned toward privatized systems as strongly as the United States.

These considerations in turn lead theorists into the study of the *political field*. The state is one element of a complex and contentious field of political and social practices and discourses. It can be unitary—controlled by a single societal force, such as the capitalist class—or a terrain of struggle. It usually includes multiple actors. Sometimes it is controlled through rigid powerful apparatuses of coercion and ideological indoctrination, but, in other situations, it can be more fluid. The political field includes civil society as well as the state, and it is linked to the fields of the media and the economy; at their capillaries, these fields extend into the micro-level of individuals and households.

Major contemporary theorists devote attention to the analysis of states and political fields. Pierre Bourdieu introduced the term 'field' and its related concepts, as we will discuss in detail in Part II. Theda Skocpol has refreshed both Marxist and Weberian approaches in order to understand twentieth-century state formation and the interplay of states and civil societies (Skocpol 1979, 2002, 2005), a topic also examined by Jeffrey Alexander (2006) from a more Durkheimian viewpoint and Saskia Sassen (2000) who is looking at the emergence of global civil society in the great global cities. An increasingly influential cluster of social-movement theorists studies the role of states in identity formation, the growth of oppositional consciousness, and the expansion or constriction of opportunities for collective action (Mansbridge and Morris 2001; Meyer, Whittier, and Robnett 2002). Stuart Hall (1988b, 1995a) has analyzed the authoritarian populism of the Thatcher government and its construction of fears of crime and ethno-racial difference, and Loïc Wacquant ([2004] 2008) is extending Bourdieu's work on politics into the analysis of the burgeoning penal activities of the neoliberal state.

Michel Foucault made key theoretical contributions in his exploration of surveillance and his introduction of the concept of 'governmentality' (a composite of 'government' and 'mentality') to mean manipulative practices of power for the management and control of complex modern societies, a topic we will explore in Part II.

CONFLICT CONSTRUCTIONISM?

Can these changes be summed up in one phrase, a term like 'structural-functionalism,' 'conflict theory,' and 'symbolic interactionism'? Or was the key characteristic of the past decades the fragmentary, jumbled nature of the ideas—little conceptual dribbles and flows oozing into each other?

Despite the theoretical fragmentation, we can discern a central tendency shared by almost all of the trends. Let's call it 'conflict constructionism.' The fact that we can sum up a central tendency suggests (paradoxically) more underlying unity—or just more blurred boundaries between the theories— than in the post-war period with its sharply differentiated triad of structural-functionalism, conflict theory, and symbolic interactionism.

The area of overlap of the contemporary theories contains three elements:

- One is that the basic categories of difference (race, gender, ethnicity, sexual orientation, and so on) are constantly created, reinforced, and deconstructed in discourses and practices. Nations became 'imagined communities' (Anderson 1983), gender is performed, and so on. These processes occur in the interactions of everyday life, in policies and regulations of the state (for example, the changing ethno-racial categories of the US census), in market transactions, and in the theoretical knowledge of disciplines such as biology, psychology and psychiatry, and the social sciences. Construction can be captured by the word 'play' with all of its connotations of looseness, contestation, amusement, and probabilistic outcomes in contrast to the rigid, fixed, earnest, and pre-determined connotations of 'structure.' This play in the construction of difference goes on at a micro-level (interactions, the self-presentation of individuals); a meso-level of organizations, agencies, and institutions; and a macro-level (state regulation).
- Second, all social processes are fluid and open-ended. Apparent fixity in social structure and in social groups' boundaries, institutions, and individual identities is illusory. The discourses, practices, and interactions that shape human action are never stable. They not only undergo major historical shifts, but also continuously change in small negotiations, in a play of definitions and counter-definitions that takes place in fields, not fixed structures.
- Third, all social categories and processes are in a state of contention, in a flow of power and resistance. No action is ever simply determined by social forces or purely coerced, but, on the other hand, no one is entirely a free agent operating outside of constantly shifting limits and boundaries. No social situation is entirely fixed by a value consensus. At the very least, actors have contending

interests, and these are usually expressions of larger collective differences in purpose and point of view. Society
is seen as nothing more than the product of contending
practices and performances within fields (such as the
field of politics or of culture) rather than being viewed as
a structure of fixed roles in permanent and stable organizations and institutions.

These elements of conflict constructionism emerge from a meeting of
symbolic interactionist and conflict perspectives (Marxism, feminism, race
theory, and, later, queer theory). But there are also surprisingly many bits of a
Durkheimian perspective folded into the mix, most directly through the contributions of Erving Goffman. Although individual and collective actors have
contending aims, they are following scripts or are constrained by discourses
that they have not invented themselves. These discourses (or scripts) limit
what they can do, how they can interact with one another, and what identities
they acquire and elaborate for themselves. The outcomes are predictable in
probabilistic terms but not certain. Convergent ideas about constraints arose
not only from Durkheim's ideas via Goffman's work but also from the theories
of Michel Foucault and Pierre Bourdieu, which have more distant affinities
with Durkheim's thought.

How did this happy ménage form? In the next part of the book, we will
trace specific individuals' theoretical contributions, but we can also spot
external influences. We can see that this shift may have been influenced
by the commodification and marketization associated with neoliberal
restructuring, a social, political, and economic transformation that broke
down many apparently solid institutions, especially in the public sector,
and relocated their functions into the rapidly changing terrain of the
marketplace.

MARXISM VERSUS POSTMODERNISM

Marxist-influenced theorists and postmodernists are two broad groups of
contemporary theorists that both subscribe to many elements of conflict
constructionism, but they do not agree on a deeper interpretation of the
new theories.

Postmodernists argue that human culture, society, and interaction have
always been processes of construction lodged in discourses and texts and
operating primarily at the local and micro-level. They are very suspicious

of any claims about broad historical trends or patterns in how this construction takes place. In the postmodernist view, these claims are themselves only narratives, not an objectively true or correct analysis of history and social processes.

Marxists are insistent that discursive and micro-level processes are shaped by the mode of production. Marxists argue that flexible capitalism and the expansion of markets have accelerated the formation of the unstable, discursive, performed, narrative self, the 'play of difference' and the fluid nature of social processes (Sennett 1998). Society itself is less structured and rigid (and less secure) than it was in pre-capitalist eras and in the period of embedded liberalism. The mode of production forms an objective bedrock of social processes, and, because capitalism is now highly fluid and market driven, it not only creates more fluidity in social construction but also heightens theorists' perception of this fluidity. In the Marxist view, postmodernism is an intellectual fashion that perfectly reflects the myths of freedom, agency, micro-level interchanges, choice, and indeterminacy that accompany markets.

This sparring could continue indefinitely, with Marxists insisting that postmodernism is only a reflection of advanced capitalism into the realm of ideas while postmodernists insist that Marxism is only a narrative, one perspective among many, a story about the determining role of the mode of production that is no truer than any other story. We can see this debate pervading many areas of sociological inquiry, such as the study of culture, the media, and the self.

The amusing paradox is that both Marxists and postmodernists are fascinated by conflict constructionist concepts. Both types of theorists have become intrigued by the 'play of difference,' the relationship between difference and dominance, the process of negotiating multiple identities, the impact of discourses and media images on societies, the micro-politics of power and resistance, and the production of deviance and marginality. For Marxists, the phenomena themselves are products of market capitalism in the information age, emerging from global flows of capital and people, flexible webs of enterprise, neoliberal state policies, and powerful new media. Even more trenchantly, for Marxists, the new theoretical attention to representation, micro-conflicts, social construction of identities, and discourses of deviance and exclusion is itself a product of the new context of neoliberal capitalism.

Postmodernists remain highly skeptical about the claims that the mode of production, and specifically capitalism and its new global patterning, offer the single most complete and powerful explanation of other changes, including changes in theories themselves. They remain agnostic on the question of how and why perspectives change.

The astute reader will have noticed that the organization of Part I with its two chapters—'real world change' and 'changes in theory'— suggests a tilt toward the Marxist perspective because we imply that changes in capitalism and the material conditions of human life provide an impetus for theoretical change or, at the very least, that they need to be considered as influences in paradigm shifts and can be discussed objectively as if they really happened. But a vigorous exchange with postmodernists is welcome (Best and Kellner 1991, Derrida 1994, Jameson 1991).

COUNTERTRENDS: PARADIGM PERSISTENCE AND RESISTANCE TO THEORY

Given that there is no stable, dominant new paradigm in sociology—more a loose collection of overlapping trends—it is not surprising that, in large parts of the field, these new theories have had little impact or have actually been resisted. We are not all conflict constructionists! We can point to several causes of resistance.

One is *paradigm persistence and revitalization*. Older paradigms remain vigorous and exciting; they can be adapted to explanations of the new external circumstances. Many theorists continue to work in the major traditions of sociology, basically the ones identified by Randall Collins: a Durkheimian one, a conflict one drawing on Marx and Weber, a micro-interactionist one, and a rationalist-utilitarian one (including exchange theory and rational choice theory). Many recent theories can still be placed within these broad rubrics, and, for many sociologists, there is no need to turn to the more new-fangled trends influenced by deconstruction, postmodernism, and so on.

A second countertrend is *the impact of policy-oriented and applied fields* on sociology. Fields such as public health and criminal justice are peopled by researchers, scholars, and activists who are not always friendly toward theory. To some, theory gets in the way of effective social practice and problem solving; it seems obscure, abstract, and unrealistically critical of existing institutions. Others accept theories as long as they are phrased in the tried and true vocabulary of roles, institutions, values, and other popular and widely diffused concepts derived from functionalist theories. Disciplinary partnerships can have a dampening effect on theoretical innovation, especially adoption of radical or surprising ideas.

A third force that leads to resistance to contemporary theories is the *impact of new data and quantitative methods*; these can even substitute for theories. Very large amounts of data are now available and can be processed by very sophisticated statistical techniques. Epidemiology and the analysis of educational achievement and attainment are two examples of areas where quantitative data are available and amenable to analysis. This new flood of information makes possible new ways of finding patterns. The discerned patterns can become substitutes for theoretical perspectives. If we can identify enough significant predictor variables for a condition, outcome, or behavior, in some sense, we have a theory for it, and many researchers find this type of theorizing more satisfying than conceptual construction.

CONCLUSION

In this chapter, we have traced processes that shaped theorizing after the 1960s. Some of these processes were internal to the enterprise of theorizing while others were more clearly associated with changes in the larger social and political environment. For example, the collapse of the Soviet system and the onset of neoliberal forms of capitalism had a big impact on Marxist theories. The clear boundaries between theories became blurrier, many types of social constructionist theories that were generally based on premises of underlying conflicts and inequalities became popular, and efforts were made to link micro-level phenomena with macro-level situations.

In the next part of the book, we will look in more detail at a key aspect of the process by which theory changes, namely the work of specific individuals. These individuals introduced new terms, concepts, ideas, and theoretical methods. Each created a large body of work, spanning many specific topics. As we trace their writing and ideas, we can see how they went about making new theories. Their work is only one part of the large shifts we discussed in this chapter, but their writing provides key insights into how these shifts in the emphasis and underlying assumptions of social theory came about. These theorists, whom we are calling 'transitional giants,' propelled theories in new directions in recent decades.

KEY TERMS

- agency
- classical theory
- community of theorists
- conflict constructionism
- conflict theories: Marxism, feminism, theories of racial dominance
- deconstruction and social construction
- difference and identity
- dominant paradigm
- fields: the political field
- frames and framing practices
- governmentality
- hybridity and transculturation
- imagined communities
- intellectual climate
- interwar period: Chicago School, Marxist theories of culture, Frankfurt Institute
- performance
- postmodern, postmodernism
- psychoanalysis
- social control and punishment
- structural-functionalism
- symbolic interactionists, micro-theories, and the dramaturgical model
- the state
- theories of representation

WORKS CONSULTED

Becker 1963

Best and Kellner 1991

Castells 1996

Collins 1994

Durkheim [1893] 1964, [1897] 1951, [1912] 1965

Feyerabend 1975

Gerth and Mills 1953

Goodman 1962

Hobsbawm, 1987, 1994

Jay 1996

Kuhn 1962

Mills 1940, [1954] 1963, [1959] 2000

Parsons [1937] 1961, [1951] 1968

Ritzer 1996

Weber [1958] 2003

PART II: TRANSITIONAL GIANTS

Introduction

What do we mean by 'transitional giants'? In Chapter 2, we treated theories as if they were disembodied anthropomorphized ideas—discussing their drift, their clashes with each other, and the way they were shaped by external forces such as globalization, neoliberalism, and social movements. This way of talking about theories makes them seem like big battling monsters—King Kong vs. Godzilla or the clash of the Titans. But of course ideas do not exist on their own, only as they are invented and expressed by human beings. We have to apply the insight of symbolic interactionism to our own thought—the only thing that's real are people doing things like writing, speaking, and interacting. Therefore, we want to look at specific people who had large roles in changing theories in the last decades of the twentieth century. We have selected four: Erving Goffman, Michel Foucault, Pierre Bourdieu, and Stuart Hall.

Our four transitional giants share the following characteristics, including being in the right place at the right time to change theoretical directions.

- They were outsiders and freer to invent and innovate. Their work broke with existing theories, especially with the triad of theories that were popular in the United States. It is probably not surprising that all four had national origins in countries other than the United States (Goffman in Canada, Foucault and Bourdieu in France, and Hall in Jamaica and later England).
- They searched for new explanations for social change. They worked in the era of turmoil—from the mid-1960s to the mid-1980s. (But we need to remember that Hall is still alive and working, and Bourdieu did much of his important work after the 1980s.) This period was a lucky moment in history for theorists. Exciting changes were taking place that influenced their ideas directly, but, even more important,

99

these changes in society were making existing theories seem tired and unconvincing and therefore inclining intellectuals to accept new ones. They were responding to the real world around them, where traditional theories started to fall apart and new explanations were needed to understand contemporary circumstances. Their responses all reflect this historical experience.

- They proposed combinations and recontextualizations of existing theories. They rejected the binaries, essentialism, and monolithic camps of existing theories and deliberately blurred boundaries that had seemed clear, such as the difference between interaction and structure, power and resistance, self and society. They reread classical theories in new ways and recombined strands from these theories to gain new insights. For example, Bourdieu drew on Marx's and Durkheim's work. Hall brought together Marx, Gramsci, theories of race, and frameworks from communications and media studies. Any one element of the transitional giants' theories often looked familiar, yet the strands from old theories were spun together in unexpected ways and placed into new contexts. Using our metaphor of theories as monsters, these recombinant forms were startlingly new. Foucault delved deep into historical studies that took him back to archaic theories of medicine; even the pre-Socratics were reread as ways of thinking anew.
- They introduced new concepts or revised the uses of old concepts in startling new ways that changed how we use and think about constructs such as 'the self' (Goffman), 'capital' (Bourdieu), 'identity' (Hall), and 'power' (Foucault).
- They invented new theoretical methods or took existing methods to startling extremes. Our readers may initially be offended by the term 'theoretical methods' because sociology curricula always contrast theory and methods, and methods are always assumed to be empirical. But, as we have pointed out, theories are made, and there are methods for making them. We will see, for instance, that Goffman's method was a rigorous observation of interaction, a micro-level approach that was already widely in use but that Goffman took to an extreme, dissecting every move and remark in an interaction. Foucault liked to study the grotesque, bizarre, and anomalous

such as the diary of a hermaphrodite and a detailed account of a torture and execution. Both Goffman and Foucault considered limit situations and confinement—the treatment of those labeled 'mad' and the incarcerated—in order to derive new ways of thinking about deviance, punishment, and regulation. Hall, a founder of cultural studies, is far more open to textual analysis than most sociologists were in the post-World War II period. Goffman meticulously analyzed hundreds of advertising images. So the objects of study, the methods of analysis, and the procedures used to invent concepts and theories shifted subtly. Under the influence of the transitional giants, there emerged a growing emphasis on limit events (madness, incarceration), discourse analysis, and micro-level power relations as keys to understanding societies.

- Previous theories had drawn overly sharp lines between structure (the realm of structural-functionalists and structural Marxists) and agency (the domain of symbolic interactionists, rational choice theorists, and other individual-level micro-theorists, as well as most conflict theorists and instrumentalist Marxists). The transitional giants developed vocabularies, concepts, and research strategies that recognized both sides of the agency-structure dialectic and did their best to transcend this binary and other either-or binaries. They thus brought startling new formulations to old concepts such as power.

- They enjoyed a moment of recognition by sociologists, scholars in related fields, and even journalists and were hailed as people who offered new and exciting views of society. They took on a legendary status so that others were more likely to read their work and use their theories. Thus, they were seen as taking the lead in paradigm shifts—in changing directions in theory.

We have tried to give the reader a few reasons that these four theorists might be considered transitional giants. Are they the only ones? Of course not. Our choice is only a starting point for answering this question: How do individual contributions change theories and shift the direction of theorizing? For each theorist, we offer a short interpretative essay that explores not only their inventions but also their continuities, breaks, and dialogs with previously established theorists.

The four chapters are not identically structured because the theoretical frameworks of the four theorists are not organized in identical ways. These differences need to be reflected in the chapter formats. Goffman, Bourdieu, and Hall provide clusters of concepts that are organized differently from each other; and Foucault's thinking shifted so markedly during his theoretical trajectory that the distinct periods of his thought must be noted.

Chapter 3

ERVING GOFFMAN (1922–1982)

Erving Goffman emerged as a major theorist at the same time that symbolic interactionists and conflict theorists were challenging structural-functionalist hegemony. The first half of the 1960s was a period of exciting new directions in sociology, and Goffman's work fascinated young scholars and graduate students. Their first encounter with his theories came through two books, *The Presentation of Self in Everyday Life* and *Asylums*.

The following discussion emphasizes Goffman as a transitional figure who switched the concept of the self in sociological theory from a stable, interior personality to a performed, manipulated, fluid external persona. He drew attention to frames as discourses of definition and construction.

MAJOR WORKS, IDEAS, AND CONCEPTS

THE PRESENTATION OF SELF IN EVERYDAY LIFE: SELF AS PERFORMANCE

In *The Presentation of Self in Everyday Life*, Goffman proposed 'the drama-turgical model' in which the self is a performance and society is revealed to be a theater production with roles, masks, and scripts. Each one of us performs our self for others, sometimes alone and sometimes with a team of fellow performers. Our performances can be either cynical or sincere and honest, but Goffman implies that there is an element of calculation in most self-presentations. The performance space—the stage of everyday life—has its front regions as well as back regions where we put on our masks and costumes. Thus, Goffman dissolves the self into the management of impressions and social structure into a myriad of performed interactional scenes.

Goffman is often seen as a symbolic interactionist, but he probably did not see himself as one (or, for that matter, as any kind of micro-theorist) though he shares symbolic interactionist premises. For him, as for the symbolic interactionists, the structure of society appears to dissolve into multiple interlinked performances. But many theorists interpret Goffman as a neo-Durkheimian fascinated by the processes of normative regulation that are built into the scripts we have learned and the norms for judging the role performances of self and others. Goffman's apparent interest in micro-situations and individual performances belies his underlying insistence on the patterning of interactions and the scriptedness of self-performances. The individual has self-interests and motivations, and certainly the ability to engage in performances, but little agency in a deeper sense.

Erving Goffman stepped out of his office (where theorizing takes place in a vacuum) and put himself at the center of activity—placing himself in the minutia and everyday pedestrian interactions that make up social life. It is the overlooked, fleeting, unexplored aspects of everyday life that Goffman documented as crucial insights into social existence. As a sociologist of ordinary life, he took taken-for-granted interactions—the way people greet each other on the street—and showed how these provided consistency and meaning to everyday existence. Setting himself apart from his contemporaries who theorized from afar with grand abstract designs, Goffman took the infinitely small details of life that go unnoticed and remain outside the realm of most theorists and brought them to the center of sociological analysis. In this way, we can see Goffman as an empirically focused micro-sociologist in practice, whose work had macro-sociological consequences for theories of society. Goffman's everyday insights into the nature of human behavior lead us to consider large theoretical questions: How is the self constructed? What are the categories that define us? How are those categories constructed and applied? How is society held together? And what role do we, as individuals, have in the construction of the social world? For Goffman, humans create society through verbal and nonverbal interaction and the exchange of symbols. By exploring the nature of everyday social interaction, Goffman led us to understand how society as a whole is a series of multiple and interlinked meaning-making micro-interactions that form the basis of social life.

THE PRESENTATION OF SELF

Goffman's dramaturgical approach is the theory, echoing Shakespeare, that 'All the world's a stage, / And all the men and women merely players'—that people perform or act in particular ways depending on specific social contexts. This performance, or presentation of oneself to the audience, is shaped by the environment (props, such as furniture, setting, and scenery) and the audience for which one is performing. The performance of self or this acting metaphor is useful for understanding how social interaction works on an everyday basis through the roles that we play, the quality of our role performance, and the audience's response. Goffman alerts us to the ways that our behavior is not only reactive but also intentional in that we desire that the presentation of ourselves is consistent with the aspired goal of who we are or want to be.

In presenting the self, a social actor gives off information, and, if this information is controlled effectively, the audience is convinced of the appropriateness of the behavior; the role is seen as sincere and authentic. The believability of the act or presentation is constructed through verbal signification and nonverbal gestures that establish and confirm intent. Presentations are made to be consistent with expectations of society. As if evaluating a play or a movie, we ask whether the performance is compelling or not. Goffman alerts us to the ways that presentation of self or our performances are always linked to social constraints and social norms through people being 'forced' to fulfill the duties and behaviors and characteristics of their social role in a consistent manner. This is not to say that acting out a performance is perfunctory; rather, we learn to read the situation and adapt to the role and grasp what to do in the moment by being sensitive to our audience and surroundings.

Goffman divides the theater or stage metaphor into two zones, the front stage and the back stage. As if a curtain separated these zones, we step out from behind the curtain to present ourselves to the audience in our roles as actors and to retreat to the back stage to change costumes and retouch our makeup. Goffman highlights the ways that our social identity is like the front stage—that part of the performance area where regulatory roles serve as the vehicle of standardization of performance. The standardization allows others to understand the individual on the basis of normative meanings. The front stage is a collective representation that establishes proper settings, appearances, and manner for the social role assumed by the actor.

If the front stage is where the action is, then the back stage serves as the unseen region where the props, costumes, makeup, and scripts to be performed at other times reside. The back stage usually has the connotation of informality, as in the place where we 'let our hair down' or 'chill out,' apparently relating to others in ways that are more spontaneous, coarse, and indiscreet. Consequently, it is often thought that the front stage is where we act according to the norms of society and the back stage is where we act as 'ourselves.' Yet 'acting ourselves' is also a scripted performance. The contrasting front and back stage, while a metaphor for the individual's behavior and personality, can be seen in less psychological terms, in an illuminating application, through a spatial analysis of an haute-cuisine restaurant. The front stage, the dining room, is the place of the formality of white tablecloths, linen napkins, and polished silver, where all must abide by the rules of decorum and consumption. Here is where well-dressed people engage in 'civil conversation' in monitored tones so that they are not bothering guests at the table next to them. The setting is pristine, serene, and orderly. As diners, patrons perform their roles according to the norms of haute-cuisine dining. Meanwhile, the kitchen is the back stage. Here is where the raw ingredients are being assembled for production. The world here is chaotic, as cooks rush to fill orders, busboys frantically clear dishes and wash them, servers come and go looking for their table's meals or to give special instructions at the last minute for a particular order, people bump into each other as they try to coordinate all the tasks required to make the restaurant run. The world here is messy, disjointed, and boisterous, as everyone shouts out orders and requests and vents candid frustrations during especially busy evenings. The dividing line between the dining room and the kitchen is more than just a wall or curtain, it is the symbolic marker of two radically distinct worlds—the visible, polished world of calmness where the finished aesthetic product is displayed and the unseen, tarnished world that scrambles to assemble that product.

Yet the back stage has its own scripts and roles. When a cook picks up a piece of meat that fell on the floor and places it on a plate the waiter will take to the diner, the cook is not simply 'being himself.' He is performing social scripts of frugality, nonchalance, or contempt for the customers. When the professor who kindly answers students' questions after class returns to her office and makes sarcastic remarks about them to a colleague, which is the real professor? Or are both characters only performed personae, each enacted for a different audience? Front stage and back stage have different audiences and scripts that are governed by different aesthetic criteria. For example, a show of sincerity, candor, and frantic preparation for the back stage is in contrast to the performed perfection, serenity, coherence, and unity of the team for the front stage. The back stage is not spontaneous, real, sincere, or genuine either, and, in fact, these terms are largely meaningless in the dramaturgical model.

Returning to the individual in interaction, we can see how the presentation of self as a front-stage and back-stage negotiation is a powerful tool to understand how we have multiple personae.

THE SELF AS A HALL OF MIRRORS

If the front stage is an area of performance for an audience, is the back stage not also a performance venue for a different kind of audience? If the formality of the front stage is dropped for informality in the back, is this substitution not just a consequence of playing to a different crowd, a matter of the substance or style of the performance rather than the absence or presence of an enacted role? If so, Goffman's analysis of front and back leads us into a hall of mirrors where the front stage has a back stage, which is really a front stage after all. Is there ever really a back stage, or does the back stage serve as an empty signifier or placeholder for the transition between performances? The questions that are evoked here force us again to rethink what we mean by the self and how one can theorize a self at all.

Goffman's distinction between the front-and back-stages offers a powerful approach for understanding contexts of action and how those contexts are always changing and unstable. As we push Goffman's metaphor to its logical conclusion, we see that the distinction provides us with a methodological entry point, but one that does not hold up analytically. If every front stage has a back stage and if, even on the back stage, there is a front stage performance going on as well, this leads us into a dizzying model of the self—a never-ending reflection of different and multiple front- and back-stage selves constantly shifting and playing off each other—the self in a hall of mirrors. As a result there is no way to pin down the 'actual' or 'original' self because we always find the self *in medias res*, in the midst of things. There is, in the end, no way to tell the performer from the masks. The performer is a never-ending set of masks constantly being changed without a face behind them. What we call the self, for Goffman, can be seen as a faceless indistinguishable entity only made visible or concrete by its wearing a mask of what it wants to be.

Ultimately, Goffman's hall of mirrors thrusts us into an infinity of images of ourselves: with so many masks, who is the real performer and what kind of performer am I as I get caught up in the ever-changing drama of life?

Goffman framed this world of performances and presentations in terms of our internal sense of self. As in Freud's tripartite dissection of the psyche (id, ego, superego), in Goffman's theory, presentations of the self are always motivated and evaluated by our sense of pride and esteem. Like Freud's superego, the site of this evaluation is an embodiment of the social norms of a particular society. Performances for Goffman are always about impression management, the control and communication of the performance, in order to avoid embarrassment and being discredited in social life. For Goffman, embarrassment, humiliation, incompetence, or any other negative or self-defeating or self-degrading emotion or feeling is to be avoided. Therefore, Goffman theorized that social interaction is always governed through an implicit normative function of saving face and acting in ways that make one appear in the best possible light.

On a side note, we should remember that, although Goffman's presentation of self appears to be disembodied theoretically, implicit in his analysis is a theory of the body. As Goffman points out, whenever we present ourselves and interact with an audience that interprets and evaluates us, there is always a dual process of the signals and the meanings that we intend to give off through our performance and those signals and meanings that are read off us by the audience. It is here, in the presenting and reading modes, that the implicit theory of the body comes through. Since these two interpretations do not always correspond, we can look to the body as a place where the non-verbal world of gestures, body language, and unconscious movements are privileged in interpreting the credibility of any performance. Our conscious and, even more so, our unconscious signals uphold or betray our performance. (These themes resonate with Bourdieu's notion of competence and capital, which we will explore in a later chapter.) While we may say all the right things, if our bodily movements don't accompany these words, this discrepancy discredits the performance. For example, if I meet someone and exclaim how happy I am about the meeting and all the while I have my arms folded and head down, it is more than likely that the person being spoken to will not believe my speech since my gestures convey no sense of pleasure. Therefore, we can see that *the body* is just as much wrapped up in presentation as the script that is recited to save face—both make a role credible to the audience.

Goffman does more than examine the role of a particular actor in the presentation of self: he extends his theoretical model to groups or 'teams' of people. Goffman emphasizes how interacting within a group is like role-playing, with each person playing his or her part. This role-playing illustrates that, without cooperating and acting together, the group members will be unable to achieve their goals. Each member must play an individual role in accordance to its function within the group. For example, on a basketball team, there is a point guard, shooting guard, small and power forwards, and a center, and all have designated assignments and tasks they must perform according to their position in order for the team to be effective. If one of the team members acts against his or her role, for example, if the point guard refuses to pass the ball to the open player or the center refuses to rebound the ball, the team will be ineffective in its goal of winning the game.

The notion of team can be dramatized even more if we examine the world of the con artist (a personal favorite focus for Goffman who, as a sardonic observer of human life, wrote an essay on con men entitled 'On Cooling the Mark Out: Some Aspects of Adaptation to Failure'). As a team, all the players must play their roles according to their tasks. The con team consists of four members: the roper, the person who lures the victim or mark in; the fixer, the person who arranges all the physical settings and props; the shill or lure, the accomplice who aids the team in making the scene believable; and the inside man, who pulls the con off by tricking the mark out of his or her money. Each member of the team must stick to the script—putting on a play in which everybody knows his or her part except the mark—in order for the confidence game to be convincing. If any one of the players' roles or front-stage performances is discredited or is not performed according to script, then the con fails. But when all players act and interact according to plan and maintain their fronts, each individual player enhances the overall group performance. Hence, the moniker 'con *artist*.' We can then bring back the front stage-back stage metaphor to frame the world of the confidence game. The back stage is where the planning takes place and the strategy is discussed, the props put into place, and the details worked out in full, while the front stage is the performance of the con itself.

OUTCOMES

Goffman's analysis of everyday life, especially the interaction of front- and back-stage roles and the presentation of self and its interaction with others, raises a host of interesting questions and problems. How can we understand the self as depicted by Goffman? Our visceral and commonsense assumptions about the world lead us to think that there is a 'real me' or an 'authentic' self that is the core of identity and that this self is distinct from the roles that we play or the performances we give. We can think of this as the two-self theory—the idea that the individual is a series of masks manipulating and hiding the real self behind them. If we accept this gut-felt folk notion of the self as a coherent, unique entity that makes each of us special, then this staves off the notion that we are always acting and 'faking it' or that our behaviors and interactions with others are always contrived. But, if we follow Goffman and bracket these asociological commonsense assumptions, we can begin to understand the social dynamics and social forces at play in social life that channel our behaviors differently in different contexts. By thinking through the performance model, we see that our behavior is often contradictory and incoherent when all our different performances for our different audiences are compiled together. And Goffman's model of performance allows for exactly those contradictions. In fact, his theory of the self helps us understand the very fragmented, disjointed, ever-changing world and our ever-changing reactions to it. In addition, rather than seeing the self as acting instrumentally or through strategic and rational choices, we can understand how performances are scripts or roles to be played out in terms not of our own design.

Why are humiliation and saving face so important for Goffman? While there may be no true underlying self for him, there is an underlying sense of normativity that needs to be explored. This happens on two levels. First, the performance of any particular role need not depend on the actor's conviction. As long as one performs well and the audience believes the performance, that is all that is required. Here, morality seems to be thrown out the window, as we need not believe in anything we say or do. Our personal beliefs and emotions are irrelevant to a good performance. For example, just because we are in a bad mood does not permit us to act offensively or disrespect others, nor can we choose to act out in any way we please. We must still perform our roles accordingly for meaning to be established and communicated according to prevailing expectations. Second, Goffman helps us explore how everyday interaction is often undertaken below the level of consciousness. We interact with many people every day without thinking twice, thereby overriding our conscious intentions or strategic deployments of self. In fact, most of the time we are interacting without thinking about the roles we are playing out since we are *in medias res* and not reflexively aware of any particular role nor of the multiple roles and performances we are switching back and forth from in response to the different audiences we encounter. Behavior is not strictly governed by explicit rules, and the notion of 'presentation' does not mean our lines are written out and we perfunctorily read them; rather our everyday behavior is undergirded with an overwhelming normativity, which maintains the social order through a constant disciplining of individuals to perform to the mandates that are dictated according to their differing roles.

Goffman's metaphors and key concepts frame our understanding of the social world and serve as critical tools to illuminate the taken-for-granted and often overlooked dynamics of interaction in everyday life. Through this investigation, Goffman provides us with new understandings and approaches to examine the subtlest of gestures in human dynamics. He also illuminates the larger theme of social control, a concern that became evident with the publication of *Asylums*, possibly his most important work.

TOTAL INSTITUTIONS AND LABELS

ASYLUMS

The second major work of this period, *Asylums*, could lead the reader to see Goffman as a micro-conflict theorist. *Asylums* lays bare the destruction of the selves of people who are trapped in total institutions as prisoners, mental patients, military recruits, or converts to rigid faiths. They are held in institutions in which their entire life is controlled, monitored, supervised, regulated, and molded. They are stripped of their identities and transformed into tractable inmates who can only rebel within the shadowy underside of the institution.

Goffman's interest in *total institutions*—those institutions that break down the barriers that separate the spheres and activities of ordinary life—leads him to study what appear to be a set of disparate unrelated institutions (such as an orphanage to care for abandoned or neglected children, a mental hospital that looks after those who are threats to themselves, a prison to protect the community from danger, a boarding school to instrumentally accomplish the task of reforming students, an army barracks to train soldiers, or a convent that functions as a retreat from the world). And he exposes how, despite their ostensive or official purposes, these institutions function in an almost isomorphic fashion and generate homologous outcomes in fulfilling their official aims. Here are the four elements of total institutions as defined by Goffman:

1. All life is conducted under a single authority in the same physical location.
2. All activity is carried out in the presence of others where all are treated alike and do all required tasks together as an amorphous group.
3. All activities are regimented and scheduled. One activity leads to the next, and all occur at prearranged times. All activities are organized and under surveillance from above.
4. All activities are brought together into a coherent design to fulfill the aims of the institutions.

In *Asylums*, Goffman describes the mortification of inmates, or the ways in which the self is broken down. He begins by specifying the defining characteristics of total institutions, such as a single authority system, a physical space that contains the entire round of life, batch processing of inmates, and the tight scheduling and formal organization of all activities. Furthermore, the inhabitants of the total institution are sharply divided between staff and powerless inmates. This setting provides the framework within which the selves of inmates are broken down in a process of mortification. Goffman describes the obvious, largely physical mortification that the inmate experiences when he or she enters the total institution—shaving of the head, stripping, humiliation and beatings, degradation, and bodily markings and defilement.

This round of mortification, in turn, sets the stage for more subtle psychological destruction of the self, such as looping.

Looping is a striking example of a process for destroying selves, and its elaboration is an excellent example of Goffman's way of thinking and writing. Goffman (1961a) describes looping as the situation in which

> an agency that creates a defensive response on the part of the inmate
> takes this very response as the target of its next attack. The individual

finds that his protective response to an assault upon the self is collapsed into the situation; he cannot defend himself in the usual way
by establishing distance between the mortifying situation and himself ... In total institutions spheres of life are desegregated, so that
an inmate's conduct in one scene of activity is thrown up to him
by staff as a comment or check upon his conduct in another context. A mental patient's effort to present himself in a well-oriented,
unantagonistic manner during a diagnostic or treatment conference
may be directly embarrassed by evidence introduced concerning his
apathy during recreation or bitter comments he made in a letter to
a sibling—a letter which the recipient has forwarded to the hospital
administrator, to be added to the patient's dossier and brought along
to the conference. (37)

Similarly, the face-saving reactive expressions that people use in ordinary
interaction—sullenness, sotto voce profanity, signs of contempt, irony, and
derision—are immediately used as grounds for further punishment. In looping everything the inmate does is held against him or her, including efforts
to rescue the self from mortification, to complain about mistreatment, or to
express any degree of distance or criticism of the staff and the institution.

While Goffman notes looping as a major way of discrediting the self in total
institutions, we are probably familiar with cases of looping in organizations. For
instance, someone who has been sexually harassed or made the subject of racist
remarks files a complaint—and then the complaint is used as evidence that this
person is hysterical, overreacts to minor problems, and fails to be collegial or a team
player. Lodging the complaint itself has become the target of the next attack.

Asylums was based on Goffman's observations of a large mental hospital,
but the more general concept of the total institution encompasses mental
hospitals, prisons, concentration camps, the military, and the closed worlds of
cults and religious indoctrination. In many ways, the total institution is not a
real place but a template, metaphor, or microcosm of the totalitarian tenden-
cies in society. Thus, his work was given a subversive reading as a critique of
all the processes that mold individuals into conformity, and, in this regard, it
parallels the theories of social control and surveillance that Michel Foucault
was developing at the same time in France, which we will encounter in the
next chapter. Like Foucault, Goffman saw the discourses surrounding mental
illness as a paradigm of classification and discreditation. But Goffman's writing was more direct and accessible than Foucault's; he was less interested in
large historical shifts and more involved in observing and describing face-to-
face interactions.

The World of the Institution

Goffman's analysis of institutions is functional in approach. He considers institutions in terms of assessing their purpose, in other words, their intention to accomplish some instrumental goal, whether it be economic, educational, medical, or punitive for the protection of the wider community. Whether for incapacitation, deterrence, rehabilitation, or reformation, the institution functions as a means of social control. This social control is worked out through a structured hierarchy between binary categories (caregivers and care receivers, guards and prisoners, doctors and patients, the well and the sick) that determine the power dynamics between groups in the institution. The authorities within any institution have the right to discipline those who are subject to its rules whenever needed. This total control creates a dynamic of inequality and increasing desensitization and distancing from the institution for the inmates; in turn, hierarchy, authority, and distance all lead to an ever-increasing control and exercise of power of one group over the other. Authorities also use a system of punishment and reward to perpetuate this hierarchy that simultaneously functions as a strategy of control through the deployment of incentives for prisoner or patient compliance. Since the authorities are always right and the inmates are always wrong or ill, these power dynamics become taken for granted and accepted as the normal functioning of the institution. In this way, Goffman's analysis leads to the exposure of total institutions as self-sustaining and self-legitimating organizations; institutions legitimate their activity through defining their aims and ideals, and those aims and ideals legitimate the activity institutions take to secure those goals. Perhaps, in this regard as well, his analysis can be read as a fable or metaphor of all institutions, not only total ones.

The World of the Inmate

For those interned, total institutions create and sustain a particular kind of tension between the outside world (of which the patient or inmate is no longer a part) and the institutional world (where the patient belongs). This tension is used to further the social control and management of those inside the institution. Total institutions work to uncover the truth of illness or crime and to strip away the layers of the prisoner or patient that deny or refuse this analysis. The inmate is unveiled to himself or herself and to others as the sick or criminal person that the institutional authorities have insisted he or she really is. At this point, alternative performances of self have been so undermined and discredited that the inmate can be corrected, reformed, or rehabilitated—made over in the image mandated by the institutional authorities. Through forced interaction and group activity, the individual is prevented from autonomous or individual decision-making or from exercising agency. This undermining of autonomous action happens primarily and most powerfully, according to Goffman, through the process of looping in which the inmates learn to condition themselves through accepting the definition of the self imposed by the institution, to conform their actions to this definition, and to adjust their behavior to that expectation. In the case of mental patients, the reactions to their situation are collapsed back on the situation itself, so there is no longer differentiation between the individual and the situation. The institution and the patient's identification with the institution are supposed to become one and the same.

How Does the Self Deal with This?

Although these institutions are total, this does not mean that the total institution is socially deterministic or that there is no room for any freedom. Those inside institutions are still able to exercise some degree of agency, however limited. A total institution tries to completely control and define those subject to its authority, but those subjected try to resist this domination through various tactics. For example, those subjected to the institution create a *situational withdrawal* in which the inmates withdraw apparent attention from everything except events immediately around the body and see these through their own perspective or daydream; in other words, they fantasize to distance themselves from this world. Another tactic is to form an *intransigent line*: the inmates intentionally challenge the institution by non-compliance with activities, thereby risking punishment and additional looping. Or they can accept a form of colonization whereby the establishment is taken as a whole and an existence is built out of maximum satisfactions procurable within the institution. And finally inmates accept *conversion* to the institution, yielding to the supervisors' or authorities' definition of self and the role of institution.

The tactics inmates use demonstrate that the exercise of power usually meets with resistance. Few inmates surrender completely to the labels, definitions, and rules imposed on them by the staff. Yet their resistance is weak, their agency very limited, and their tactics of resistance often lead to further punishment and humiliation. We will return to these themes in our discussion of Michel Foucault.

The Consequences for the Inmate

When an individual is removed from the outside world and becomes an inmate, he or she must construct a new self-narrative. Time incarcerated is time wasted or time taken away from life. Without the acknowledgement of the outside world, the inmate loses corroboration of the former pre-institutional self. All sense of autonomy or self-determination is annulled inside the total institution. Confined to a total institution, the subject loses the tool kit for identity construction, as he or she no longer has mirrors to reflect back anything other than the monolithic and negative identity the institution imposes. The institution offers few resources for the creation or definition of self. Within the total institution, all times and spaces are under surveillance; there is no privacy or place to hide in embarrassment. This constant unveiling without recourse to some other definition of self ultimately crushes self-worth and individualism, as there is no self other than the one defined by the institution.

Questions That Remain

If the self that is brought into the institution is disarticulated, stripped down, and resocialized for life inside the institution, what happens to those released back into the outside world? Is it possible that, for an inmate released from a total institution that has redefined his or her identity, the threat of stigma, of being forever classified as sick or deviant, creates an overwhelming state of anxiety in which the released inmate may be too weak or broken down to resume coping back in the outside world free of the total institution's regulation? Does the total institution strip us bare—cause a complete disassociation—so that we may lose the ability to acquire the habits and norms required in mainstream society? Is there a self to be had in a world totally under surveillance? If there is no back stage to be had, can we claim a self at all that is ours and not the product of the total institution? Finally, how does the institution create the symptoms it is designed to treat? (Later, we will see the same question posed in a more explicit fashion by Foucault in his critique of institutions.)

STIGMA: DISFIGURED, DISCREDITED, AND SECRET SELVES

All of Goffman's work, including *Asylums*, focuses on the self and the ways in which each person tries to present the self—often cynically and dishonestly in order to keep identities consistent—and on the way other people perceive and discredit these performances and seek to humiliate, mortify, and destroy the self. *Stigma*, published in 1963, continued Goffman's observation of self-presentation, focusing on those selves that could not be candidly presented. Those identities that could not be shown were constantly subjected to being unveiled and therefore exposed for their deficiencies. Some stigmas are readily apparent—a disfigured face, physical disabilities, or the 'wrong' racial identity; other stigmas can be kept secret—a record of incarceration or an autobiography of racial passing. Because one is always in the precarious position of having an identity spoiled or discredited, or of having a false presentation revealed, Goffman dissects the multiple strategies people deploy in coping with these hidden or visible spoiled identities.

Goffman theorizes stigma as a process whereby constructed or physical characteristics are valued or devalued (arbitrarily), and he examines how these stigmas become taken-for-granted meanings. Stigma, in effect, can be seen as turning culturally based meanings into naturalized or inherent meanings about different groups of people. This process works through the binary classification of self and other, or normal and deviant.

Goffman's theory of stigma forces us to think about the ways that we interact both consciously and unconsciously with others, as well as to confront the visceral effects of stigmas not as abstractions but as real influences on the identities and life chances of those stigmatized. Within the framework of stigma, we can consider how members of different groups compete and struggle for the power of normalcy, to be legitimated, or to have the stigma removed from their group; this could be along racial, gender, sexual orientation, or physical lines. Stigma is not a predetermined process; stigmas are the result of cultural labor and the exercise of power by one group over another. Here again, we can see Goffman as a conflict theorist of sorts because those who are able to wield more power are able to stigmatize others with greater ability or to control discrediting information being circulated about themselves and others.

Linking stigma to frames of reference, we can think of stigma as the use of categories to regulate our modes of interaction and behavior in face-to-face interaction. Stigma functions as a regulatory or socializing power of self-management and self-presentation to others. In this way, we can see how looping relates to stigma. By internalizing and regulating behavior through self-monitoring, individuals reproduce the dominant social distinctions without the need for coercion to reproduce the hegemonic social order. Through the sense of stigma, we can see how Goffman was also a theorist of power, not the power of coercion or the direct power one group wields over another but power that operates underneath consciousness in the very categories through which we apprehend the world. Stigma, the difference between the normal and abnormal, forms the frames of reference and becomes the natural perspective on the world. Goffman's theory of stigma ultimately offers us an explanation of how face-to-face interaction between individuals and groups in everyday life links to much larger structural patterns of inequality by allowing us to draw out the implications for much broader macro patterns of social interaction.

Stigma evolves out of both *Presentation of Self* and *Asylums*. In the theory developed in *Stigma*, we see a combination of how people present themselves and are classified by others that is context dependent. Goffman focuses again on the control of discrediting information, on the normative regulation of behavior through the use or non-application of stigma, on how 'proven' identities and projected identities are kept consistent, on how stigma functions as both a regulatory and disciplinary socializing power through self-management, and on the self's social relations to others. This whole process is a continuous activity that is always precarious because of the possibility of its being revealed, which, at the limit, creates a sense of paranoia. This is also like the micro-practices of power because people internalize and regulate their behavior down to the smallest level of detail. These minute power processes become more efficient the more self-monitoring takes place, so no coercion is necessary to keep people in their places, and people reproduce and assent to the hegemonic social order.

All three of these works are about the self, despite the superficially different subject matter of *Asylums*. They are about the ways in which people try to present their selves—often cynically and dishonestly—and the way other people discredit these performances and seek to humiliate, mortify, and destroy the self.

INTERACTION ORDER AND BEHAVIOR

In Goffman's analysis, the self is not just an isolated set of performances that can be believed or discredited in micro-interactions alone. For him, the presentation of self occurs in public in what he refers to as the 'interaction order.' He defines society as a reification of interactions, rituals, and performances (an idea shared with symbolic interactionists). Goffman's sociology of everyday life posits that micro-interactions and everyday behavior are as serious a subject as problems of the state and economy. Attention to the rules of interaction in public demands constant awareness. The risk of losing face and being discredited becomes greater as one moves from the small group exchange to the public itself. Again, in public, the primary mode of comportment is to save face. In many ways, Goffman's view of public interaction (as seen in *Behavior in Public Places*, *Relations in Public*, and *Interaction Ritual*) communicates an existential angst, as one is constantly subjected to the terrifying fact that there is no meaning other than the despair that may result from one's embarrassment.

In addition, in *Behavior in Public Places*, Goffman suggests that there is an irony in that, to be civil and obey the social norms, one must be in many ways antisocial. Goffman discusses strategies of interaction almost always in defensive modes of conduct: deterrence, avoidance, shields, distractions, and diversions. The commonsense emotions and social bonds we assume people strive for in everyday life—love, intimacy, and connection and relation to one's community—seem not to have any place in Goffman's world. For Goffman, it is best to make one's behavior as innocuous as possible so that you always have deniability for your actions. In his view, there is no reward or adulation— rather, the act of saving face is as good as it gets. The non-engagement of people in public places takes on the motions of avoidance of people, distance and spacing from others, and inattention to other people. These strategies serve to save face and avoid embarrassment. These defensive actions are the regulatory norms that undermine the establishment of any and all social connection but, for Goffman, create and sustain the social organization.

The ways we interact always are precarious; we need successful engagement to save face. Goffman outlines several sets of strategies for interaction. One of them is the strategy of 'supportive rituals' in which we act in supportive ways, such as extending concern, sympathy, and comfort to others. These supportive actions are reassurance displays; through congratulations, condolences, greetings and acknowledgements, and other rituals, we reconfirm the status of the relationship. Contact occurs by means of participating in the same social occasion, such as a business, an accident, or a ceremony, which all provide the reminder and need for supportive expressions and thus become rituals that sustain the social order and the basis of social interaction.

Just as Goffman discusses the presentation of self, he also discusses the multiple roles a self can play. In *Encounters*, Goffman defines a role as an activity the actor engages in based on the normative demands upon that position within society. A role differs from a performance because a role comprises the actual conduct of particular individuals in this position as a cycle of face-to-face social situations with others that is in relation to relevant audiences; a role is not a one-time event. A 'role set' is a group of norms relating to the multiple roles in the ways we relate to others. Through roles, tasks in society are allocated and arrangements are made to enforce these repetitive performances.

However, the manner in which individuals manage their multiple roles may conflict with each other. Goffman offers two possibilities when performing a role—that of embracing the role and that of distancing oneself from the role. Role embracement is a complete involvement in the role; the activity is seen and made seamless in one's actions. Role distance is a complete or an attempted separation from role communicated through a release of tension, acknowledgement that the role is beneath you.

As in the performance of self, there is constant failure around the corner; in role enactment, we cannot completely control the information given off and taken in by others about ourselves. Roles, if consistent, get sanctioned; roles are contingent upon the responses and reactions of others, and one may have trouble changing them once they are established and identified with the performer. Goffman further discusses role performance in relation to the body or, as he terms it, 'the body idiom.' For Goffman, the body idiom is bodily behavior that conveys complex information to others, even when words are not spoken. For example, dress, body language, facial gestures, and emotional expressions all comprise the body idiom. All express one's social attributes and one's sense of self, of others, and of the setting. The body idiom involves more than a non-significant conversation; Goffman considered the body idiom a 'conventionalized discourse' because an individual can never stop communicating through the body idiom. Although people are not always conscious of the signals or meanings they are giving off, they will quickly become self aware if communication is out of the ordinary or the body idiom is in direct contradiction to what is being spoken. Just like the words we utter, our bodies are also linked directly to the normative order, either conforming to what others are doing or failing to do so and/or losing face and being discredited in the process. By bringing the body into the center of the presentation of self, Goffman once again raises the specter of anxiety; while words may deceive us, the body never lies.

Following Durkheim, Goffman sees role performance in everyday social life as normatively stable yet evanescent in that every social gathering or social situation is temporal and open to the possibility of change. The primacy of temporality, the fleeting nature of time, is at the center of Goffman's analysis. For Goffman, it is not people and the moments they have but rather the flux of life and the people that are caught up in it that matter most. As we see in the presentation of self, in the interaction order there is a minimal model of self: the self is a placeholder, like a chess piece, a faceless and fleeting pawn, whose interaction with other faceless actors is a momentarily stable incident within the larger world that is constantly in flux. Through interaction rituals, the self is an image pieced together from the full flow of events that occur; this image establishes one's reputation in good or bad play, and it may be part of the face saving that any particular player must maintain in order to stay in the game.

We must ensure a particular interaction order to sustain consistency. This consistency happens not only through the judgments and sanctions of others but also through each individual developing a repertoire of face-saving practices to guard against possible threats and contingencies, through constant self-reflexivity and micro-management (the panopticon effect, a term we will encounter in Foucault's work too). If we apply the panopticon effect to the affairs of everyday interaction, where everyone is always performing, always on camera, where there are no dress rehearsals and everything is under the microscope, there is the constant possibility of being discredited in one's role or of unintentionally discrediting oneself at any moment.

Therefore, for Goffman, the world is never neutral; in fact, Goffman's world is a brutal world where face-work (the avoidance of embarrassment and discreditation and the maintenance of a credible front) can be seen as an arena of contest and combat, not just acceptance and mutual consideration. Here one scores points and makes gains for oneself, displaying as much capital as possible favorable to oneself and damaging to others, in all social spheres. Two questions linger: What ultimately holds the moral order together, and why is it not torn apart by individual self-interest in an anxiety-riddled theater of life?

FRAMES OF REFERENCE AND DISCOURSE

FRAME ANALYSIS, FORMS OF TALK, AND GENDER ADVERTISEMENTS

Frames: How We Learn to Limit What We See

Eventually, Goffman became intrigued by the way that discourses and images in the media shape thought. As empirical material to support this theoretical direction, he analyzed hundreds of advertising images to show how gender is constructed in these images in simple elements such as the positions or expressions of the models in the pictures. He contributed the terms 'framing' and 'frame analysis' to the theoretical analysis of the media. The words and images of the media are frames that limit our ability to see realities.

For Goffman, social experience is organized by the frames—the principles of organization we apply that govern the subjective meaning we give to events. In this way, all experience is relational, lodged in the ways that we relate to a particular event. Frames are not personal or individual creations, yet experiences are built upon the use of frames because frames comprise a mutually agreed upon or socially accepted orientation to life. In addition, Goffman explores how experience is interpreted through one of the two *primary frameworks* that underlie all experience—the natural and the social. Natural occurrences happen through the natural framework and are not morally judged, but those that occur through the social framework are morally judged. Relational refers to how we relate to events and to people. These relations are not individual or idiosyncratic creations, but are built up with frames, the ways we organize and understand our experiences. Also, Goffman argues that experiences can be *keyed* or have a *key* to them in that they may be interpreted in different ways depending on context. Finally, Goffman looks at the *designs* and *fabrications* that are intentional efforts to manage activity, to create a false belief in others as to what is going on, or to frame events and experiences in a particular way in order to obtain a particular meaning or outcome.

Goffman thought that frames are part of all human interaction, as they are anchored to everyday life, but frames are not bound to an objective reality because all frames rely on layers of other frames of social meanings. Although all frames allow us a sense of reality, their operation does not imply that the world is transparent. Any person or situation can be misconstrued or misunderstood. Just as Goffman argued in *Stigma*, there is no objective certainty that the frame used to interpret a person or situation is correct. It is quite possible that a person or occurrence may be viewed through a distorted or ill-fitting frame or be *misframed*. As in any presentation of self, there is always the possibility that something can go wrong or that others may interpret our performance incorrectly. Again, we can see Goffman as a micro-conflict theorist because frames themselves, like stigmas, are exercised with greater authority and power by those in the dominant positions to establish them and apply them as the correct frameworks through which to interpret the world.

Frame analysis makes the implicit assumptions we share about the world explicit. Frames prevent us from having to guess what is to be done in any situation because we share a common pre-established point of reference. Frames serve as the ultimate backdrop for all of Goffman's theorizing in that they are the basis within which any social interaction or exchange of meaning can occur. Without frames, every situation would have to be defined consensually down to the minute details. Every social interaction would then take excruciating time and labor to reach the assumed intersubjective understanding that frames provide. For example, if I enter a restaurant, I expect to be seated and have a menu presented to me. Without these basic frames, the idea of a restaurant—of host, patron, and the interaction that is assumed when one walks in the door—could not exist.

Goffman's extension of the concept of frame is worked out in his two late works *Forms of Talk* and *Gender Advertisements*. In *Forms of Talk*, Goffman argues that all communication is governed by social conventions and mutually shared understandings and presuppositions upon which we draw collectively and which always depend on social context, that talk is always a form of social interaction, and that talk is aimed at establishing meaning in relation to our own utterances and social interactions. In the case of talk, framing is always at work in the way that people express themselves and are interpreted by others.

In *Gender Advertisements*, Goffman applies frames to explain how social interaction is framed to produce the meaning of gender. Through socialization, people learn to express gender in social situations that reinscribe the natural sex differences that appear important. Similar to Goffman's argument about the presentation of self, the idea here is that gender is given expression through *displays*, which, like presentations, are not backed by any underlying human nature or biology but are learned cultural acts or framed expressions. From the things we use to the places we go, in all situations, gender is an organized set of roles permeating the entire social organization. As these gender differences are replicated throughout all spheres of society, they become, in turn, legitimating tools of social differences and social inequality. (It is interesting to note that Goffman outlines the different positions but suggests no opportunities nor desire for social change. An explicitly critical perspective on these naturalized displays of gender awaited the work of Judith Butler, which we will discuss at the end of the chapter on Foucault.)

The constant possibility of miscommunication, of spoiled identities, of failed performances, of discredited roles, and of misframing underscores the isolation and alienation that all individuals are faced with in every social encounter because miscommunication and misunderstanding lie in every encounter. Despite humans' professed need for love, intimacy, and meaningful relationships, these goals are not real possibilities in Goffman's world. The best we can do is to try and save face in this theater of the absurd—a theater encompassing both the comedic and tragic.

Normativity Overrides Morality

Goffman's ultimate concern with the normative order that shapes all social interaction becomes a theoretical thread to link Durkheim, Goffman, and Foucault together. All three thinkers, starting with Durkheim, argue that normativity overrides morality. For all three, morality is built into the normative order; morality is not something over and above it, which somehow regulates the normative order. For all three thinkers, whether people act out of virtue or against their will or desire, as long as the norms of a society are upheld, that is all that matters within the society. (The sociologist can have a personal code of ethics or morality—both Durkheim and Foucault certainly expressed theirs—but it is essentially on hold during the process of sociological inquiry.) All three theorize a world where it does not matter if actions are undertaken for moral or sincere intentions as long as you play your role according to the audience. This is a world without morals—with only performed roles and prescribed rituals of interaction. The power of normativity expressed in Durkheim's work on crime, deviance, social structures, and social organization reappears in the world Goffman theorizes at the micro-level of face-to-face interaction; and it eventually resurfaces in Foucault's concept of 'bio-power'— the idea that socialization and social control are one and the same.

BEHAVIOR IN PUBLIC PLACES

Goffman's observations of self-performance and total institutions became the basis for *Behavior in Public Places*. He was beginning to insist that society is lodged in the rules of interaction, in intentional and unintentional communication expressed through words, rituals, gestures, and body language on an ongoing, everyday basis. In other words, we speak of society, but this expression is only a misleading shortcut for referring to ongoing rule-guided actions and interactions. Reification is a term that means the false representation of processes or actions as a concrete, material thing, such as a desk, a tree, or a person. Society, according to Goffman, does not exist as a thing.

Goffman's fieldwork for *Asylums* (as an observer in a mental hospital) contributed to his view that micro-interactions and everyday behavior are as serious a subject for sociology as problems of the state and economy. These interactions are the sites of mortification, inequality, and power. *Behavior in Public Places* and his work on interaction rituals expanded his observations from self-performance and total institutions to many other situations.

THE POLITICS AND FEELING-TONE OF GOFFMAN'S WORK

In his engaging personal thoughts on Erving Goffman, Gary Marx (1984) remembers Goffman's opening remarks to a class: 'With a wry smile he said "we will try and keep you entertained."' Marx (1984) describes Goffman in the following terms:

> Goffman presented himself as a detached, hardboiled intellectual
> cynic; the sociologist as 1940s private eye. His was a hip, existential,
> cool, essentially apolitical (at least in terms of the prevailing ideolo-
> gies) personal style. As a Canadian Jew of short stature working at
> the margins (or perhaps better, frontiers) of a marginal discipline,
> he was clearly an outsider. His brilliance and marginality meant an
> acute eye and a powerful imagination. He had a fascination with
> other people's chutzpah, weirdness, and perhaps even degradation.
> (653)

These qualities made him a spellbinding lecturer. Roberta Garner remembers two hours flying by at the University of Chicago as we heard him dissect
casino gambling and reveal the myths and illusions that gamblers cannot
shake even as they lose their life savings.

There is an unsettling and even sinister quality to Goffman's perspective,
and this feeling-tone is an area of convergence with Foucault, paralleling
Foucault's fascination with freaks, limit experiences, and extreme situations.
For Goffman, in social interaction, many things are not as they seem but
are cynically and consciously manipulated in the performances of everyday
life, in the impression management in which all individuals engage. Most
performances are deliberate stagings, created to gain advantage and to hide
stigmas and secrets; few performances are 'from the heart.' Most observers
of these performances are in turn skeptical of what they see, and, especially
in total institutions, the identity and self of the inmate are constantly discredited by the audiences. In the larger society, the media use their ample
resources and the power to create images in order to shape our perceptions
and our selves.

The structural foundation to the play of performances lies in the fact
that they are tightly scripted and must follow strict rules to be convincing. The guiding norms are not moral precepts but aesthetic judgments.
Goffman plays with the idea that performances must follow rules, and
the more rule-bound the performance, the more likely that nothing is as
it seems. The more calculated, cynical, and even antisocial the purpose
of a team or individual, the more closely the performance must fit the
rules of interaction, the criterion of aesthetic coherence, and the script
of sincerity.

Goffman's own writing style conveys despair and detached amusement
at the same time. We are not quite sure if we are meant to feel sad about
the mortification and self-dismantling that inmates and the stigmatized
undergo—or be merely intrigued and entertained.

RUPTURE AND CONTINUITY: GOFFMAN AS A TRANSITIONAL GIANT AND POSTMODERNIST

Goffman's emphasis on interaction and performance shows a sharp break not only with structural-functional theory but also with the conflict theories of the 1960s. It rejects stable structure and predictable lines of identity formation and cleavage in societies. The dramaturgical model makes society seem fluid, unstable, and as ephemeral as an evening of theater. We are all Tinkerbells who can survive only if the audience applauds hard and long enough.

If the self exists in performance and is easily discredited, it suggests that the self and other apparently stable aspects of social reality are the products of certain types of discourses and practices. Goffman does not use these terms, but his analysis converges with the work of Foucault and others who do, and his observations of media framing also converge with the analysis of discourse.

Goffman's work suggests that there is a current of conflict running through all interactions. There may be consensus on what constitutes a convincing performance, but there is little consensus on anything else. Performance suggests aesthetic criteria rather than moral consensus. Unlike the conflict theorists of his day, Goffman does not take sides on what appear to be the major struggles of the times. In *Asylums,* he reveals clearly enough who the underdogs are—inmates—but this is not the same as signaling his allegiances on major political issues of the day, let alone identifying with particular movements or parties.

Goffman's work elicits contradictory interpretations. Was he sort of a symbolic interactionist or sort of a structural-functionalist in the tradition of Durkheim—or a micro-conflict theorist defending the mad, stigmatized, and incarcerated? Was he cool and ironic or a passionate champion of the most marginalized and humiliated people in modern societies?

Goffman has selected certain limiting situations and cases to reveal the general processes of self-performance and discrediting, namely, the situations of the 'mad' and the stigmatized. For structural-functionalists, these situations were at the margin of society, to be considered under the rubric of deviance and dysfunction. For Goffman, no one is safely immune from having the self discredited; most people have secrets to hide and dubious performances to offer to skeptical publics. Furthermore, psychiatric perspectives are key examples of coherent, organized ways of discrediting the self; psychiatry is not a professional practice to help deviants at the margins of society (the structural-functional view) but the contemporary paradigm and template for discourses and rituals of discrediting. Goffman shares this interest in madness and the construction of normality and insanity with Foucault.

Though breaking with the structural-functional theories of his day, Goffman returns to Durkheim and the roots of sociology. One of the ways in which Goffman was a transitional giant was his astonishing reconceptualization of Durkheim's legacy. Most structural-functionalists considered themselves Durkheim's heirs because of their emphasis on social structure and the functions of social institutions (not to be confused with total institutions). Goffman transformed Durkheim's legacy from a view of a framework of structure and functions into the study of normative regulation built into performance scripts and media frames—that is, into highly constrained interactions and discourses. Individuals and teams can only attain their essentially primitive, self-interested aims if they adhere to these scripts or, in unusual cases, succeed in developing effective new ones that meet the largely aesthetic criteria for guiding a good performance. Their performances must be convincing.

This model is a powerful alternative interpretation of Durkheim that contrasts with the conventional structural-functional reading of Durkheim, which had envisioned society as a system composed of institutions functioning to maintain stability. Goffman shares Durkheim's view of the self as empty and fundamentally irrelevant, but he does not substitute 'institution' for 'self' as a basic unit of society. Rather, he pursues Durkheim's concept of normative regulation to its logical extreme. Regulation is revealed—made manifest—in the scripted interactions and the ongoing judgment of performances as convincing and credible or unconvincing. Goffman's dramaturgical reconceptualization of Durkheim's radically sociological vision avoids the reification inherent in phrases such as 'collective conscience' and 'institution.'

Also, Goffman shows more of an interest in the body than previous theorists. Structural-functionalist theory had been curiously disembodied (the messy body had been left to structural-functionalism's psychological partner, psychoanalysis). People had roles and statuses but not bodies. Marxists were interested in how factories and machineries warped the body, but, apart from a few throwaway lines on sensual pleasure in the communist future, there was little about the body in Marxism either. It was feminists who opened up this area of theory most decisively, but we can already see its outlines—of a mostly repulsive and gruesome turn—in Goffman's observations of performance, stigmatized and disfigured bodies, and bodily defilement in total institutions.

Finally, relatively late in his career, Goffman was intrigued by the media and media framing, showing that he too was caught up in looking at the explosion of media in society, one of the key trends in the new paradigms, as we indicated in Chapter 2.

All of these themes and perspectives reveal Goffman as an explorer pointing sociological theorists toward a new terrain.

KEY TERMS

- dramaturgical model
- everyday life
- frames
- impression management
- interaction order
- intransigent line
- looping
- presentation of self
- saving face/discrediting
- situational withdrawal
- stigma
- total institutions

Chapter 4

MICHEL FOUCAULT (1926–1984)

The work of Michel Foucault transformed social theory by the end of the century. All the categories of Marxist analysis, conflict theories, and mainstream thinking were seemingly 'melted into air' by the radical innovations of the French theorist, a professor at elite institutions at the top of the French system of higher education. It is difficult to write about Foucault without constant use of the word 'yet' because the conclusions of his early writing are different from those of his later writing, and he is not afraid of contradicting himself. His initial work shows strong continuity with the ideas of the conservative reaction, Comte, and Durkheim—a French tradition that de-emphasizes the individual and highlights the compelling and external character of culture. While Foucault is considered a post-structuralist, he shares the structuralists' dismissal of theories based on individual action and agency. Like the structuralists, he is a perpetrator of 'the death of the subject'—the rejection of theories that focus on individual choices and the effects of human actions. Yet his later work was primarily about the self.

Foucault is the French Goffman, but his work is more difficult to read, more obviously influenced by European philosophy—especially Nietzsche and Heidegger—and more attuned to large-scale changes in the structure of thought. The many similarities between his work and Goffman's suggest that their ideas were influenced by the climate of the times and reflect changes in society itself. What was the climate of the times, and how did the work of Goffman and Foucault signal a shift? In both men's writing, we can discern a turning away from existentialism, a popular orientation after World War II. Existentialism, most notably associated with Jean-Paul Sartre, emphasized individual choice, the authentic self, and the creation of a world through human action. In contrast, both Foucault and Goffman were inclined to de-emphasize the human subject and to look at society as the product of a template or script acted out by people who had interests without responsibility. Yet, especially for

Foucault, the apparent rejection of Sartre's perspective masks an existential affirmation of existence without a normative foundation, a possibility of self construction that becomes clearer in his later work.

Both Foucault and Goffman rejected another popular orientation of the times, psychoanalysis. In the psychoanalytic perspective, individuals have a deep core of the self, which must be discovered or unearthed through therapy, and they are able to expand their spheres of rational action as they became more aware of their unconscious impulses. The work of both Goffman and Foucault dismisses this fundamentally hopeful view of human nature. For all its emphasis on the dark side of the unconscious, psychoanalytic theory always retained the hope that, by bringing unconscious drives into light, humans could evolve toward freedom. For Goffman and Foucault, these hopes seemed unlikely to be realized. Thus, their work, although different, shares a loss of faith in progress toward freedom, a stance that was in line with the emergent ideologies of postmodernism. Their writings share a strangely playful foreboding tone. Yet, throughout his life, Foucault's focus on domination suggests attention to its opposite—freedom—and the possibility of freedom becomes clearer in his last works on care of the self.

MAJOR WORKS, IDEAS, AND CONCEPTS

Key concepts in Foucault's writing include discursive formation, discipline, punishment, power and knowledge, the body, surveillance and policing, the state and governmentality, and the care and regulation of the self. This list of concepts follows a roughly chronological order that corresponds to shifts in his ideas. It would be mistaken to identify these shifts as an evolution or as steps in a path of conceptual development. The trajectory of his ideas is not clear and straightforward, his methods are not conventional empirical research methods, he takes apparently contradictory positions on many fundamental issues, and the reader is constantly left with the task of making a coherent mosaic out of many fragments. One scholar sums up the situation in this way:

> Foucault's work is at root ad hoc, fragmentary and incomplete. Each of
> his books is determined by concerns and approaches specific to it and
> should not be understood as developing a theory or method that is a
> general instrument of intellectual progress. (Gutting 1994: 2)

Foucault's ideas changed as he wrote a series of books, including *Madness and Civilization* (1965), *Archaeology of Knowledge* (1969), *Discipline and Punish* (1979), and *History of Sexuality* (1980). The titles recall Durkheim's *Suicide* and his work on crime and punishment. Like Durkheim, Foucault focused on deviance and on acts and conditions that appear to be highly personal and individually unique—sex and insanity. Like Durkheim, Foucault was intent on showing that these apparently individual behaviors can only be understood by examining prevailing cultural frameworks or, as Foucault referred to them, discursive formations.

Foucault's *Madness and Civilization* is one of his first efforts to introduce the concept of discursive formation and the changing definitions of madness and normality that are imposed through a historical sequence of discursive formations. His next works of sociological relevance are *Archaeology of Knowledge* and *Discipline and Punish*, writing focused on punishment and regulation, the relationship between knowledge and the exercise of power, and the body as the locus of these processes. Foucault sought to understand the interlocking relationships between these processes by asking how truth is produced, circulated, and controlled, as well as how truth is used through particular channels, manipulations, and streams of power that distribute it.

Foucault coined and introduced the term 'governmentality,' a word that fused *government* and *mentality* to encapsulate a new consent-inducing art of governing. This concept allowed Foucault to raise issues concerning historically grounded practices that can be said to constitute government and to consider debates over what forms government can take, who is to govern, as well as who is to be governed. Governmentality involves positive incentives, manipulated consent, coordination of various public and private stakeholders, harnessing of expertise, a shift from public-sector funding to the coordination of multiple funding streams, and a constant redefinition of goals and priorities in public discourse. This process has enabled states to administer large societies with a relatively low level of coercion and an equally low level of government spending. The current mode of governmentality, neoliberalism, is defined by the withdrawal of the state from direct intervention in society and the state's shift to a role of manipulating and managing multiple private partnerships (Light 2001). The market becomes the main mechanism for inducing self-regulation.

The theme of regulation of the self grew larger in his later work. Toward the end of his life, he wrote a history of sexuality that explored social control and the self. One theme was the sequence of shifts in the understanding of same-sex relations in ancient Greece, Christian Europe, and modern Western culture. But the real topic of the book (and of other late writing) is technologies of the self, the different ways in which the self is taken as an object of regulation in successive historical periods, and, above all, the contrast between autonomous self-regulation and self-regulation imposed or manipulated by others.

These striking new concepts transformed theories in the social sciences, cultural studies, comparative literature, gender studies, and many other fields.

DISCURSIVE FORMATIONS

A discursive formation is a way of representing the nature of society and human beings. It is a framework of words and images, as well as practices, a framework that constitutes the internal social organization of any historical period. At any point in time, we see ourselves primarily through these words and images. These words and images are shared by the entire society (and by groups of societies such as the Western world). In some societies, they are said to be religious, while in others they claim to be scientific. In all cases, the discursive formations are systems of knowledge, claims to understand the nature of human beings and the practices that comprise the world in which we live. Historical change involves change in discursive formations, major shifts from one to another form.

Foucault's method for understanding these shifts was not to research and write an orderly, chronological history of ideas in conventional form, but to engage in 'archaeology.' This term means an unearthing of structures of thought that continue to affect our ways of thinking; these structures are usually excavated in fragmentary forms, just as an archaeologist finds pieces of old walls or little potsherds, possibly in dusty forgotten places. Foucault often found these fragments in old medical texts or the diaries of mad people. Later, Foucault revised this archaeological approach to include 'genealogy,' a term he drew from the work of Nietzsche to refer to the method of tracing origins and subsequent historical shifts and transformations of structures of thought that dominate our orientations today.

A discursive formation can be seen as a set of round holes into which the unpredictable, multi-shaped pegs of human experience are crammed. The round holes define what is normal and deviant, sane and insane, natural and unnatural. The discourses form the objects of which they speak; we create 'madness,' 'deviance,' or 'perversion' by creating and naming these categories. As a pedagogical tool, these words are put in quotations since they have no essence or intrinsic meaning. The cramming of human acts and experiences into the categories of the discursive formation always involves the exercise of power, of action taken in order to have an effect on others' actions. It often requires enactment of punishments. Power is always met by some degree of resistance. Although discourses and labels appear to be only words, they are tightly linked to the exercise of power differences and ultimately to practices, including physical ones enacted on the body, such as torture, executions, incarceration, corporal punishment, insulin shock and electroshock, and many other treatments invented by the medical profession past and present or exercised by the system of 'corrections.' Even non-violent acts of power linked to definitions and classifications have a physical or bodily component, and this non-violent regulation of bodies for the purpose of productivity is especially a feature of capitalist societies. For instance, some workers are assigned offices with windows while others are in windowless cubicles; and different people are assigned different work schedules that organize their daily cycle of wakefulness and sleeping, eating, moving around freely, or commuting in a cramped, slow-moving vehicle.

The force of discursive formations is well illustrated by a topic that Foucault turned to later in his work, the history of human sexuality. Foucault argued that human sexuality is an historical form of discourse and practice that emerged through the personalization, medicalization, and signification of sex, which defines the core of personal identity (Dreyfus and Rabinow 1982). In other words, human sexuality is a construct derived from personal views, practices, and experiences (personalization); from the knowledge of doctors and psychiatrists (medicalization); and from the production and circulation of discourses about sex (signification). He used the phrase 'bodies and pleasures' for the fundamental and unorganized ground of sexuality. He meant that people fantasize, they are sexually aroused, and they engage in activities by themselves or with partners. Beyond these experiences and acts, sexuality has no intrinsic or natural organization. The discursive formations of successive epochs impose categories such as good and evil, natural and unnatural, virtuous and sinful, homosexual and heterosexual, or true/authentic and false/hypocritical on these experiences and acts—on bodies. The categories and terms are claims to knowing and classifying the true nature of sexuality. In different times and places, different rules govern sexual behavior. These rules are learned by individuals, shared in interaction, and sometimes formally codified.

A couple of examples may help clarify this viewpoint. In classical antiquity, sexuality was believed to be an expression of dominance. Penetration was seen as an act of dominance, engaged in by adult men with women, slaves, or adolescent boys of one's own social class. Some men felt ambivalent about relations with youth, because boys were going to mature into a category of social equals, unlike women and slaves. Christian teachings radically rearranged the categories and the meaning of the acts, defining all same-sex relations as sinful. Among the Sambia in Papua New Guinea (a case that Foucault did not discuss, but that illustrates his contention), the rules are different from both the ancient Greek and the Christian formations. Ingestion of semen is required for the attainment of manhood. In adolescent initiation rites, boys perform fellatio on older youths, a stage the initiate eventually attains himself. When a youth reaches adulthood, he marries a woman and, in most cases, engages exclusively in heterosexual sex thereafter. Men who continue to have sex with boys are seen not as immoral but as immature (Herdt 1987).

In modern Western societies, the classification rules are that people are either heterosexual (straight) or homosexual (gay or lesbian), that these are largely mutually exclusive categories, that if a person engages in same-sex activities or has same-sex fantasies, he or she is 'really' homosexual, and that, although homosexuality is some people's 'true identity,' it is nevertheless less natural than heterosexuality. Some people (generally fundamentalist Christians or Jews) believe that this deep homosexual identity can nevertheless be changed or 'cured' and transformed into a heterosexual one; others deny this possibility. In the contemporary discussion of homosexuality, rules and knowledge are in dispute. Foucault suggested that rules are, above all, rules of knowledge and classification; in most cases, they are also linked to judgments about morality vs. immorality, naturalness vs. unnaturalness, maturity vs. immaturity, or authenticity vs. hypocrisy. When a contemporary North American man admits to sexual acts with another man, but denies that he is gay, he is accused in only some communities of being immoral because of the acts themselves, but, in almost all circles, he is thought to be a liar and a hypocrite. Ancient Greeks would not have used these classifications. Their categories, rules, and evaluations of sexual acts were organized quite differently, in ways that did not match modern Western categories of true and false identities or moral and immoral acts.

Foucault's analysis of the discursive formation of 'madness' is similar. In all ages, some people's behavior fails to fit a norm. Those labeled 'mad' may be allowed to roam around freely or, as in modern times until the de-institutionalization of the 1970s, they may be placed in prison-like insane asylums. They may be defined in religious terms or, in modern times, subjected to medical analysis and treatment. These terms and definitions are intimately linked to practice, to material life (for example, the architecture of the prison and asylum), and, above all, to regimes imposed on bodies.

PUNISHMENT, DISCIPLINE, AND POWER

The definition of crime and the punishments it receives also vary. In the period of European history before the French Revolution, criminals were punished by corporal and capital punishment, subjected to gruesome tortures, and exhibited in public spectacles. The Enlightenment and the French Revolution marked the start of new ways of thinking about crime and punishment. After this turning point, criminals are incarcerated, separated and isolated from society. Emerging human sciences such as medicine, psychology, and sociology claim to understand the causes of crime and to be able to effect rehabilitation, the transformation of the character and behavior of criminals. The emphasis in regulatory regimes shifted to rehabilitation or 'corrections'—to the imposition of order and self-control on the imprisoned criminal.

Foucault saw these changes in the treatment of the mad and the criminal as a central feature of modern discursive formation, a topic that he elaborated in his writings on discipline, specifically, the human disciplines, such as medical practice and the social sciences, but, more generally, he used the term 'discipline' to mean the intertwining of power and knowledge. For Foucault, knowledge is never neutral or arbitrary; rather, knowledge is produced, circulated, and utilized for particular ends. In this way, knowledge exercises power over the decisions people make, the categories through which they think and classify the world, and the practices that define everyday life. Discipline operationalizes the active regulatory and normalizing effect of this intertwining relationship.

Modern discursive formation, then, is characterized by the dominance of the sciences—biology, economics, psychology, sociology—and by the translation of these disciplines' claims into fields of practice, such as medicine, psychotherapy, and social work. All these fields constitute disciplines of power; that is, they are focused on the imposition of order, social control, and the regulation of behavior and bodies. Technologies of all kinds—medication, electroshock, lobotomies, behavior modification, management practices, and computerized surveillance and record keeping—are put to the service of social regulation.

Like all systems of power, these disciplines employ a 'gaze,' a form of scrutiny exercised by those with power upon those with less power. Doctors examine patients, psychotherapists look at the disordered and the troubled, educators monitor children for signs of attention deficit and behavioral problems: These are all examples of surveillance. Foucault thus distances himself from the social sciences. He is not a social scientist and not complicit in the functions of the social sciences, which offer tools of normative regulation. He is especially critical of the well-intentioned efforts in all the contemporary human disciplines to make social regulation more refined and less brutal.

Although power operates from the top down, in both institutions and authorities, it also works from the bottom up and laterally. By viewing power as multidimensional, Foucault demonstrates that power is not something one has or wields over others; rather, it is constitutive of all social relations, norms, and practices, working on the dominant as well as the dominated. In this way, we can see that power is not centralized, not restricted to political institutions nor reducible to them; rather, power circulates in a web in which we are all enmeshed. This position raises enormous questions for the reader struggling with the question, what is theory good for?

THE BODY AND POWER

The Body

Foucault argues that the body is the basis of existence. (This position is implicit in much of Goffman's work and explicit in that of feminist theorists and Pierre Bourdieu, as we will see later; the body had been curiously absent from much sociological theory, which had often appeared to be written about disembodied selves, groups with roles and identities but no bodies, and mental orientations without a carnal basis.) Foucault's genealogical analyses, especially those on power, describe how the body is constructed and deconstructed. The body is the locus where the minutest social practices link up, intertwine, and connect to larger organizations of power. Power, here, is closer to the sociological term 'socialization.' Whereas sociologists use the concept neutrally, to define the processes by which we become human beings, or members of particular cultures or communities, the linkage of the term 'power' with 'socialization' here is to demonstrate the understanding that socialization is never neutral but a form of discipline by which particular definitions of identity and normalcy of behavior are defined. The multiple technologies, networks, and workings of power are articulated on and through bodies where dispositions, attitudes, orientations, and understandings of the world are embodied. By thinking about 'power' as 'socialization,' we can move from what appears to be abstract to the concrete empirical reality that Foucault is invested in revealing; as well, this view forces us to rethink our taken-for-granted sociological assumptions about what socialization means for social analysis. The body is not a fixed structure with fixed needs, nor is it a universal invariant or essence; it is the physical basis of culturally and historically situated constructions. In analyzing the body, Foucault seeks to understand both how the body can be divided up, manipulated, and rendered docile by society and also how to resist these societal practices through one's own practices.

Power

Power is not a position that one individual holds and another lacks. It is neither clearly subjective ('I feel I am a powerful/powerless person') nor objective (to be observed and measured by an external scientific researcher). Foucault's use of power is closely related to the sociological concept of socialization, the formation of certain dispositions. Not only are individuals socialized through institutions, but they come to be complicit in this regulation and transformation of the self. This complicity has become particularly noticeable in modern societies because management, governmentality, capitalist practices of enhancing productivity, and the use of the human disciplines to induce self-regulation have become practices of power, replacing more violent and brutal ones.

The construction of capitalism dovetails with and depends on the creation of docile and useful bodies that make possible productive activities. Foucault can be read as providing an innovative and fundamental layer in the Marxist analysis of capitalism, despite his apparent break with Marxism. Marx had certainly noted physical regulation and drudgery as an aspect of alienation from species-being and trenchantly remarks that modern industry converts the worker 'into a living appendage of the machine' (Marx as quoted in Tucker 1999: 412). But Foucault takes this analysis further.

Through modern techniques of power, the individual emerges as an object of inquiry within the scientific, political, and economic spheres of life. Power operates on the body as a form of social regulation; although power may be coercive in terms of discipline, it is not always coercive; it is regulatory and order maintaining of the norms, codes, and rules through which the social organization is produced and reproduced. Foucault's use of the term 'power' gives a critical edge to processes that structural-functionalists had treated more delicately under the rubric of 'socialization.'

Power is not a commodity, a position, or a prize, nor is it a zero-sum game that some exercise over others in a system of relations; it is not even a matter of consent or the renunciation of freedom. Rather, power operates throughout society, down to the very micro-practices of everyday life. It is multidimensional in that it circulates through institutions but is not reducible to institutions, not even to those that are considered political or even to the state. It is illusory to think that power is applied only by those on the top to those on the bottom; it is exercised on the dominant as well as on the dominated. Power cannot be looked at in terms of consensus or ideology; rather, power must be analyzed by answering the question, how does power operate? The focus must be on the relations of power, not on power as an object, and on ways that it shapes social action, social structures, and social relations. (In this regard, power is similar to 'relations of production' in Marxist thought; class is not a characteristic or property of individuals or groups—it is a relation among them.)

Power cannot be exercised without freedom; freedom is the necessary structural condition by which power can operate. Without spaces of autonomy, where resistance or free movement can occur, power would be equivalent to physical determination or pure domination. The relationship between power and freedom must be seen as an agonistic one that is reciprocal in a permanent provocation. The sociologist's role is to analyze power, its manifestations, and its relations to freedom as a political task in all aspects of social life.

Although Foucault argues that the state is the most important form and specific situation of the exercise of power, the diverse forms of power that circulate through society (pedagogical, juridical, economic, and so on) are not reducible to state power or always derived from it. While power relations have come more and more under control of the state through this historical process, this development has not been simple or uniform. Foucault argues that power relations have increasingly governmentalized, developed, rationalized, and centralized under the aegis of state institutions, as we will discuss below.

The Microphysics of Power and the 'Capillary Level'

Foucault, like Goffman and feminist theorists, placed a strong emphasis on the micro-level of power relations. Power is not simply coercion exercised by the state or a few large organizations or apparatuses. Rather it flows through all human interactions, for example, in the relationship between a professor and a student, a husband and wife, a police officer and a suspect, a supervisor and a worker, and a doctor and a patient.

Foucault used a couple of striking metaphors to emphasize this diffusion of power into all interactions. One was the phrase 'capillaries of power.' Power not only flows through the big arteries of the large organizations of the political and economic system—the military, the police, the large corporations, and so on—but also seeps into interactions between individuals. The state has power over individuals ultimately at the capillary level, in the interaction between a police officer and a suspect, for example, and the corporation's power is exemplified and manifested in the relationship between an employee of an insurance company and the patient who is denied benefits.

A second, related metaphor Foucault used was the 'microphysics of power,' meaning that it is necessary to chart power relations at the smallest level of individuals and their interactions (rather like the level of interactions between subatomic particles), where the body is turned into an object to be manipulated, molded, or controlled. Here, the body is subjected to a field of forces that constantly acts to reduce the body into a state of complete docility.

By the same logic, resistance was also expressed at the micro-level and not just in large-scale movements of the oppressed such as the civil-rights movement, revolutions, and the national liberation movements to gain independence from colonial rulers. Power and resistance formed a pair in Foucault's thought, and, wherever power was exercised, some degree of resistance would emerge. This formulation resonated with empirical research in the 1970s and 1980s that examined the 'resistance of the weak'—for example, resistance among peasants against landowners, slaves against masters, or workers against employers in situations in which it was too dangerous to form movements and undertake organized collective action (Scott 1987). In these situations, sloppy workmanship, a movement in a dance, a song lyric, the tilt of a man's hat, or a wooden clog (sabot) jammed into machinery ('sabotage') could signal resistance; each was a tiny claim to autonomy. The power and resistance thesis also resonated with research by feminist historians who found ways in which women had resisted patriarchy even in societies with extremely oppressive institutions of male dominance.

Later in his life, Foucault moved in two apparently divergent directions. One was an analysis of the state and the practices of power, such as surveillance, policing, and, above all, governmentality as a process of penetration into the capillary level, the interactions of civil society, and self-regulation. The other path he explored was care of the self, by which one's own personal existence took on a new aesthetic and ethical turn.

THE STATE AND CONTEMPORARY GOVERNMENTALITY

Foucault's project is to construct a genealogical history of the modern state and its different modes of governmentality or governmental rationality. The term 'governmentality' refers to the practices of government not the institution as such. Contemporary governmentality does not refer to objectifying power that turns bodies into docile objects but rather to subjectivizing power that constructs individuals who are capable of choice and action. Governmentality is a process of turning individuals into active subjects, who appear to initiate actions and make choices. Governmentality is a form of rationality that seeks to align personal or individual choices with governmental goals. Through this new mode of conceptualizing and acting in the world, citizens take on an active role in their own subjectification by their own complicity. Governmental rationality therefore simultaneously totalizes and individuates. Foucault's analysis connects a particular mode of rationality to the specific modes of securing, observing, monitoring, shaping, and controlling individuals. Thus, it is not focused on the state but rather on all particular practices of governing locally in multiple and local sites, such as the family, the school, or places of worship, which are all points of socialization as well as social regulation.

Once again, despite Foucault's break with Marxism and structuralism, we can see convergence here with structural-Marxist Louis Althusser's observation that capitalist ideology works by 'interpellating' the individual—insisting on individual or personal responsibility within a capitalist system of social relationships that allow very little autonomous action; the magic of the market is that it is ruled by the invisible hand, yet individuals feel they can and must take personal responsibility for their destinies. Althusser and other Marxists emphasize the fundamental role of the capitalist mode of production in this sleight of hand, whereas Foucault sees it pervading all practices of power in contemporary society and especially the state.

The modern state emerged out of the previous historical period when the state governed by the pervasive intervention into the everyday conduct of each individual in order to create blind obedience to authority, or what Foucault refers to as 'pastoral power.' As the state became ever more secularized and less ruled by church doctrine, it required a new raison d'être, a new autonomous rationale or secular justification for government that was not based on religion. For Foucault, the emergence of the modern state came through three forms of rationality, or what Foucault refers to as a triangle of interlocking forces: sovereignty, discipline, and governmental management. Governmentality as a set of practices has 'population' as its target of scrutiny, political economy as its major form of knowledge, and apparatuses of security as the central instrument of social regulation.

Police

Foucault defines 'police' or 'discipline' as a program of regulation rather than a specialized institution (the commonsense notion we have of police today). Policing is a mode of administration by which police and disciplinary techniques generate a 'state of prosperity' by grounding the state's wealth and power in the productivity of all individuals that make up the population (Pasquino 1991: 105). Policing oversees the population through detailed and continuous monitoring of population activities and dynamics (e.g., the efficiency of trade, communication, wealth, health, territorial distribution, and population birth and death rates). By establishing a detailed knowledge of the population's activities, policing serves as a regulatory control over all social practices in order to promote happiness. As a result of these practices, the concept of population emerges as a new object for governmental rationality to exercise itself over.

Self-Regulation and the Human Disciplines

The shift to modern formations of governmentality left behind the totalizing society of coercive practices and replaced it with practices based on self-monitoring and self-control. The ideal modern person suppresses impulses of all kinds, especially sexual, violent, and unruly ones. The gaze of surveillance is turned upon oneself, and this self-scrutiny is the most pervasive and effective form of social control. Foucault drew on the metaphor of the panopticon, a prison proposed by Jeremy Bentham, the utilitarian philosopher; the prisoners are locked in tiers of a structure that is observed from a central vantage point. They can be seen at all times by the guard, and the knowledge of their visibility leads them to monitor and regulate their own actions. Historically, prisons were actually built on this model, but Foucault was less interested in the specifics of prison design and more intrigued by the panopticon as a template for all of modern society, a society that was increasingly becoming a carceral system, a society in which surveillance, self-surveillance, and social regulation are diffused throughout all institutions of society. If people cannot monitor and curb impulses on their own, they turn to the physicians and what are sometimes called the 'helping professions' for treatment. The surge in recent decades in administering prescription drugs as a way of regulating problems of mood adds a new twist to Foucault's reflections.

In short, knowledge in modern times is organized in terms of scientific claims rather than religious judgments, and power is exercised in the context of expertise and scientific knowledge. The 'gaze' in modern societies is always a detached, affectively neutral, scientific gaze—the gaze of the researcher and the dispassionate diagnostician.

The emphasis on self-regulation at the individual level and the use of the human disciplines in modern societies is now joined by governmentality, the penetration of regimes of self-regulation and coordination throughout society. This process shifts government functions from coercion and public spending (the obvious stick and carrots available to the state) to the manipulation of individual self-regulation and the coordination of organizations such as private enterprises and non-profits. A couple of contemporary examples may help demonstrate the way governments use individual self-regulation and organizational management to reduce state intervention. The establishment and uses of governmentality can be seen quite clearly in the area of health care, where governments spend less and less on individual health care and instead try to substitute a web of third-party payers and competing providers, in a system sometimes called 'managed competition' (Light 2001). In the schooling of their children, parents in most major cities in developed nations are now faced with a bewildering array of choices, some private and some public. Parents feel that they have only themselves to blame if their children's education turns out badly, and the state is increasingly relieved of having to address educational disparities and no longer has to force people to attend schools in their residential district (Oberti 2007; Maloutas 2007).

Liberalism

Liberalism as a new form of rationality emerged in opposition to the totalizing control of the police. Against the imposition of regulation over all spheres of social life, liberalism stressed the necessity of the autonomy of spheres of life upon which social prosperity depends. In particular, liberalism stressed the autonomy of the economy and the political arena and saw both as specific cases in which an intrinsic logic makes self-regulation the most appropriate form of regulation. Within these arenas actors are self-invested, so they cannot be controlled or directed without undermining the growth of these fields and the betterment of the state. Liberalism became a specific technique of governing through promoting the free circulation of transactional processes within these two arenas. Liberalism entailed the exercise of a laissez-faire form of government over the dynamics of the autonomous subjects that made up the population. Here, mechanisms of security or modes of state intervention secure the free functioning of political and economic processes. Opposition to both authority and to abuses of power are now offered up in liberalism as new citizenship rights. Yet these liberties are incorporated into techniques by which security is exercised over the population; the existence and exercise of liberties creates a more adaptable and flexible form of management than was possible in a rigidly controlled state.

Security of the State

At the heart of Foucault's argument about governmentality is the development of governing authorities to promote security and prosperity. Rather than secure complete control the practice of governmentality governs a population by promoting the well being of the subjects in both political and economic life. Foucault argues that the governmentalized state is one that emerges alongside new objects of governance, such as the population and the economy, and new knowledge and modes of understanding these objects, specifically the social sciences. This governmental rationality is individualizing and totalizing as it seeks to govern both the individuals and populations of a society. The main technique in this regulation is security, which Foucault sees as a form of governmental rationality based on calculations of the possible and the probable. The logic of security is not purely functional in stabilizing all aspects of society-maintaining stasis: rather, security structures government as an active practice of problematization. Through problematizing the population (as too numerous or too few, not healthy enough, not educated enough, not prepared for some emergency, not productive, not compliant, and so on), the state develops new techniques of management in order to calculate its strength and to promote the wealth and efficiency of its internal organization.

THE TURN TO THE CARE OF THE SELF

Foucault's work after both *Discipline and Punish* and the first volume of *The History of Sexuality* took two divergent paths: one more sociological and political and the other more historical and philosophical. The first is his work around power, surveillance and governmentality; the second examines the ethical concern about how to live one's life. Although this second, more philosophical reading of the last two volumes of *The History of Sexuality* is often neglected in the social sciences, it will be reconsidered here with the following sociological question in mind: How does one negotiate everyday life in the face of mass society, nihilism, the implosion of meaning, and the alienation of existence?

The last two volumes of *The History of Sexuality* (*The Uses of Pleasure* and *The Care of the Self*) are not primarily an analysis of sex in ancient Greek thought and in the first and second centuries in Greece and Rome but an exegesis on ethics or what has been termed an 'aesthetics of existence.' Foucault was seeking to understand morality in terms of the self's relationship to itself.

While many postmodernists proclaimed the death of the self or subject, Foucault returned to the self as a mode of social transformation and resistance to the disciplinary normalizing power of society. Foucault did not seek to know the self in the traditional sense of cognition or of discerning one's inner truth or identity; rather, he sought to care for one's self, to create an aesthetics of existence, or, in other words, to create the self as a work of art.

Strategies of Self-Constitution

The project of the self that Foucault formulates in *The Care of the Self* is about the subject working actively on his or her self through practices of self-constitution. Knowledge is not defined as cognition, but as a way of altering one's mode of 'being-in-the-world.' Knowledge is not simply self-reflection, but becomes an embodied practice of working through one's own identity. The return to the ancient Greek view provides an alternative understanding of self, one that has been lost through the ages but that can become a resource for self-transfiguration. In this project of Foucault's, we can spot engagement with Nietzsche's ideas about the self as well as with the meaning of Socrates' admonition to 'know thyself,' which influenced Foucault both directly and indirectly via Nietzsche's own love-hate relationship with Socrates. Although Foucault is drawing on these earlier views of the self, he is keenly aware of new challenges to self-knowledge and self-construction in contemporary society.

For Foucault, the subject is fragmented and unceasingly changing. The self is a plurality of changing masks or faces, many selves that can change, be in contradiction to each other, and alter their contents over time. Foucault argued for a desubjectification of the self so that there was no longer one type of subject one could be but rather a constantly changing plurality of selves, a concept that both allows for the possibility of transforming oneself and parallels the experience one has of one's self. This desubjectification makes possible trying out new forms of the self through new modes of thinking, talking, acting, and experiencing. This transformation takes place within the historically situated context in which we find ourselves. The concept of desubjectification marks a return to agency and places the self in an active stance toward itself, a position that was missing from Foucault's earlier works. Turning one's self into an active player in one's life allows one to create a style of life or an aesthetics of existence through self-practices—not in relation to contemporary laws or morals or to traditional ideas on chastity or purity—but through an alternative mode of conduct and precepts.

The care of the self took on four strategies for which Foucault uses the Greek terms: *aphrodisia, chresis, enkrateia,* and the *telos* of freedom and truth. *Aphrodisia* means determining the part of oneself that is in need of moral care. What is the ethical substance that needs to be problematized or is in need of correction or development? *Chresis* refers to the codes of conduct that one will follow and to which one submits oneself to achieve proper conduct. *Enkrateia* is the active and critical labor one performs on the self to transform oneself into a moral subject; this is the constant activity of gaining command over oneself by continuously confronting one's self with what one is doing. This activity means being free from rigid rules or propositions and being free to enter into new relationships by means of thought, experimentation, and philosophizing, as new modes of living. *Telos,* the final aspect, is the goal of directedness or the constant striving toward an aesthetics of existence. This stylization cannot be given in advance, for we create ourselves into works of art as we live.

This aesthetic demands attention to the care of oneself. The stance is not that of the traditional *flâneur,* the idle observer of life, but close to what Simmel referred to as sociability or as 'the free-playing interacting interdependence of individuals' (Simmel [1911] 1949: 158). And care of the self resonates with what Lévi-Strauss called the *bricoleur,* one who takes whatever is ready to hand as resources to work upon the self as a constantly ongoing project of creating the self. This self-creation is a way of existing in the world, a mode of survival, which, if it were consistently practiced, would transform the social life of both individuals and society. For Foucault, this project resonates with thinking differently; one undergoes change in order to think differently and live differently—not as theoretical doctrine or cognitive understanding but as a practical mode of engagement in everyday life. Care of the self is not ego centered but rather a creation of oneself beyond what one is in order to understand oneself and one's place in the world, to achieve an inner tranquility in a world of constant motion and anomie. To attain this tranquility requires exercises and practices. Foucault's ideal of knowing one's self is not defined by any modern understanding of subjectivity—an impossibility now that the postmodernists have declared the death of the subject. Instead, Foucault went in the opposite direction, trying to theorize how one could fashion oneself into a new type of subject.

Foucault sought a mode of subjecting our selves to a critical scrutiny of the conditions of the present in order to understand how the limits of our experiences could be transgressed and how we could become something other or more than these boundaries. We need to transgress the very limits of ourselves—along the lines described by Nietzsche—'to become who we are' or to create ourselves (Nietzsche [1887] 2001: 189). In response to disciplinary power (Foucault's term for current conditions and especially the contemporary social forces of docilization and productivity), he takes an oppositional and resistive stance. The task of thinking is to question, critique, and transform the reality that defines us. We must make a commitment away from domination toward freedom.

Care of the Self as a Sociological Project

The task of social critique or sociology is to free ourselves from the forms of identity and subjectivity to which we are currently bound. This emancipation is not a complete detachment or break but a transformation, the *telos* or goal of which is freedom; it is a freeing to the conditions of possibility. The aim of the techniques or practices of self lead to an art of living that is also and always ethical work. Here ethics and aesthetics are intertwined in the goal of transcending current conditions of existence.

This is a non-normative, non-foundational, non-universal, non-totalizing, and open-ended project. Readers may see similarities between this concept and the ideas of other theorists and philosophers: Freedom is like Heidegger's nothingness, Nietzsche's will to power, Simmel's sociability, Kierkegaard's thrownness. Foucault's freedom is not a nihilistic response. On the contrary, Foucault offers an existential affirmation of existence without a normative foundation, definitives, or prescriptions of what one should do or be. It is not a politics of narcissism or relativism. It is similar to Nietzsche's self-overcoming to become a better and more exceptional human being, an affirmation of existence in the face of the automatism of everyday life.

What value does thinking genealogically about the body have? A history of the self and the possibility of resistance are the answers here. Genealogical analysis is a mode of self-creation and a means of resistance. If the body or self can be lived differently at different historical periods, then change is always a possibility that remains open. While we cannot live outside our own historical period, these different genealogical periods may offer up insights into alternative ways of being or the possibility of using these insights as resources to undertake such a transformative project within our own times. For Foucault, the aesthetics of existence is not a search for inner truth but rather a response to the contemporary malaise of everyday life. Thus the project revealed in his work on care of the self is a sociological one, not only an existential one.

Foucault argues that the art of living potentially endows all individuals with the right and ability to define their existence to themselves and to others.

To care for the self or develop an art of living is to desubjugate one's self from the disciplinary power and dominant discourses that reify and objectify the subject into particular and predefined forms. Social transformation is linked to individuals creating themselves as works of art.

Technologies of the self would help create new cultural forms, new social relations, new forms of art put into action through our sexual, political, and ethical choices. This is an affirmation of existence not to uncover the authentic self but to create new forms of being, to practice the art of living. The aesthetics of existence is an existential ethic—not to seek one's truth but to create one's self as an open-ended project, dispensing with truths about the self. This was not the deep truth of the self offered up by psychoanalysis, nor was it the authentic self created through existential decisions as advocated by Sartre. Nor does it mean artistic production in the conventional sense of creating works of art, but it means creating ourselves as works of art. Foucault argues that the modernist conception is to understand the present as it really is, to grasp the hidden truth of reality. His project is different: he advocates for a self-creation that takes oneself as the object of transformation at the individual level. The individual transformation heightens the possibility of autonomy so that, at the social level, the project can take as its aim the goal of freedom from domination.

FOUCAULT AND THE TRADITIONS OF SOCIAL THEORY

It may be useful to begin this section by identifying continuities and breaks between Foucault's thought and that of classical social theorists and philosophers. This perspective helps us to understand how theories are changed and how fundamental concepts and even large fragments of theoretical frameworks may be incorporated into the brand new structures of social thought. In short, we can do a bit of archaeological excavation of Foucault's ideas. Although Foucault's thought transformed social theory at the end of the twentieth century, it was not an entirely new creation, and it converged with themes that radical feminists such as Judith Butler were starting to articulate.

DURKHEIM AND FRENCH SOCIOLOGY

Foucault's startling new ideas have a foundation in classical French social thought. They are in line with Durkheim's analysis of the shift away from repressive laws. But where Durkheim was at least moderately optimistic about evolution toward a more humane and less rigid system of social control, Foucault saw the oppressiveness of the new forms as well. For Foucault, there was no narrative of progress; rather, there were different historical periods with different forms and mechanisms of social regulation and control. At one point, Foucault appeared to break with the Enlightenment, implying that the apparent advances of scientific thought and human rights cloaked new forms of oppression and societal regulation. But, later in his life, he conceded that there was at least a small degree of progress and humanity in the effort to abolish torture and religious obscurantism.

Also, Foucault sees society in ways that are similar to the ideas of the conservative reaction, Comte, and Durkheim, but he turns each of their values upside down. The conservative reaction celebrated social compulsion; Foucault loathes it in both its traditional and modern forms. Comte hailed the emergence of the human sciences, the exercise of expertise, and the prospect of 'order and progress'; Foucault attacks them. Durkheim believed modern structures of normative regulation to be more humane than old ones; Foucault (at least early in his career) sees them merely as different types of social control at different historical periods.

He agrees with the French tradition of analyzing the external and compelling character of culture. Society is not a conglomerate of individuals each motivated by desires and self-interests, jostling against equally atomistic and willful others. Society is formed by patterns of regulation. For Durkheim, these could be summed up as the collective conscience or consciousness. For Goffman, they are manifested in the scripts that govern interaction and self-performance and in the aesthetic judgments that render performances as credible or unconvincing. For Foucault, they are lodged in discourses and practices that interlock with each other into discursive formations that change over time. He also agrees with Durkheim's perspective on crime and social deviance, in which these phenomena are not seen as social problems but as fundamental expressions of society. Taking Foucault's work seriously leads us to place social control and regulation at the core of sociological theory, reinforcing Durkheim's original insight that sociology is about normative regulation, crime, and the organization of the collective conscience. Deviance, punishment, and social control and societal regulation are not just interesting topics in sociology—they are the essential substance of sociology.

Foucault points to these constraints in order to induce us to consider breaking them, a position that is distinctly different from the layers of resignation to regulation found in Durkheim and Goffman's writing.

WEBER, SIMMEL, AND NIETZSCHE

Foucault's ideas are close to Weber's concerns about the 'iron cage' of formal rationality and instrumental reason. Like Weber, Foucault foresees a society in which rationality becomes a repressive and inhumane force. Science's claim to the complete understanding of nature gives its practitioners a hold on human action that is hard to break. Foucault's emphasis on capitalism's base in the manufacture of docile, productive bodies converges with Weber's discussion of this-worldly asceticism as a precondition of capitalist accumulation; Weber associated discipline and renunciation with the Protestant ethic (a connection not fully explored by Foucault) and was less interested in the details of its embodiment, but a large overlap of ideas can be discerned.

Weber, as well as Foucault, was influenced by the work of Friedrich Nietzsche, a nineteenth-century critic of liberal rationalism, and Foucault was almost certainly also directly influenced by Weber's work, as well as sharing with Weber a common inspiration from Nietzsche.

Nietzsche had also profoundly influenced Georg Simmel, inspiring Simmel's pessimism about the money economy, its calculated pseudo-rationality, the growing weight of objective culture that forms hardened and institutionalized constraints external to individuals, and the shrinking autonomy and creativity of the individual. As we saw in the section on care of the self, Foucault tried to address this increasing loss of individual autonomy and creativity, as well as the ways in which we are complicit in our own domination through the subtle mechanisms of disciplinary power and governmentality.

CHALLENGING FREUD

Foucault is in a confrontational dialogue with two other social theorists, Sigmund Freud and Karl Marx. His work on sexuality is a direct challenge to Freud's view that each individual's self is formed around repressed and unconscious infantile sexual impulses. Freud's view implies that there is a true self and that psychoanalysis can uncover it, restoring a person to health in the process of discovery itself. The person can never, of course, return to the world of infantile sexuality, but he or she can, at least, understand how they were forced out of paradise. This understanding cannot make an individual happy, but it does provide a limited type of freedom. Foucault does not believe there is such a thing as the true self, nor does he think there is a consistent, universally human process of repressing infantile sexual impulses. Sexuality is a cultural product, varying among cultures. It has no true form, repressed, infantile, or whatever. The subject—each individual's sense of self—is constituted by processes of power and knowledge within a discursive formation. The concept of a true self, formed by repression of sexual impulses but accessible with the help of a psychoanalyst, is the target of Foucault's attack in *The History of Sexuality*. Foucault argues that the essentialism inherent in the concept of a true self leads to a confused notion that a true self can be discovered, contained, corrected, and improved. Foucault instead takes Nietzsche's position that one is what one becomes and that becoming is not predetermined, defined, or limited by any a priori (whether it is a demographic category or a particular set of unconscious drives).

CHALLENGING MARX AND ENGELS

Foucault challenges Marx and Engels in several ways. First, Foucault believes power is exercised at many sites; the mode of production is certainly one of them, but it is not necessarily the determining or most important one. Power is not lodged only or even primarily in a distinct social group with a strong subjective identity that we could term the 'ruling class' or even in a distinct social category such as the economically dominant class. Second, resistance is omnipresent not focused in a movement, let alone one led by the proletariat. Like power, resistance appears always and everywhere. Power is always met by resistance, and the two processes appear throughout the formation. Resistance is as strong in the university lecture hall, in school, at the office water cooler, in bed, in prison, in the mental hospital day room, and at the rock concert as it is on the factory floor or the socialist party headquarters. Resistance is an ongoing micro-process. It has no particular endpoint. Third, Foucault shared a view with many other French intellectuals in the 1960s and 1970s—that the effort to channel resistance into an oppositional movement of proletarians against capitalism had disastrous consequences, namely the formation of rigid Communist parties and one-party states. Foucault was writing at a time when left-wing intellectuals were growing disillusioned with 'real socialism' in the Soviet bloc and China and becoming disengaged from the western European Communist parties. Foucault was politically active in the prisoners' rights movement in France, supporting the civil rights of the incarcerated. Sharing Marx and Engels' vision of human emancipation, he did not pursue it in contemporary Marxist theory and practice (apart from a tentative fling with Maoism) but with the more individual and anarchic perspective of the outsider and deviant.

Although the social and political circumstances of late twentieth-century France led to Foucault's turning away from Marxism as a leading paradigm of social thought, he contributed to the critical understanding of capitalism, especially through his analysis of the creation of docile and useful bodies in capitalist production, a topic Marx had broached but not fully explored in his discussion of the impact of machinery and the factory system on the bodies of the workers.

FOUCAULT'S IMPACT AND METHOD

Foucault's work revolutionized social theory by its radical social construction-ism, its pairing of the concepts of power and knowledge, its critique of the human sciences, and its thesis that resistance is a pervasive phenomenon. These elements of Foucault's thought were incorporated into feminist theory, revisions in Marxist theory, and mainstream cultural studies. For example, they resonate with the thought of Judith Butler and other feminists that repression, control, normative orders, and domination are closely linked to all forms of classification and that categorization (such as assigning gender categories and categories of sexual orientation) must be met with transgression.

FEMINISM AND JUDITH BUTLER: TRANSGRESSING CATEGORIES

Foucault's relationship to feminist theory requires comment. Foucault's ideas converged with and influenced feminist theory strongly, although he showed little interest in the women's movements or the work of women intellectuals in France. The establishment of categories through discourse, the association of these categories with oppression and marginalization, the use of the gaze, the complicity of the human sciences in legitimating classification and subordination as natural, and the microphysics of power (coercion lodged in everyday interactions rather than in only class relations and state apparatuses)—all of these themes appeared in both Foucault's theory and the theories of the radical feminists. Especially the work of Judith Butler, with its emphasis on the establishment of categories of gender and of sexual normality and deviance, converges with Foucault's perspective, and so does her work's transgressive tone.

Schemas of categorization that discipline, normalize, and regulate bodies are key for Butler. For her, as for Foucault, the microphysics of power regulates the movement of bodies, and, in *Gender Trouble* and *Bodies That Matter*, she ties power to the categories of sexuality. A convergence in their work can also be found in the analysis of discourses of sexuality. These discourses limit what be said—what can be articulated in a speech act. Speech acts define what bodies can be talked about and whether these bodies are normal or deviant—and some bodies cannot be talked about at all. (The more psychoanalytically inclined reader might want to recall Harry Sullivan's discussion of how parental speech and behavior constitute body parts of the child as 'good me,' 'bad me,' and 'not me' and how the third of these parental responses is associated with feelings of dissociation and uncanniness.) Discourse thus brings into being embodiedness, an actual embodied, material state. Finally and most important is the issue of resistance. Where there is power there is resistance; where there is normality, deviance will always push back against it. Butler utilizes Foucault's notion of power and resistance to pinpoint specific aspects of gender and sexuality performances and their transgressions.

Judith Butler's work transformed gender theory by encouraging a growing emphasis on gender as performance and an increasingly radical subversion of the concept of identity (1990, 1993, 2004). Butler argues that the construction of gender is the binding together of sex, gender, and heterosexuality into a single package. This packaged identity is then inscribed on the body in a process that appears to be natural. We expect anatomy, gender, and sexual orientation to be aligned with each other and each component to be 'normal.' Even gay and lesbian identities, though not normative, are expected to follow certain conventions of performance and naturalized identity. As Foucault pointed out in his history of sexuality and as D'Emilio (1983) elaborates in his discussion of gay identity in capitalist society, gay and lesbian identity has not always been a coherent and stable category of self and identity.

Butler sees gender as performance. It is 'a stylized repetition of acts' (Butler 1990: 178). One could say that gender is an act, with all the double meaning inherent in the expression.

On the one hand, gender is an embodied practice. We hold our bodies in a certain way, we move our limbs and our torsos, we have certain expressions on our faces, we gesture in one way and not another, and we dress our bodies 'appropriately.' Gender is 'styles of the flesh' (Butler 1990: 139), stylized acts that are repetitively performed by bodies and inscribed on bodies. In this way, we perform or act out gender according to rules that make a practice normative. The specific rules vary among societies in their content, intensity, and the harshness of punishments associated with transgressions.

Gender is also an act in a second sense—it may not correspond at all to the thoughts and feelings of the actor. Butler emphasizes that the performance—the acting—of gender must be self-concealing. This concealment is important because it creates the illusion of naturalness and necessity, the impression that 'one could not possibly be otherwise.' If the performance draws attention

to itself, it may undermine rather than enhance this impression of naturalness. A woman who wears too much perfume or very long false eyelashes
may be perceived as trying too hard and so might a man who always wears
camouflage combat gear.

As in Goffman's dramaturgical model of the self, gender performance
is judged as credible or non-credible. Non-credible performances include
a large range of transgressive acts such as dressing in drag, tomboyish
behavior, and stereotypical homosexual mannerisms. These acts are seen
as unnatural, and they fail (or refuse) to lock together sex, gender, and
sexual orientation seamlessly. They disrupt the links that are supposed to
exist among these components of the performance. Transgression involves
rendering incredible that which is supposed to be credible; the ludicrous,
unsettling, and mismatched acts put the entire understanding of gender
as natural into question. Sometimes, transgression may be recuperated by
placing these acts into the category of the carnivalesque. For Halloween or
Mardi Gras, it is okay for a man to wear a dress—in fact, his funny appearance reaffirms that this style is not appropriate for men. At what point does
transgression become really transgressive, going beyond play and carnival
performance?

Ultimately, gender performance is linked to macro power differences. The
naturalization of gender—its correct performance and the way the correct
performance conceals the performed and 'unnatural' stylization—sustains
masculine dominance and compulsory heterosexuality. Because convincing
gender performance makes us feel that gender (and its link to sex category) is
to be taken for granted, it takes gender arrangements off the agenda of reflection, discussion, contestation, and possible collective action. By showing how
the dualism man/woman and its mapping to the pair dominant/subaltern
is created in our speech, discourses, thoughts, practices, and performances,
Butler seeks to undermine them.

Butler particularly parted ways with some conflict feminists in her insistence that gender is not a stable identity at all. Many feminists had sought to
raise women's consciousness, to increase the salience of gender for women who
might otherwise have remained complicit in their own inequality. They had
'interpellated' women as women, demanding a public identity commitment.
But they had left intact the naturalism and dualism of gender construction,
simply shifting the positive value away from men to women. Butler argues
that her critique of gender arrangements is more profound and ultimately
undermines the foundation of gender hierarchy and hetero-normativity more
thoroughly than identity politics can. She argues that her analysis points to
a more complete restoration of agency, in the sense of a freeing of human

beings from the oppressive category of gender itself. The point is not to emancipate women from men, but to emancipate human beings from compulsory
gender identity and hetero-normativity.

THE SOCIOLOGY OF DEVIANCE AND PUNISHMENT

Discipline and Punish (actually *Surveillance and Punishment*, in the French
title) had a particularly powerful impact on sociology. It addresses the ongoing interest of sociologists in crime and punishment and reveals Foucault's
unconventional methods of research. He likes to proceed by investigating
unusual and bizarre historical materials, reconstructing the histories of
deviance and punishment with fragmentary, quasi-anecdotal evidence that
highlights those phenomena he believes are most important. For example, he
might examine the accounts of a particularly bizarre murder, the gruesome
details of an execution, records of a reform school, or the personal memoirs
of a hermaphrodite. These strange, unsystematically accumulated details are
like the intense light of a search beam thrown back into the darkness of history, illuminating key elements of landscapes of deviance, crime, madness,
and punishment.

In the opening pages of *Discipline and Punish*, Foucault shows us images
of before and after the shift from pre-modern to modern punishment. Before:
The attempted regicide, Robert Damien, is torn apart in a horrifying public
spectacle of torture and execution. After: Punishment in post-Revolutionary
France is replaced by 'corrections'; the timetable of a reformatory exemplifies
the new order. The deviant is hidden away, incarcerated in a prison or insane
asylum. Order is imposed on an unruly body; every motion is prescribed and
monitored. Control over the deviant's time is essential to the imposition of
order; every minute of the day is accounted for. The deviant is subjected to
constant surveillance. The prison and reform school become the starting points
of a carceral society in which all behavior and thought is under surveillance
and subject to social control by medical and social professionals as a first line of
defense against unruliness and by security forces in more extreme situations.

Another influential image of Foucault's was the metaphor of the panopticon, a prison of total and constant surveillance, as an image of modern
society. The gaze of the prison guards can be turned upon all prisoners at all
times, eventually inducing them to monitor themselves. Although utilitarian
philosopher Jeremy Bentham had actually first proposed the panopticon, it
was Foucault who turned it into a metaphor of modern forms of social control
in which the human disciplines induce us constantly to monitor our own

thought and actions, which become the new mode of societal regulation and normative order. Everything can be held against us. Notice the convergence with Goffman's analysis of total institutions and the processes of regulating and discrediting the self, especially with looping.

FOUCAULT'S POLITICS

What is the meaning of resistance in Foucault's work? He made little effort to spell it out, theorize what it is, or suggest how to do it. Does resistance mean engaging in transgressive actions as an individual or in a collective, for example by shattering the category system of man/woman or homosexual/heterosexual, as Judith Butler and other feminists seem to imply? Does it mean more organized political engagement, such as, for example, Foucault's own activism on behalf of the incarcerated? Does it mean an ongoing cultural offense—and offensiveness—as in musical forms or clothing styles that express disgust with corporate culture? Is absenteeism from the office or rudeness to customers a form of resistance? At what point is organized political action a form of resistance and at what point is it—regardless of its oppositional content—a strategy that is already hopelessly co-opted into the system? Why engage in organized political protest and activism when the historical record suggests that movements, when they succeed, become as repressive as the regimes they opposed? And how is resistance related to the aesthetic, creative, and even crypto-existentialist ideals proposed in his work on care of the self? Like Marx and Engels' vision of proletarian revolution and the road to communism, Foucault's view of resistance leaves much to the imagination of the reader.

Foucault was a physician's son, and perhaps this social origin inspired his fascination with quarantine, medicine as a regulatory practice, definitions of health and illness, the power of medical professionals, anatomical anomalies, sexualities, and, above all, embodiedness. On the other hand, it would be quite an oversimplification to label him as gay and suggest that his sexual orientation was the key to his startling new theories. He eschewed this easy labeling of his identity and kept his personal life private, though it is known that he experimented with drugs, including LSD, and sadomasochism and other bodily 'limit experiences' in San Francisco; he died of AIDS in 1984 (Miller 1994). He was politically engaged throughout his life, but he moved from an early fringe involvement with the French Communist Party to new types of activism on behalf of the marginalized and incarcerated. One of his most notable acts was participating in the founding of the Groupe d'Information sur les Prisons (GIP) in 1971, a radical anti-prison movement. This activism was linked to the core of his theoretical work on punishment and the carceral system. Although he had disparaged the Enlightenment for ushering in scientific techniques of social control, he ultimately embraced many of its central themes—the right to life, liberty, and the pursuit of happiness; critical thinking; individual rights; and the right to challenge governments and place limitations on state power.

In his academic career, Foucault followed the ideal typical path of brilliant French intellectuals, progressing from the demanding Lycée Henri IV (one of France's most prestigious high schools) to success in the rigorous entrance exams to the École Normale Supérieure, the pinnacle of the French education system at that time. He advanced (not always smoothly) to appointments in leading institutions of higher education in France as well as visiting appointments and lecture series at Stanford and the University of California at Berkeley.

His political trajectory is not easily summed up. In a broad sense, he was part of the left, though he criticized not only the French Communist Party but Marxism as a whole, arguing that, when it was linked to practice in the Soviet Union and China, it contributed to the substitution of new regimes of surveillance, power, punishment, and control for the old ones. At one point, he was close to Maoist factions in Paris, but eventually he broke with them. He strongly opposed France's effort to hold on to Algeria in the later 1950s and 1960s and supported the rights of North African immigrants. His relationship to feminists was generally hostile and dismissive, though their insights on society converged. Feminists found many of his concepts—discourses, the gaze, the use of human disciplines as instruments of control—very useful in their analyses.

Foucault's pattern of political engagement—with its individualism and vacillation, distance from established parties of the left, lack of enthusiasm for revolutionary socialist regimes, and championing of the most oppressed and marginalized people, especially the incarcerated—marked a new direction among politically engaged intellectuals. It was linked to the transitional nature of Foucault's thought and shows the active side of his role in creating and not only reflecting the intellectual climate of our times (Macey 1993).

CONCLUSION: FOUCAULT AND THE TRANSITION TO CONTEMPORARY THEORY

In so far as Foucault's project can be summed up, it is to construct a mode of analysis of the cultural practices and cultural formation that are instrumental in the production of the modern individual as both subject and object of analysis. This formative process works through and on the body. Foucault offers a history of the present in which power and knowledge intersect and understandings of ourselves are produced. Knowledge is never separated from power. Power and knowledge operate in mutually generative fashion and are not reducible to each other.

In closing, let's look at four major perspectives that Foucault shared with Goffman and with feminist theory, perspectives that were incorporated into many contemporary social theories.

- Micro-processes: Although he was not a micro-sociologist, he had an interest in micro-processes, the microphysics of power, power exercised in interaction, and the resistance to power that also takes place continuously in interactions and micro-environments, in the 'capillaries.'
- Discourses (scripts and framing in Goffman): Foucault was interested in the way in which discourses, or framing in Goffman's terms, impose order and limits on experience and thought. These categories, in turn, are linked to laws, institutions and their practices, experiences of everyday life, and regimes imposed on the body. They create stigma and deviance. In contemporary societies, the human disciplines are major forces in social construction, as Goffman pointed out in his analysis of the career of mental patients and as feminists found when they traced the complicity of psychologists and sociologists in defining 'normal' sex roles.
- Madness, deviance, punishment, and incarceration (total institutions in Goffman): Foucault focused on 'madness' as a key situation in societies, brought into being by discourses and definitions (rather than existing as an illness or a consistent set of deviant behaviors). These discourses serve as metaphors or templates for all kinds of categorizing, normalizing, and regulating mechanisms of control; they maintain the normative order of society. Categorization and social construction are most dramatically apparent when we study extreme cases, such as treatment of inter-sex individuals or the mentally disordered. Goffman, Foucault, and feminist theorists agree that the state is a major player in categorization, differentiation, and punishment.

- The regulation and manipulation of the body were key elements of Foucault's theory, and these resonated with feminist theorists who were interested in the way power, difference, and domination are inscribed on the body.

KEY TERMS

- carceral system
- care of the self
- discourse and discursive formation
- the gaze
- governmentality
- human disciplines
- microphysics of power
- panopticon
- power and resistance
- punishment
- regulation of the body
- surveillance

Chapter 5

PIERRE BOURDIEU (1930–2002)

THE CRAFT OF SOCIOLOGY

In *The Craft of Sociology*, Bourdieu outlines his program for sociology. He begins with a critique of both objectivism and subjectivism, which define philosophical and social science paradigms (from existentialism to structuralism to neo-classical economics to rational choice theory) as modes of knowledge that are either independent from individual consciousness and wills or too invested in explaining the world through the conscious making of informed decisions. Instead, he argues for a sociology grounded in *epistemic reflexivity*, a practice-based model for explaining the experiential relationships that subjects have with the structures of objective relations that shape everyday life.

We must therefore look at the main aspects of Bourdieu's contribution to social theory and sociological practice. As is often the case in the formation of new theories, he begins with a critique of existing theoretical work. He engages in an empirical refutation of a whole series of scholastic dualisms, such as the distinction between the objective and the subjective; he offers a critique of the epistemological arbitrariness (and historical causes) of the division between sociology and anthropology; he decries the autonomization—the disconnect of theory from actual empirical work. Finally, he considers the way cognitive, practical, and political logics are embedded in social metaphysics, practices, and forms of domination.

BREAKING SUBJECTIVISM/OBJECTIVISM

Bourdieu examines the contentious place that social science occupies. Is the discipline 'social' or 'science'? Sociology seems to straddle a divide between looking at the world as social observers using science-based principles and scientifically studying the social world as scientists. Bourdieu (1990c) argues that, regardless of which position one takes, most sociological work fails to break away from the dichotomy between subjectivity and objectivity in the 'theoretical modes of knowledge' (25). Neither does it avoid a whole series of other scholastic dualisms such as structure vs. agency and micro vs. macro.

Bourdieu (1990c) discusses 'the imaginary anthropology of subjectivism' (42). The subjectivist viewpoint is closely related to rational actor theory (RAT). Rational actor theory, used most frequently in economics, assumes (and advocates) that people (agents or actors) make decisions based on a pseudo-statistical calculation after obtaining all of the pertinent facts associated with the impending decision. Applied to society, RAT and its close relative, subjectivism, hold that social beings are making rational, subjective decisions during their action and interaction and that the sum total of these decisions or choices constitutes society. RAT is subjectivist because it makes the agency of individuals the driving force of social outcomes (one of the myths we criticized in Chapter 1).

Applied to sociology, subjectivity is the mode of knowledge creation that aims to 'reflect an experience since subjectivists see the primary experience as immediate understanding of the social world' (Bourdieu, Chamboredon, and Passeron 1991: 26). Bourdieu sees limits in subjectivity as a sociological mode of knowledge because the social world is not made up of rational actors making informed decisions that can be reflected a priori into sociological texts after observing the actions of social agents. 'Spontaneous sociology' is what he calls this naïve philosophy of the social, in which reflected experience (subjectivism) is deemed to represent the truth. The social world is much more complex than straight subjectivity allows. For Bourdieu, if one fails to recognize any form of action other than rational action, it is impossible to understand the logic of any actions that are reasonable without being the product of rational calculation.

Objectivity as a theoretical mode of knowledge rejects RAT and the reflection of lived experience as incompatible with the reality of the social world. Instead, objectivism seeks to establish objective regularities (e.g., structures, laws, systems of relationships) independent of individual consciousness and agency. Yet objectivism has potential shortcomings as well. By condemning subjectivism and overemphasizing the power of social structures, objectivism faces the danger of falling into the trap of not allowing for individual or collective participation and complicity in the system.

Bourdieu's critique of spontaneous sociology appears to pull him in the direction of objectivism, but this is merely a provisional move in order to form a complete understanding of the experiential relationships and experiences that the subjects have embedded in an objective system of relations. This detour through objectivity is necessary for the break from spontaneous sociology, and, once the break has been completed, the 'pure' form of objectivism must also be rejected because subjects' experience of meaning is always part of the larger totality of the meaning of experience.

Bourdieu calls for sociologists to break from the subjectivity-objectivity dichotomy because both positions are equally opposed to the practical mode of knowledge, which is the basis of ordinary experience of the social world. Bourdieu argues that, by breaking from this false dualism, we can develop a scientific theory and verify its possibility of being represented in the field under study; we can accomplish this by moving beyond immediate networks of relationships in order to find those higher-order relations that give rise to the immediate ones.

CONSTRUCTING THE OBJECT

For Bourdieu, 'constructing the object' is the key to sociological research (Bourdieu, Chamboredon, and Passeron 1991: 147). Constructing the object means constructing a theoretical problematic that makes possible the investigation of those aspects of the world that are brought into relief when the object is investigated through the lens of this problematic. The lens cannot be held too closely to the empirical world, nor should it be identical to any type of conventional research method. Without a scientific construction of the object of study, the project will deteriorate because of the sociologist's lack of distance from what is being studied and the possible personal biases that the researcher brings to bear upon that object of analysis. As a result, the scientific construction of the object of study is necessary in order to avoid constructing facts based on hyper-empiricism. Hyper-empiricism means observation without theory, and it leads to illogical questions that do not address the object properly, as well as to uncritical acceptance of statements as factual when they are provided by the object of study. In other words, hyper-empiricism means an unquestioning and atheoretical recording of experiences and utterances that are encountered while doing research. In place of hyper-empiricism, the sociologist should use the theoretical problematic as the basis of methodology, and this commitment means constantly considering the ways in which the method illuminates the object and the theoretical significance of the questions asked.

For Bourdieu, sociologists must reconstruct the system of constructed relations in a way that is analogous with Weber's use of the 'ideal type.' Here, the ideal type is not the limiting case of the relations in question; instead, the ideal type is conceptualized as the 'pure type,' which allows the whole system of relations to be grasped by their relation to the ideal type. The ideal type does not represent the system; it represents a sample of the system with which the rest of the system can be developed by difference.

For example, one might be interested in studying segregation and the exclusion of ethno-racial groups as a general social process. The ghetto in which African Americans were historically confined in US cities by violence, real-estate practices, mortgage markets, and public housing policies represents a powerful form of segregation; other patterns of exclusion and segregation—such as the concentration of people of North African descent in the French urban periphery—can then be understood in terms of their similarities and differences to the US pattern (Wacquant [1993] 2005, 2008a). In making this comparison, we are forced to understand the similarities and differences in the conditions and in the historical forces that shaped the two distinct forms. We can't simply apply the word 'ghetto' to the French periphery because these areas are quite different from the ghettos of the United States. The French periphery is much more diverse and was formed by different historical processes than was the segregated ghetto of the United States. We constantly have to bring together and examine critically empirical observations, historical understandings of the systems of relationships, and the theoretical constructs we want to use to talk about the situations.

Bourdieu argues that comparison guided by the hypothesis of analogies provides the instrument for breaking with pre-constructed data and offers a model to construct the relationship between relations that define any social world under analysis. Analogies are used to reveal the underlying systems of relationships and thereby explain the empirical observations, while, in turn, empirical observation must be encompassed by the concepts and terms we develop. This method helps the sociologist avoid pitfalls such as hyper-empiricism (what we observe is all there is to know), positivism (if we can observe and measure something, we don't have to interpret it or understand its historical sources), and reliance on intuition (the best interpretation is the one that feels right to me). Bourdieu defines the method of comparison guided by analogies and theoretical construction as applied rationalism.

APPLIED RATIONALISM

Applied rationalism is the approach of reversing the relationship between theory and experiment. In the typical research process (observation, hypothesis, experimentation, theory, observation), which is also the basis of the false duality of subjectivism and objectivism in science, theory is developed after the initial observation and experimentation. This approach is specifically touted in grounded theory, a position of assuming that theory will emerge from observation.

Bourdieu argues that social scientific research must begin with a reasoned theory, at least a preliminary theory, before the researcher can head out to the field to make observations. Given the epistemological primacy of reason over experience, theory illuminates aspects of the world that would remain unperceived without it. Theory is simultaneously a construction and a break—because one needs to have broken free of preconceptions in order to construct analogies. One must break down the appearances or surface relations in order to construct an understanding of deeper relations among the shattered appearances.

REFLEXIVITY

The break with spontaneous sociology is always a difficult one because the sociologist is a part of the social world. As such, his or her experience seems to confirm the naturalness of the objective system. This taken-for-granted understanding can lead to naïve representations of society, based not in scientific methodology but in positivism and intuitionism, which is popular with the masses since it reflects both commonsense understandings and understanding the world through common sense. Reflexivity is the practice that protects the sociologist against common sense, positivism, and intuitionism; through reflexivity, sociologists conduct a sociology of sociology. This practice means objectifying the relationship of the observer to the observed in order to break with the subject's preconceived notions of the object and the system of relations in which the object exists.

Furthermore, and possibly more important, reflexivity means breaking with the scholastic and intellectual preconceptions that exist in the institutions in which sociology was developed and is currently practiced. Sociologists must go into the field having bracketed—put on hold—their own assumptions about the world. For example, if they fail to acknowledge and bracket their commitment to a Marxist paradigm, they are likely to see class divisions and class struggles everywhere, a viewpoint that is common among European intellectuals. In the United States, they are likely to see the world through the lens of mainstream sociology and positivism unless they make an effort to bracket this predisposition. Without reflexivity, the sociologist will likely misrecognize the systems and practices of the objects of study by seeing them as taken-for-granted conditions because of following a pre-reflexive 'logic' in conducting the research. Ultimately, reflexivity figures at the heart of Bourdieu's approach because sociologists operating without reflexivity are likely to create self-fulfilling prophesies by finding exactly what they were looking for.

In undertaking sociological research, a person must remember that there is a transcendent dialectic operating between two elements. One element is composed of the subjects' situated viewpoints on their world, that is, the world seen through their eyes. The second element is composed of the larger social structures within which subjects are embedded and of which they are not yet fully aware. This second element constitutes the objective conditions of their existence. In order to understand subjects on their own terms, social scientists must take into account their subjects' knowledge, experience, and understanding. In this way, the researchers can document how people understand the world on their terms and in their language, how they assign meanings, and what is salient in their everyday lives. In this way, one can learn what a situation means to them on a practical level and grasp their intentions and subjective perceptions, as well as their immediate, unmonitored, and unreconstructed interactions, actions, and practices. Insider accounts explain getting along in that social world and are strategies for coping and accommodation.

At the same time, the interviews themselves must be placed within a context in order to understand and analyze them. We need an interpretive framework to understand symbolic power and see the limitations of the subjects' understanding of their world. As Bourdieu argues, we cannot mistake what people say about their worlds as the truth of those worlds. We cannot accept spontaneous utterances nor can we accept their ideas and classifications as true subjective accounts of the world; we cannot focus on the perceptions and reflections of the participants as being the truth of that world. Their explanations are always disembodied reconstructions of their practical activity. Just because our subjects are embedded and situated in the social world that we are studying does not mean that they will provide the truth about this social world or know the full context of their actions. Structures are beyond immediate grasp, and people live within conditions not of their own making. Bourdieu's position has major implications for ethnographers; ethnographers always have an intellectual responsibility to provide a theoretical interpretation for what their subjects tell them—it is not enough just to repeat the subjects' views and opinions as if they grasped the whole truth.

In order to have a science of what people actually do and how they understand and act in the world, we must take account of how those actions occur within the external structures that, although not formally conceptualized, still shape and mold social life. Only by making explicit this gap between the subjective knowledge that actors have of the world and the objective knowledge gained through structural analysis, can we begin to construct a reflexive theory of society that combines the objective and the subjective in the construction of knowledge without falling into a false dualism.

HABITUS, BODY, PRACTICE

HABITUS

Bourdieu seeks to explain social action without reducing it to either free, open-ended, conscious choice or predetermination by obedience to rules, roles, and norms. For Bourdieu, the goal is to theorize a way out of explaining patterns of social behavior without reliance on external structures or conscious choice alone. In order to transcend these dualisms, he theorizes the relationship between individuals and society in terms of the concept of habitus. Rather than argue that the individual and society are diametrically opposed, Bourdieu argues that social reality is both inside and outside of individuals. There is no real separation between the individual and society. The social is in the body and the body is in the social.

In this way, habitus represents dialectical or interpenetrating realities of subjective experience and the objective social world. Habitus emphasizes the internalized set of practices, schemas, and knowledges (Bourdieu uses the plural) and competences of the world that shapes, conditions, and structures perception of the world as well as social interaction. Habitus can also be considered the past socialization of individuals, an historical orientation that shapes their present and future perceptions, appreciation, and social practices. As the orienting social disposition toward the world, habitus operates below the level of consciousness and reflexivity.

Habitus can be understood as a 'structuring structure' in that habitus is a template for reproducing perceptions and actions and for continuing to induce individuals to perform practices as if they remained within the context in which habitus was first produced (Bourdieu 1977b: 72). Thereby habitus reproduces the existing structures that socialize habitus. However, this is not just a blind reproduction; one's experiences are internalized and turned into expectations and orientations that become externalized in action, which, in turn, reproduces the objective structures within which action takes place. For example, a child learns to be obedient and submissive to authority; the habitus that is produced in the child by these practices then is reproduced as the child grows up and becomes an adult who is authoritarian toward subordinates, submissive to authority figures, and demanding of similar perceptions and behaviors in others, for example in his or her own children, students, or new recruits to an organization, although the contexts and specific commands and expectations may change.

This structuring aspect illuminates how habitus is mutable and adaptable rather than predetermined; habitus can be altered as new dispositions and forms of knowledge are acquired through new experiences and new social

theory of the development of sexuality

contexts. Because it is a set of dispositions, the structuring structure in turn organizes other dispositions, practices, and orientations. This aspect enables Bourdieu to define action as something undertaken without being conscious, calculating, or rule obeying. In this way, society is not reproduced mechanistically; rather, society socializes the individual while simultaneously society is reproduced through individual action and practice.

Bourdieu emphasizes the role of competence and allows for both strategic action and action undertaken habitually. Action can occur without being reduced to blind obedience. Nor are skill, insight, and improvisation curtailed in pursuing goals. Bourdieu (2000a) points out that there are two kinds of logic: 'practical comprehension' (incorporated logic), which can be understood as the logic of practice or habitus (the almost instinctual and reflexive feel for the game) and 'conscious, intellectual comprehension' (130).

Habitus can create 'durable solidarities' because groups of people inhabiting a similar social or physical space share dispositions, although these dispositions are also individualized, incorporated, and unconscious (Bourdieu 2000a: 256). The individuals are not consciously enacting solidarity; it is created by their shared habitus—by shared individual interests. Because individuals belong to multiple groups (race, class, gender, age, and so on) and develop their habits and attitudes from contact with others in these groups, the individual habitus expresses these influences. – *still one single "habitus"*

It is not coincidence that one's position is reproduced in society because habitus reflects and reproduces the very habitat from which it emerged. The historical alignment of 'habitus and habitat' is formed through social mechanisms that ensure the adjustment of one's dispositions to the positions one occupies in social life (Bourdieu and Wacquant 1992: 128). Habitus underlies the predisposition to react a certain way in certain situations and in new or unforeseen situations as well. The behaviors of youngsters on their first day of school reflect their habitus rather than individual personalities; children can be rambunctious and unruly, quiet and docile, or outgoing and friendly with their classmates and teacher. These ways of acting are patterns that reflect a habitus formed in family and neighborhood environments, even though, in conventional thinking, the behaviors are often seen as personality traits. The learned and embodied habitus, emerging from shared social mechanisms, does not result in automatic or fully predictable behaviors, only in a general predisposition or patterning.

Habitus disproves two epistemologies: *mechanism*, which holds that we act like machines set in motion by external structural constraints, and *finalism*, which, similar to the rational actor theory, holds that we act freely and are consciously aware of the consequences. Habitus is the practical sense of what you should do, incorporated and unconscious, the 'feel for the game.'

Being attuned to the game allows you to anticipate future events in the game, even if they are not fully predictable. Habitus, being socially constructed and imbued in the body, acts without our consciousness, producing the 'correct' action within the social constraints in which the body exists. This application of the concept of habitus refutes the concepts of class consciousness and false consciousness because there is no conscious decision to participate in a class; one inhabits it due to historical, temporal positioning, because of the times and places within which one has been and is situated.

similar to the "me"

BODY

Bourdieu argues that we are biological individuals, with bodies that hold all of our learning. The body is exposed to the world and conditioned by the material and cultural conditions of the world within which it exists. The body includes the mind and the senses, and we acquire habitus through the body's position in the social world. As habitus is embodied and becomes body, and therefore is enacted by the body, it provides a practical comprehension of the world quite different from rational or conscious comprehension. These arbitrary socially constructed distinctions are then experienced as naturalized, essentialized, and institutionalized in the body.

Sports trainers can teach the intellect, but they must teach the body, in which practical mastery needs to be learned in order for athletes to be effective. However, by learning the movements that must be executed, the body can learn how to react unconsciously by practicing. The movement then becomes a reflex. Sometimes, the habitus is thrown off a bit and misfires. For example, tennis players may become rusty by taking time off and then have to return to consciously working on a flawed stroke, which is adjusted through the body. However, since the habitus is continually adapting, there is always the possibility that individuals may be out of line with the social context they find themselves in; they may be mismatched to the situation. For those who have matched dispositions with position, habitus and social context are in alignment, and they can then rely on their habitus as dispositions without reflection. When habitus and context are mis-matched, dispositions can be inappropriate and therefore require more conscious adjustment and attunement to what are the proper dispositions and perceptions. A person unaccustomed to the bourgeois lifestyle attending a wine-tasting event must give careful attention to his movements and gestures.

The body is where our physical, mental, symbolic, and lived experience, i.e., culture, is reproduced and manifested. It is in and through the body that our knowledge and understanding of the world exists; however, the body is not a static receptacle of knowledge. Because we are social beings acting and interacting in social space, the body becomes an active instrument of learning in which the social order inscribes itself through constant confrontation. The body effectively serves as a 'memory pad' in which the most serious and essential knowledges (Bourdieu uses the plural) that we have of the world are rooted. These socialized and internalized practical knowledges are not states of mind or consciousness but 'a state of the body' that leads the mind unconsciously along with it (Bourdieu 1990c: 68). The body contains the *in-corporated* or embodied history of its experience, and it is through the body's existence in social space that cultural forms and cultural practices are learned and enacted. Through this socialization, the body develops dispositions suited to comprehend, act, anticipate, and respond in the world. Corporeal knowledge is quite different from the intentional act of consciousness or mental comprehension. This bodily knowledge is a preverbal, a priori understanding of the world that flows from being socialized into the world. Bodies appear as if they were naturally talented or as if they possessed some innate knowledge because those cultural knowledges are so firmly embedded that they appear instinctual in their enactment when viewed by both practitioners and observers. In this way, corporeal knowledge is the product of the subject's entire history, which becomes second nature in the present and then forgotten as history.

While initial stages of learning may be conscious, as these knowledges become increasingly embodied they become more natural, efficient, and transparent. As a result, corporeal knowledges are not the product of conscious understanding; rather, they are arduously acquired through inculcation, labor, and training. The habitus does not orient our social interaction through rule following or rational choice but rather on the basis of a previously internalized and developed practical sense of the particular cultural practices in which it is engaged.

PRACTICE

Bourdieu seeks to analyze society through the prism of practices, to study what human beings do as active agents on a regular basis. Bourdieu places emphasis on practice because human activity—not actions—is practical. Social life is lived through the ways that people understand their worlds and act according to those understandings. Practices emanate from habitus, from the dispositions, orientations, and schemas through which people apprehend and appreciate the world around them. Bourdieu is seeking to move past the overemphasis on rational conscious action, especially the RAT and the rational choice paradigm. On the other hand, he also rejects deterministic and functionalist paradigms in which all human behavior is determined by social structures. Instead of either paradigm, he offers a picture of patterned regularities of social interaction that happen on multiple levels of recognition and awareness. This study of the economy of practices, whether cultural, economic, political, or academic, charts the habitual ways of acting in and responding to the world within which the individuals and their practices are situated.

It is integral to Bourdieu's position, however, that practices are also collective or shared and 'structured'; the ways in which agents act and reason tend to be similar within particular societies, historical periods, and social groups, and actions and thought tend to be manifested in durable patterns and regularities. As a result, practices are contextually specific so that different groups or societies or classes have different practices; that is, they have modes of social interaction specific to them that differentiate them from other groups and other societies. Bourdieu looks at human interaction through a relative lens—this lens is not a moral, evaluative one but one that must be used to understand those practices relative to the specific group that undertakes those types of interactions. *Specificity like Foucault*

Bourdieu distinguishes practices from rules. Although practices provide a normative foundation for interaction, he does not interpret them as rules, as functionalists are inclined to do. Practices are general ways of doings things, but they do not specify exactly what is to be done in any situation or how it is to be done. Rules suggest obedience and rigidity—they are to be followed; whereas, for Bourdieu, practice allows for improvization, creativity, and strategy—all aspects of agency that cannot be discounted in explaining human behavior. According to Bourdieu, human interaction is based on comprehension and a feel for the game whereby people act, react, and interact based on their knowledge of their worlds, and yet they are often not aware of that knowledge. In Bourdieu's framework, we do not act as rule followers or because rules force us into action, even if our actions are constrained or defined within accepted parameters (e.g., style, morality, civility). Practice allows us to analyze the world in terms of regularities and ordered patterns of interaction without sacrificing strategy and innovation and the primary modes by which people negotiate the terrain of everyday life.

SYMBOLIC POWER, SYMBOLIC VIOLENCE, AND MISRECOGNITION

Like other theorists (most notably Goffman, Foucault, and Butler), Bourdieu sees classification as a form of power. The relationship between symbolic classifications and social structures becomes a dominant theme in Bourdieu's work. Bourdieu argues that theorists must go beyond economic power, the traditional Marxist mode of explaining domination and subordination, in order to examine the role of symbolic power and the way in which classification, cultural practices, cultural products, and institutions play a role in generating and maintaining inequality in contemporary societies. This move to the symbolic is also a return to the role of culture and away from the role of coercion and physical force, a reaffirmation of the role of beliefs, attitudes, and understanding. This move is very much a Gramscian move toward the analysis of how hegemony is created and maintained rather than an argument about power being founded on manipulation or false consciousness. Through an analysis of all symbolic systems, Bourdieu seeks to understand how these forms of classification compose the intelligibility structures through which we understand the world; they serve as the basis of communication and the formation of knowledge and function as modes of differentiation and of assigning social values, hierarchies, and rankings.

Most important for Bourdieu, symbolic systems serve as modes or mechanisms of domination, as they are the dominant symbolic meanings or categories through which we understand the world. Those with the ability to impose their views upon the world, the dominant groups, are able to set the standards, values, aesthetics, rankings, and hierarchies. They induce the dominated to accept those hierarchies as legitimate and taken-for-granted reality. By highlighting how symbolic systems are arbitrary social constructions, Bourdieu illuminates their political functions as mechanisms of social power. By accepting the dominant, legitimized, institutionalized classifications as the natural order, people accept their place in the dominant system and participate in their own domination. Symbolic power is the power to define social reality.

This is not an argument about false consciousness; rather, it is a mode of analysis that seeks to free us from such arguments. For Bourdieu, ideology is the mode of comprehending the world, and it operates through the power that symbolic systems wield by masking economic and political power in taken-for-granted understandings. Symbolic power thus legitimates existing political and economic relations and establishes and reproduces existing modes of social domination. This is not simply a top-down imposition; both the dominant and the dominated come to accept these classifications as the natural taken-for-granted order of the world. Bourdieu argues that symbolic violence occurs through the imposition of particular values, ideas, and classifications as universal, ahistorical, and natural. Symbolic violence occurs through inculcating these very categories into the habitus, making them the ways that people comprehend the world. As people accept these distinctions, they come to misrecognize or fail to see the arbitrary character of these classifications. They do not grasp that the classifications serve particular political and economic interests and instead view them as disinterested or neutral. Symbolic power is able to disguise invested cultural distinctions as disinterested, and thereby it helps reinforce the social order within which they operate. Classifications, practices, and institutional perspectives gain their effectiveness and legitimacy by going misrecognized as they become separated from their particular investments.

Bourdieu's definitions of symbolic power and misrecognition have implications for social research. They suggest that researchers must go beyond a faithful reporting of what research subjects say about the world, no matter how respectful researchers would like to be of the views of the people they interview or encounter in a field study. The opinions, ideas, and cognitive maps of the research subjects almost undoubtedly contain misrecognitions, and the researchers must be prepared to discuss these misrecognitions when they interpret data.

Symbolic violence cannot be overcome by raising awareness because the violence is exerted upon the body, inscribed in the form of dispositions, and perpetuated as belief comes to match observation. Bourdieu defines this process as the two-fold naturalization of the world, that is, the inscription of particular classifications in the body and in structures of the social and political order. The effect is symbolic violence—the system of domination goes on without question, with everyone participating in its perpetuation.

FIELDS, SPACES, AND CAPITALS

The concept of field contributes to overcoming the scholarly opposition between materialism and idealism by grasping dynamically an 'economy of symbolic goods' that extends to social spaces as 'non-economic' as art or religion (Bourdieu 1993c: 74). A field, for Bourdieu, is any social arena having its own internally defined logic of practice and rewards for participation and competence of participation. We suggest that you read the next few pages with a specific field in mind—for example, the university, professional sports, or the mortgage lending business—and use experiences in that field to illustrate Bourdieu's concepts.

The field or 'the game,' as Bourdieu refers to it, is the social context within which the habitus operates. In order to play the game correctly or move within the field with ease, one must have the proper habitus or have one's habitus in alignment with the game being played. This alignment requires one to have the requisite skills, knowledges, and aptitudes relative and specific to that particular field. In this way, we can see how habitus, practices, the body, and the field all are interrelated concepts within Bourdieu's theory of action. For Bourdieu, the embodiment of practices in the habitus relative to the field allows one to move more or less adroitly, more smoothly or roughly, and to play the game better or worse than others. Habitus thus mediates the practices of the field and, as it becomes more and more competent at mastering those specific practices, one becomes a more effective player of the game—more in tune with the logic of the practice of that field.

By participating in the field, the habitus learns to adapt and to act in accord with the demands and norms of the field. As the habitus learns the rules of the game and refashions itself as a player in the game, it becomes more and more competent and compatible with the field. Through this participation combined with bodily labor and training, the agent develops a feel for the game, a feeling for how to operate practically within the field, that functions at a level below consciousness. In this way, people operate within any particular field with greater or lesser skill given the dispositions, competence, and resources that they have relative to the particular field under analysis.

Fields are not neutral spaces of interaction; rather, they are structured around struggle over different forms of capital (different values, resources, and assets, for example). Fields are arenas of the production, circulation, and consumption of goods or knowledges, and this circumstance allows actors to position themselves in better or worse positions within the field in relation to others. The structured spaces of dominant and subordinated positions are based on types and amounts of capital, which is always distributed unequally. Power is in the distribution of capital. For Bourdieu, this inequality is not about the personal attributes of the players; rather, his is a structural analysis of the volume and types of capital at any position within the space, which are always relational to other positions and capitals.

The current unequal distribution of capital has a history because this distribution is the outcome of past struggles over capital accumulation. The present unequal distribution, in turn, defines the field of future struggles and future strategies. The whole history of the game is thus present in each move of the game.

Those with established capitals try to conserve their position; through orthodoxy, they try to reproduce these positions, the dominant position for them, and to define legitimate knowledge to match the knowledge they have. These guardians of orthodoxy are the curators of culture. Newcomers can be seen as subversive; they are the creators of culture, they invent new forms of knowledge, and their challenges force conservatives to make defensive moves. Subversion is carried out by those who expect to gain little from the dominant structuring of the field. Often, subversion takes the form of challenging the dominant group's legitimacy and its claims that standards of the field correspond to the existing orthodoxy.

Fields are always networks of relations of domination and subordination. Positions within any field are always objective positions in that they are always determined by their influence (the amounts and types of capital they possess) and the influence they employ in their present position and in possible positions in relation to other positions in the field. Through the accumulation of capital by individual players and institutions, the field is organized unequally, with power differentials within it. The concept of the field enables us to grasp how fields are organized around competition and therefore how power functions to shape the social system.

The concept of the field helps us accomplish five theoretical aims:

1. Thinking relationally: We recognize that invisible relations that are not properties of individuals or groups shape the patterns of interest and struggle and define the conflict-based character of social life. We can analyze the positions independently from the characteristics of the occupants of those positions. Properties depend on position within the spaces of the field.

2. Avoiding class reductionism: Class, like all other social factors, is mediated through fields; classes are refracted through fields and are never products of direct conditioning or logic. They are always mediated through the dynamics of the field's power and hierarchy. Fields are not reducible to other fields. In this way, we have a break or split between macro-level analysis and micro-level analysis—we can understand how both social structural arrangements, such as power, economy, and racial domination, impinge on the interaction of specific actors in specific contexts, which, in turn, reinforce those structures. We become able to see immediate environments of everyday life and the broader societal structures and forces that structure them. Domination in fields is not necessarily about money, but it is subject to economic pressures.

3. Discerning social conditions that shape cultural production: Fields have their own laws of governance—specific to the field itself. Each type of field is defined by its own types of stakes and interests.

4. Recognizing struggle: Rank, hierarchy, and exchanges between positions in interaction are shaped by the relative location in the hierarchy of position. All positions are struggled over; even the boundaries of the field itself are objects of struggle.

5. Solving the problem of autonomy vs. interconnection: In Bourdieu's framework, cultural fields are relatively autonomous, yet they are still interconnected with external forces. The term 'relative autonomy' means that fields are always situated within larger economic and power dynamics; culture and economy are never distinct, always interconnected.

FIELD HOMOLOGIES

Fields are also homologous in that they develop isomorphic or correspond-ing properties, such as positions of dominance and subordination, strategies of exclusion and usurpation, and mechanisms of reproduction and change. Bourdieu draws this metaphor from mathematics; it means that we can establish a mapping between fields and that they share certain features of underlying structure or organization.

We can understand these homologies in two ways. In an abstract sense, they refer to similarities in the organization or structure of the fields and in the pro-cesses that take place in them, such as domination, exclusion, and reproduction. At a more concrete level, the homologies can be seen in the structural correspon-dence that exists between social classes, economic capital, and cultural capital. A position of legitimacy, visibility, and domination in one social hierarchy often means that its occupants will hold similar positions in another field. For example, Donald Trump has a lot of money (economic capital), and he is also visible as a celebrity (symbolic capital) and enjoys political influence in urban development decisions (social capital and influence in the political field).

The struggles in the cultural field produce a euphemized or 'veiled' form of ideological struggle between social classes or racial groups. Field homologies reinforce patterns of conflict across different fields—the effect is the reproduc-tion of common patterns of hierarchy from one field to another. Class or race becomes translated into euphemized forms specific to other fields: the domi-nant racial structure is reinforced by the operation of the euphemized processes in a different field. For example, an activist professor who has written newspaper articles that challenge racial discrimination in a community's school system is denied tenure at the local college because he 'hasn't published enough in peer-reviewed journals.' In this example, the euphemized struggles in the cultural field of academic publication serve the interests of racial domination.

THE POLITICAL FIELD

Bourdieu's analysis of the political field deserves special attention and has impli-cations for political sociology and the borders between sociology and political science. Bourdieu suggests that we need to replace terms that were inherited from the period of structural Marxist analysis without dumping its insights about conflict and contention. In place of the rigid concept of apparatus (as in school-ing or the military as apparatuses of the state), he suggests the term 'field.' The image is of an open expanse in which can be found various elements that might include organizations not only of the state but also of the private sector and society. These elements can move around, change, connect to each other, or become more distant. For example, the field of education can contain public schools but also private ones, religious institutions, textbook publishers, and parts of the media. In some ways, 'field' is akin to Parsons' concept of function. The parts that carry out educational functions are not a single institution, structure, or apparatus but multiple organizations and practices. In this new geography of fields, social movements and collective action also form fields and appear within other fields—as when activists seek to make changes in school curricula.

Bourdieu's political field is a terrain of actors and practices rather than of institutions and apparatuses, in contrast to the more fixed concepts of structural-functionalists and structural Marxists. The political field is organized by the logic of power and domination. It includes the formation of parties and social movements, socialization and political comportment, and the production of political products such as policies, events, and mobilizations. The capture of state power can be the aim of practice. The political field overlaps in actors and practices with fields such as the media, culture and education, and the economy. It has its own types of capital—especially social capital formed by networks of political actors. But other kinds of capital, such as money and the symbolic capital of media influence, are also in circulation.

Bourdieu's concept of the political field dissolves political science into sociology by defining politics as one type of social practice. Key terms of political philosophy such as legitimacy, authority, sovereignty, citizenship, and even politics itself are transformed by sociological analysis based on empirical study that is informed by a theory of the social world and practice. For Bourdieu, practices in the political field are Durkheimian 'social facts' and part of the subject matter of sociology (Bourdieu, Chamboredon, and Passeron 1991: 154). At the same time, the concept of the political field avoids the reduction of political analysis to economic causation, avoiding both 'vulgar Marxist' explanations and narrowly economistic utilitarian and rational choice treatments. (For example, the George W. Bush administration's handling of US foreign and military policies contained a logic of power and global dominance that is not reducible to the control of oil, though oil is certainly part of it.)

SOCIAL SPACE: THE GENESIS OF GROUPS AND SYMBOLIC POWER

Bourdieu deploys the term 'social space' in order to break from Marxist conceptions of group relations by distinguishing between a theoretical class and an actual group of people out there in the world. Bourdieu distinguishes between groups on paper and groups actually embedded in society by emphasizing the networks of relations that these latter groups have. Second, Bourdieu wants to break with models of economism, whereby economics becomes the sole defining principle of social organization and social position. By breaking with the objectivism of the economy, Bourdieu shows how, in addition to economic struggles, symbolic struggles also characterize social fields of relations. In these struggles, what is at stake is the representation of the social world and the particular classifications and social-cultural hierarchies that shape and define each field.

It should be noted that social space is not something added on to the economic structure of society, as if it were some sort of Marxist superstructure that reflects and reinforces the economic structure a posteriori; nor is it in an a priori relationship to the economic structure. It is intertwined with and constitutive of the economic structure.

Following Bourdieu's model for an analysis of social space requires that we theorize social space as the relational differences and distribution of properties and resources active within a particular social universe that allows agents to define their relative positions within that space with greater or lesser leverage. Social space is not a group of individuals gathered together, nor is it the amalgamation of groups in a particular geographic area; rather, social space is an objective set of power relations, normative orientations, and dispositions that define the particular social field in question and impose themselves on all who enter that field. These power relations between different positions and possible positions to be taken up in social space are defined through the amounts and types of capital that define that social space (both the types of capital that individuals and groups possess and the volume of each type). For example, in the housing market, if I want to purchase a condominium and belong to a wealthy condominium association, I must have enough economic capital to buy in, the social capital to know when a unit is or will be on the market, and the symbolic capital or status to be accepted by the board for ownership.

The concept of social space enables us to grasp how different agents (in terms of race, gender, and sexual orientation) can occupy similar positions in geographical space (in terms of where they desire to buy housing) and, because they are immersed in similar social and material conditions within social space, are likely to have similar dispositions and interests. They therefore buy in particular neighborhoods for particular reasons (such as schools, restaurants, and entertainment) and adopt similar cultural practices and stances toward the world around them (habitus). These groups are not self-conscious or mobilized as a unit for struggle; on the contrary, individuals within these groups may not even consider themselves as part of any unit. Nevertheless, the concept of social space makes it possible to explain and predict the practices and properties of these groups. We can specify the probability of individuals constituting themselves as part of those groups because they are closer in social space. Because they share similar positions in social space, the subjective categories through which they perceive the world are the product of the internalization of the objective structures of social space. These perceptions then become taken for granted as their mental maps of the world correspond to the material conditions within which they are situated. The sense of one's place within the social space is homologous to a sense of distances and distinctions to be marked and maintained, which, in turn, reproduces the dominant divisions of the world both in the objective structures of the world and in the very categories of perception and appreciation through which those structures are understood.

For Bourdieu, social space can be compared to a geographic space within which regions are divided up. Social space is constructed in such a way that the closer the agents, groups, or institutions are situated within this space, the more properties (specifically types and volumes of particular capital) they have in common; and the farther apart, the fewer. Spatial distances on paper (e.g., between the wealthy and the poor) coincide with actual social distances in reality. Such is not the case in the actual lived space of everyday life. Those who are close together in social space—by choice or by necessity because of their position in social space—often will be close together in geographic space, thereby generating a sense of segregation among groups because distinctions of social space mirror those of geographical space. People from very different social spaces may briefly interact or cross paths in geographical or actual physical space, yet these interactions are fleeting.

Five examples will clarify these concepts: 1) In terms of social space and geographical space, overlap exists in downtown financial districts where wealthy business people cross paths with clerical staff, janitors, maintenance workers, and the homeless, for example. However, beyond the business district, geographical space mirrors social space in residential patterns and in the dispositions and orientation people have toward other groups. 2) Gated communities are another example showing how the dominant groups in social space are those who posses the most capital; members of the executive strata live with a shared social space and a shared vision of the good life, safety, housing, neighborhood, and desirable neighbors. 3) Conversely, consider public-housing projects in both the United States and western Europe. These are places of relegation for people who are placed in the lowest or most marginalized positions in social space and who are also the most geographically marginalized. In the marginalized geographical space of public housing, people develop shared views of being excluded, marginalized, and stigmatized, and often they internalize these views, reproducing the dominant vision and beliefs about those communities (Venkatesh 2002, 2006; Wacquant [1993] 2005, 2008a). 4) Consider the relationship between suburbs and cities (especially certain parts of cities) and the way people in the middle classes in the United States feel about cities and position themselves at a distance from the city through their conceptualizations of it, which associate the city with images of fear, danger, and a lack of safety. In the 'imaginary' of many US suburban dwellers, the city is stigmatized as dirty and crime infested in contrast to the open green spaces and idyllic conditions of suburban life. 5) Finally, consider borderland and hybridized spaces where different social groups intersect and interact, such as the Mexican-US border or the edges of Spanish territory in Ceuta and the Canary Islands, where African migrants hope to enter European space as undocumented workers. What is the mapping between these borderlands, these cultural fields of racial categorization and fields of economic dominance? How rare are the borderlands? Where are they, and what are their characteristics?

For Bourdieu, scientific work maps out the objective relations and oppositions between the different positions constituting the field as well as between the points of view on that space, all of which play a part in the construction, conservation, or transformation of the social space and, in turn, the geographical space through which people move. In mapping these positions, we must be mindful of the effect of homologies: those who occupy the dominant position in social space occupy the dominant positions of symbolic production and the dominant viewpoints that define that space. In doing so, it is necessary to ensure that these positions and viewpoints are not reducible to the economy; rather, social space is multidimensional, and, in it, different actors or groups (not necessarily as 'groups-for-themselves' in the Marxist sense of conscious agents) are engaged in different struggles in different dimensions over that social space. Like Bourdieu's notion of the field, mental space, geographical space, and social space come to form homologies as people's mental categories influence them to interpret the world around them both socially and geographically and instill the illusions of naturalness and common sense into these interpretations. As each sphere reinforces or mirrors the others, people come to find themselves 'at home' in their particular situations because they share commonalities with others situated near them (socially and geographically), and they therefore, ultimately, share similar dispositions on the world—or mental and cognitive maps that form their understanding of the world.

CAPITALS IN THE FIELD

For Bourdieu, 'capitals' (again he uses the plural) are social relations of power. Capitals are the resources, knowledges, objects, practices, and skills relative to any particular field that a person utilizes to advance his or her position in the social order through their acquisition and distribution. Capitals come in multiple forms, and one's position and one's future orientation in any particular social arena is based on the types and volumes of capital that agents or institutions possess in relation to other agents and institutions. In addition, capitals may be exchanged and converted through various strategies and techniques of augmentation.

Capitals function not only as relations of power but also as objects of struggle through which the social world is defined. For Bourdieu, capitals are defined as having value, or being valuable insofar as they are agreed upon socially for their value; capitals are only valuable in that they depend on our recognition and definition of their value. Bourdieu's theory of capitals provides a way around reducing all forms of power or domination to the arena of economics and instead offers a multidimensional sense by which different types of power define different spheres of life. For Bourdieu, there are four major types of capital—economic, cultural, social, and symbolic; however, he also writes about other types, such as juridical and linguistic capital.

Economic capital, for Bourdieu, entails all income, savings, and assets that have a monetary value, defined in terms of that value. Economic capital has an independent existence, in the form of money, which allows it to be accumulated, calculated, invested, transmitted, and translated into other types of capital. As such, it tends to serve as a model against which other forms of capital are compared and conceived. Economic capital forms the basis upon which other capitals can be accumulated by providing the resource and the time needed for accumulation. For example, in the United States, the percentage of college graduates among people with low test scores from high-income homes is higher than the percentage of college graduates among people with high test scores from low-income homes, 30 per cent and 25 per cent, respectively (Mishell 2008). In this stark example, economic capital can buy cultural capital—or at least credentials; the process can be a bit subtler, for example, when wealthy parents buy homes in neighborhoods with excellent schools signaled by high standardized test scores.

Cultural capital, for Bourdieu, comes in the form of educational credentials; knowledge of objects, practices, and customs; and the manners, dispositions, and tastes one displays in the modes of perception and appreciation of the world. Cultural capital can be converted into economic capital depending on the market and the exchanges that may take place. Knowledge of Impressionist painting can boost an art dealer's prestige with wealthy clients and his or her income.

Social capital, for Bourdieu, is the networks and acquaintances that an agent can call upon in her or his effort to achieve a specified goal. The 'old boy' networks of the elite university systems that pave the way for admissions or for employment in prestigious firms are examples that clearly demarcate the effects of social capital (Khurana 2002). In different circuits, such as local government, political appointments are made on the basis of social networks.

Symbolic capital, for Bourdieu, is the power of being able to define legitimate authority. It is the power of being taken for granted as authority figures and perceived as natural claimants to status or recognition. Symbolic capital may have an objectified or institutionalized form. Various awards and prizes are measures of symbolic capital, for example, degrees from institutions, the Nobel Peace Prize, and the Pulitzer.

TASTE, DISTINCTION, AND NATURALIZED CATEGORIES

Two central questions drive Bourdieu's analysis of culture: 1) How do cultural resources, practices of cultural consumption, and cultural institutions serve as mechanisms of domination? 2) How are a person's tastes, cultural practices, and cultural knowledges a reflection of position and orientation within the hierarchy of the social structure? For Bourdieu, the misrecognition of the role of culture is the necessary condition for the exercise of power, as culture serves as a euphemism to mask economic domination.

Bourdieu stresses the arbitrariness of culture and of cultural categories. In doing so, he problematizes both what counts as culture in general (or as 'elite culture,' 'popular culture,' or the 'vulgar') and how these distinctions serve to reinforce hierarchies in society. Through cultural analysis (based on photography, painting, household items, manners, and tastes), he problematizes not only what counts as culture but also how culture functions. Bourdieu defines this analysis of culture through the term 'distinction'—also the title of his most widely read book—because he is interested in the process of making something distinct and different from others and the ability to distinguish between things by making distinctions. This twofold process exposes not only what is valued but also who is valued in being able to make certain objects and practices distinct and who has the ability to understand the distinctions being made. This analysis links back to Bourdieu's theory of capitals, especially that of cultural capital, because it is those who have the ability to make cultural distinctions who are holders of cultural capital. It also is connected to his concepts of symbolic power, symbolic violence, and misrecognition in terms of how power operates to legitimate some values, tastes, and preferences and to denigrate or deny others.

Bourdieu links his theory of culture to an understanding of the habitus and how positions within the social structure are normalized through the acceptance of one's position. Bourdieu defines this as the acceptance and rejection of certain material circumstances, which shape the ways that people come to understand *what is* 'for the likes of us' as opposed to *what is not* (Bourdieu and Wacquant 1992: 130). Specifically, he analyzes the notions of possibility versus probability when it comes to understanding what people's preferences and tastes may be. For example, he notes that someone from a working-class background, without formal training in art history, will probably not appreciate a Jackson Pollock painting because she or he does not have the cultural capital (cultural competence, aesthetic disposition and appreciation) to understand abstract art. It is possible that this person could have been self taught, but unlikely given the individual's cultural capital. In this way, Bourdieu is pointing out that people's positions in society are linked to resources to which they have access and to those that they do not have available; and he comments that this observation is a way to objectively assess how what is denied is often disdained, whereas what is available is desired.

Cosmopolitan and educated elites have the cultural capital of appreciating abstract art and distinguish themselves from the middle and lower classes by making understanding abstract art a premium and a badge of cultural sophistication. Because they have the capital, namely, the economic and cultural resources to appreciate and the time to consume such art, they are also in possession of the symbolic capital to make enjoyment of abstract art the privileged position while denying a 'badge of distinction' to products to which everyone has access, such as commercial television. On the surface, these appearances come off as natural because we take for granted the cultural hierarchies in place and misrecognize that they are the views imposed upon society by an elite group; there is nothing natural (or more sophisticated or inherently valuable) about preferring abstract painting over television. It is the culturally and historically constructed categories that go misrecognized as such and appear as ahistorical transcendental categories outside of historical and social conditions that define the good, the tasteful, and so on.

Bourdieu defines cultural consumption as mirroring aesthetic dispositions. Through consumption, positions are taken within the field and identities defined through those positions taken. It is not only the categories through which we perceive the world but also the things we do and acquire through those categories. Just as knowledge of painting distinguishes one observer from another in terms of her or his cultural capital, the display and consumption of culture through participation in events or activities, ownership, and connoisseurship are also ways in which culture makes us aware of cultural boundaries that serve as class boundaries and boundaries of exclusion that keep others out. The more wealth one has, the more one can separate culture from economics, as in the case of leisure time versus work time. The separation of leisure from work is a key measure that defines claims to social position and social domination. All art draws distinctions, and it naturalizes distinctions that society has drawn to hide the socio-economic system that makes them. People use culture and taste to distinguish themselves, and they are always already distinguished because they have already staked a claim to the right to make and use these distinctions. Bourdieu's project is to demystify high culture's claims to be necessarily better than working-class culture; he criticizes the structures of legitimacy and shows the workings of power—symbolic power, symbolic violence, and the misrecognition of legitimation—that define the cultural sphere as a mode of masking economic domination.

PUBLIC INTELLECTUALS AND POLITICS

Sociologists have a longstanding tradition of examining elites, collective action, and the distribution of power and resources in a society, often under the rubric of political sociology. In the post-war period, this analysis (influenced by Weber and Marx among the classical theorists) assumed the existence of relatively coherent organizations and stable state structures and policies over which the actors contended; the actors included competing elites, parties and interest groups, and organized mass movements. The neoliberal change in state functions and new transnational communication media have made political forms more fluid and network-like, and less likely to be conceived as fixed organizational apparatuses.

Bourdieu was a pioneer in redefining concepts and posing new questions in this area. His analysis begins with a debate with Althusser's structural Marxism; Bourdieu identifies fields in which power is exercised, rather than rigid state apparatuses. The contending actors in these fields hold varying amounts of four types of capital (economic capital, cultural capital, social capital, and symbolic capital). To some extent, these forms of capital can be exchanged for each other—for example, rich people (holders of economic capital) can send their children to elite universities where they will learn the right things (cultural capital) and meet the right people (social capital). The process is, however, fluid and not deterministic.

Bourdieu's exploration of forms of capital converges with Robert Putnam's work on social capital (itself connected to James Coleman's use of the concept). Putnam believes that communities that lack economic capital can compensate by developing and using social capital; but he also believes that voluntary association has weakened in the United States—the controversial 'bowling alone' thesis (Putnam 2001).

This thinning out of voluntary associations in the United States is also evident among social movements that are less inclined to form large, permanent organizations with a defined mass base and a political party structure. Indeed, observations of political and social movements in a number of other societies also suggest a fragmentation of popular movements. Yet this fragmentation does not mean an end to movement activity. Movements have taken the form of social networks—many of them transnational—rather than coherent organizations. They seek to influence state policies while they develop a base through redefining or creating new identities. A substantial number use and transform traditional religious identity and affiliation, most noticeably into fundamentalism as a modern movement. Also prominent is the activism of conscience constituencies, for instance, PETA, environmental movements, and the human-rights movement; these movements are often transnational, and, like the religious movements, they create identities that are quite different from the class or ethnic identities of earlier periods (Tarrow 1998; Meyer, Whittier, and Robnett 2002).

Community-based participatory or action research may be designed to rebuild or form community social capital. Community practice as a form of reflexive sociology creates interesting challenges to theory and traditional methods.

In his later work, Bourdieu associated the analysis of fields and types of capital with a more active stance of intellectual intervention, as he developed a critique of imperialist reason, globalization, and the impoverishment of the nation-state. He increasingly chose to address the public and to emphasize the relevance of sociology to everyday life, not to be the public intellectual as heroic celebrity but to encourage a critical view of society.

THE CRITIQUE OF NEOLIBERALISM

Neoliberalism is viewed by Bourdieu as the discourse and program of a pure and perfect free market framed under notions of human rights, liberties, progress, and science. He argues that it actually serves mega-capital interests and transnational corporations; it operates through financial deregulation and privatization and the extension of this program into the policies of the International Monetary Fund (IMF) and the Organisation for Economic Co-operation and Development (OECD). In his assessment, the policy that these interests and organizations impose is growing so strong that it can call into question any and all collective structures that would impede the political program or place obstacles in the way of expansion of the free market. In neoliberalism, the state abdicates its responsibility to regulate the economy for social ends; thus neoliberalism is a utopian project of denying the existence of social realities beyond the market.

Neoliberalism is a social Darwinism of the globalization of financial markets. The ever-increasing importance of information technology ensures the mobility of capital, the power of the market, the triumph of economic efficiency over all other values, and profit based on competition and power. In this analysis, 'informationalism' and 'the new information age' are not autonomous social forces but key mechanisms by which finance capital imposes its dominance not only on society but also on other forms of capital (and other fractions of the capitalist class).

The discourse of freedom supports neoliberal policies. (In *The German Ideology*, Marx and Engels had already noted that freedom is a key term of capitalist ideology, just as honor and loyalty were in feudal ideology.) Free trade, flexibility, and management's freedom to impose its initiatives on labor are portrayed as universal, natural imperatives that are indispensable to the functioning and survival of capitalism. Bourdieu argues that this symbolic violence of neoliberalism is not recognized because the discourse has been so successfully diffused and the conditions made to appear as natural. Through misrecognition, people have become complicit in their own domination. Precarious economic conditions strike increasing numbers of workers, and the reserve army of labor expands because many individuals become permanently unemployed or precariously employed in insecure low-wage work and temp jobs. The social processes that create these precarious conditions simultaneously generate responses of docility, acceptance, and consent to what is made to appear as a natural and inevitable state of affairs.

The effects of the logic of neoliberalism are exploitation of world labor; privatization of public services creating reduced labor costs and a reduction in public expenditures; the destruction of unions and association collectives, which adds to the precarious nature of jobs; the obsolescence of the welfare state; mass unemployment; the destruction of welfare legislation; and the suppression of democracy.

Next, Bourdieu argues for a social-democratic model of social develop-ment, a genuine economy of happiness that would take into consideration all profits and costs, privileging those of human life. The model would operate through the formation of a social movement as an alternative to neoliberalism, and the role of intellectuals would be to become engaged and to aid in the creation of such a movement, so as to defend society from the threats of complete neoliberal hegemony. Bourdieu argues that intel-lectual autonomy and civic engagement must be joined in a synergistic relationship such that scientists, writers, and artists increase the efficacy of their political interventions in and through the vigorous defense of their independence from economic and political powers. In this way, he advocates what he refers to as the 'collective intellectual': a collective of intellectuals who share collective attitudes (a collective habitus) working together as a research team to both 1) produce and disseminate instruments of defense against symbolic domination—against pre-packaged politics and established politics—and 2) contribute to the 'political intervention' work necessary to renew critical thought and enable it to combine sociol-ogy with civic utopianism.

A first step in intellectuals' political intervention must be the illumination of the twofold existence of history objectified in things (a royal crown, a con-stitution, a sacred text, an emperor's sword, a national boundary marked by a border post) and history incarnate in bodies, in the memories and habitus of individuals who lived through it. When the connection between reified and embodied history is made visible, we can recognize that what we call history is a naturalized social construction of knowledge and truth. We are conve-niently made to forget this process of social construction. (If our Canadian and US readers compared their understanding of events that took place in North America from 1754 to 1783, they would quickly notice this process of the social construction of history, even down to the names of the events believed to be important.) Intellectuals must expose how the construction of history is forgotten and how the constructed categories and institutions ap-pear to be natural and neutral in terms of the politics of everyday life. Bourdieu believes that the intellectual labor of identifying specific mechanisms by which power operates and defines relations of dominance is necessary in order to understand how domination can persist long after its legal and juridical forms have been abolished, for example in US racial stratification in the post-civil-rights era.

Through the notions of symbolic power, representation, and misrec-ognition, Bourdieu's categories provide an alternative for thinking about the relations between freedom, justice, and politics. For Bourdieu, it is not raising consciousness or establishing new ideas or discourses; rather, it is in the 'double naturalization' of the social world resulting from the dominant understandings of the world being in the things around us and in our own bodies (Wacquant 2005: 20). In this way, there is an isomorphic agreement between social structures and mental structures. When we look at the habitus dominated by the dominant system of relations and the somatized social relations, the law of the social body is converted into the law of the physical body and therefore reproduces that social body in our actions. Bourdieu argues that this cannot be suspended by a 'mere awakening of consciousness' because of the unconscious consent to the injunctions of the social world through the embodiment of the relations of domination (Wacquant 2005: 20). For Bourdieu, this is no less so among the dominated than among the dominant. Therefore, any politics must attack both the symbolic and material mechanisms of domination and must also, necessarily, be a politics of embodiment aimed at the dispositions and orientations of habitus.

As Wacquant (2005) has pointed out, Bourdieu's approach to the political has four practical implications:

1. Intellectuals play a new role in contemporary political struggles.
2. Political actions involve not just institutions but also a 'politics of habitus' at the individual level.
3. A 'politics of recognition' is necessary, in which the reflexivity of scientific instruments of knowledge and culture must be accounted for as they analyze the vision and division of the world through categories of thought that serve as symbolic forms of power and domination.
4. The social world is anchored in unequal distribution of symbolic capital or power, and democracy is not an *affirmative* state for a world of equality, legality, and the capacity for shared freedom. Instead, the state is an historical process of the *negation* of social negation processes; it is an effort to make social processes *less unequal, less arbitrary, and less unjust* in the distribution of resources.

Bourdieu's ultimate goal was to universalize the accessibility of resources and the political means to access the particular historical embodiment of the universal that defines democratic politics. In this way, Bourdieu advocated for 'sociology as a martial art' not to attack others but to defend oneself and others from the tyranny of social domination (Carles 2001).

CONCLUSION: A NOTE ON FOUCAULT AND BOURDIEU

While Bourdieu and Foucault appear to be very different thinkers on the surface, they share several underlying themes. Because both Bourdieu and Foucault are influenced by the Durkheimian tradition, they can be read in complementary fashion, as two sides of the same coin. Their ideas are not completely congruous or reducible to each other, but analyzing them in relation to one another aids us in understanding them in a novel way.

It is useful to think of Foucault as the philosopher of big systems of thought and Bourdieu as the sociologist analyzing their particular everyday manifestations. Both thinkers were interested in the conceptual categories through which we understand the world. Foucault sought to bring this to light by undertaking a genealogical analysis and exploring how the discourses of any particular period (*episteme*) are the modes of thought we can have. The limits of discourse are the limits of thought. As Foucault has argued, power or knowledge regimes impose a certain version of truth on the world. In this way language or thought or discourses are never neutral or arbitrary. Like Foucault, Bourdieu explored the conceptual categories of thought through which we think; he made his exploration by analyzing the symbolic power and violence that discourses contain within them. Those who are able to implement their categories of thought produce dominant modes of viewing the world, and these dominant modes are then misrecognized and taken as self-evident. Foucault examined how the discourses of economics and psychoanalysis brought about new modes of understanding people while Bourdieu's analysis focused on the different classifications of taste among lower, middle, and upper classes, but both were theorists of classification and conceptualized it as always a mechanism of social control.

Although they were concerned with categories of thought, neither was an idealist; both Foucault and Bourdieu were concerned with practices, the body, and the multiple mechanisms of socialization. For Foucault, the notion of power (whether in its disciplinary, bio-power, or governmentality forms) enabled him to explore the multiple ways that we are socialized. He focused on the pervasiveness of power as a regulating system of social relations. The notion of power as diffused into the capillaries and microphysics of everyday life illuminates how social practices that focus on the body produce us as particular types of subjects at different historical periods. Like Foucault, Bourdieu explored the notion of practices and their relation to the body. Bourdieu's notion of habitus can be seen as the sociological outgrowth of the same stream of thought. Habitus allowed him to explore different types of subjects or bodies or tastes and preferences by exploring where they were situated and socialized in society.

Like Foucault's analysis of power, Bourdieu's concept of field explained how systems of relations provide a way to explore the different positions and dispositions in society based on specific forms of capital. Foucault discusses the panopticon as a mechanism to regulate people's behaviors through inculcating constant self-monitoring. This notion can be seen as kindred to Bourdieu's focus on particular fields of relations and the habitus situated within them. Both analyses point to the ways in which people are often complicit in their own social domination.

These are just some of the parallels one can tease out of the two thinkers; our discussion is by no means exhaustive. We are providing a few examples of their similarities in a generative spirit of attempting to understand how two very different thinkers approach similar topics through very different means yet remain complementary to each other. One can probably find origins of their similarities in their shared French culture and education, as well as in the intellectual 'spirit of the times' in France as the nation moved into an era of advanced capitalist modernity—or postmodernity (Debray 1979; Derrida 1994; Macey 1993).

KEY TERMS

- applied rationalism
- body
- capitals
- constructing the object
- craft of sociology
- fields or spaces
- habitus
- neoliberalism
- practice
- public intellectuals
- reflexivity
- subjectivism and objectivism
- symbolic power, violence, misrecognition
- taste or distinction

Chapter 6

STUART HALL (1932–)

Stuart Hall is the most famous face of that 'mongrel discipline' known as cultural studies—the interdisciplinary approach to the study of language, popular culture, ideology, and social life that emerged in the United Kingdom in the 1960s. Cultural studies grew out of a series of social and economic shifts in everyday life that posed new challenges from beyond traditional disciplinary boundaries and questions that could not be answered within the pre-established approaches of any one traditional academic field of inquiry.

Stuart Hall is a transitional giant because he is rewriting and reconstructing concepts in the Marxist lexicon and framework and then applying them to the new conditions of society, such as the transformation of European nations into multicultural societies, the emergence of new media, the meaning of race and racial domination, the situation and identities of intellectuals in post-colonial regions, and the ideologies that accompanied the shift to neoliberal policies. As a public intellectual, he aims to develop concepts in order to clarify, synthesize, and agitate political discourse that addresses the issues of our times without losing the fundamental insights of the Marxist paradigm.

His numerous lectures, media appearances, published papers (both collective and individual), interviews, and mentoring all contribute to the popularity and global influence of his thought. Although Hall's work is often discussed and read as canonical in communications departments in the United States, because of disciplinary boundaries he has never been rightfully claimed and celebrated by sociology departments there, as he should be. Hall's approach to sociology is historical anti-essentialist, and anti-reductionist. In his cultural analysis, his approach is to question everything—a multidimensional and dialogic mode of contesting different knowledges—and he accomplishes this through an analysis of subfields as diverse as culture, media, political hegemony, and race and ethnicity. It is not just his contributions to these substantive areas that make Hall a seminal thinker; it is the breadth and depth of his thinking across boundaries and disciplines, which create a unique body of work that cannot be summed up neatly. Hall describes himself as a public intellectual committed to social change. In his role as public intellectual, Hall never proffers theoretical work as a substitute for politics, yet he insists that politics be informed by intellectual labor. The purpose of the intellectual, for Hall, is to speak truth to power—to challenge power at every turn through challenging it with knowledge and to predicate intellectual work on the dialogic relationship between cultural and political intervention. For Hall, the value of theory is judged by the purchase that it gives us for understanding the complex and contradictory structure of any field of practices, for seeing beyond the taken-for-granted conditions to ongoing struggles against domination, and for cultivating and executing forms of resistance.

We offer an overview of the key areas and concepts of his work. In doing so, we bracket the emergence and history of cultural studies, the school of thought Hall is most associated with, as well as the specific socio-economic relations and political struggles that define the context of his ideas at the time they surfaced in the United Kingdom. Nevertheless, the reader should keep in mind throughout our somewhat abstract exposition that Hall uses these concepts to address very down-to-earth political issues, above all the question of why substantial segments of the British public embraced Thatcherism and neoliberal policies when the concrete consequences of these policies did not appear to be in their economic or 'rational' self-interest. We identify the ideas that form an interrelated conceptual matrix, but we need to remain aware that Hall is a thinker grounded in the material conditions of everyday life and critically engaged with the political, economic, and social events and trends of the times.

HEGEMONY

Hall is most noted for his use of Antonio Gramsci's theory of hegemony to explain the relationship between culture and power and how culture serves a constitutive role in the establishment and reproduction of social and political domination. Gramsci originally used the term to refer to the notion of leadership and its role in the relationship between classes—the winning of consent to construct and maintain power. (Gramsci was influenced by Niccolò Machiavelli's belief, articulated in *The Prince* [1513], that one can rule as a lion, by coercion, or as a fox, by cunningly creating consent.) Hegemony is always a constant struggle over consent, and it is not coercion or a top-down ruling-class imposition. Therefore, the term always implies a sense of instability and resistance. Hegemony is not the property of one particular class; rather, it is a way of understanding or making sense of the relation of domination and subordination. The forces in play are not objective social classes, not fixed pigeonholed groups in a rigid structure, but rather fluid groupings of interests and agencies contending to establish a dominant worldview that becomes the common sense of everyday life.

Rather than accept an economic reductionist view in a materialist Marxist sense, Hall reworks this concept of hegemony, comprehending it as the struggle of competing forces and interests within the cultural realm by focusing on language, media, issues of representation, discourses, institutions and agents, and their interdependent relations that serve to create consensus. A key element of hegemony is active complicity with the dominant worldview that serves as a structure of dominance over a whole social formation, including both the dominant and dominated classes. For Hall, hegemony helps us to undermine reductionist readings of social relations as purely economic organizations and to understand how certain social formations are historically constructed and structured in relations of dominance and subordination. The theory of hegemony helps unearth how these social formations appear as natural and inevitable, unchangeable, eternalized and naturalized and yet, in fact, are culturally specific and historically grounded conventions. Hegemony is always an historically specific and temporary moment in the life of society, not something permanent or guaranteed, and therefore it must be actively constructed and maintained. Because the battle over what is hegemonic is never achieved or maintained on one front alone, hegemony must be constructed through multiple positions. Within the paradigm of hegemony, there is no simple correspondence between what is hegemonic and a person's class position. Hegemony operates within a wider winning of consent, a broad attainment of voluntary acceptance and compliance in multiple spheres of society as a whole. Hegemony does not mean simply the winning of consent but the taking of subordinate interests and rotating them into alignment with the interests of the dominant by articulating the latter as common sense. In this way, hegemony establishes the parameters of debate and, in doing so, shapes and positions people within larger structures of domination.

For Hall, the theory of hegemony offers up an alternative way of conceptualizing social differentiations, social divisions, and social contradictions, and, because it is built around struggle, it also offers the opening for possible social change.

IDEOLOGY

Stuart Hall also draws heavily upon the philosophical work of Louis Althusser, specifically on Althusser's notion of ideology and interpellation. *Ideology* is a system of representations, concepts, ideas, images, myths, and stories in which people live their relations to the real conditions of their existence. Ideologies are the systems of categories through which we represent the world to ourselves and to others, as well as the practices involved in the production, circulation, and consumption of those meanings. There is nothing outside of ideology since everything is mediated through ideological categories, which, in turn, become the legitimated horizon within which we think, live, and understand ourselves. Therefore, the world takes on the specific connotations provided through that particular ideological framework. Ideology, as a system of representation, is not free floating but grounded and materialized in practices in the concrete reality of everyday life. Ideology is manifested in all aspects of practices and life, which cement and unify practical and popular forms of consciousness that organizes our understanding of the world.

Hall's theoretical project is to identify the specific concrete historical practices that give rise to particular ideological formations. Ideology is not hidden but open and at the surface; what is concealed are the foundations of those practices, which operate in a way that hides the very roots of their functioning. The dominant ideology works by framing thought within a particular set of parameters within which people think.

Ideologies have a relative autonomy, and adherence to one or another of them is not determined by class position alone. They are not the ideas of the ruling class only but ideas that have diffused throughout society. Much like hegemony, ideology is an active winning of consent of the subordinated so that special interests (those of the economically dominant classes and their allies) are made to seem equivalent to the general interests of the majority; and the process concludes in consensus and the production of consent. Often, it operates by injecting and blending these ideas into pre-existing frameworks of ideology. For Hall, ideology, as a system of representations, circulates throughout all realms of society (cultural, political, economic, and so on) in an overdetermining way in which no one sphere dominates; rather, they all overlap and reinforce each other.

ARTICULATION

Articulation refers to the specific meanings that are attached to particular categories (e.g., races, classes) and how those meanings connect together or are linked to form a set of social meanings that contributes to the reproduction of social and economic order. Articulation serves the role within ideology of actively expressing the totality of society, which often appears contradictory, and making it appear unified and whole. Articulation also serves as a move that is necessary to conceal the fragmented, fractured, subject positions and social relations that make the world appear contradictory at times. By connecting these meanings and making them appear coherent, articulation is an active force of power in maintaining the dominant meanings of society, the social relations that constitute society. Articulation serves to interconnect multiple discourses, practices, and representations into a coherent system of meaning that serves the hegemonic power bloc and reproduces domination. In this way, articulation is multi-accentual in that it works to synchronize multiple layers of society together and set them working toward a particular end. Through articulation, we can come to understand how language and signifying systems determine the meaning of culture; they do not mirror the world nor can they be reduced to a reflection of the economic.

Hall argues that the politics of articulation removes all forms of finalism and essentialism: social, political, and class formations do not exist a priori; they are the products of articulation. Therefore, Hall is arguing that ideology is a site of struggle just as much in the symbolic realm as it is in the economic or political realm. For Hall, ideology is not transformed or changed by replacing one whole ideology with another, as if one could trade them wholesale. If meanings are historical constructions, they can be re-articulated in different ways. Because there is no fixity to language or meaning, there are always possibilities of reworking and transforming them, thus providing the opportunity to point out the contradictions around which strategies of resistance and struggles can be organized.

OVERDETERMINATION

Hall argues that we cannot simply fuse a particular ideology to a particular class (or even to a sector of a class) because of that class's position within socio-economic relations. Hall uses the term 'overdetermination,' borrowing again from Althusser, to explain processes by which society achieves a coherent wholeness. For Hall, wholeness based on the overlap of spheres allows us to escape any sense of economic determinism, as all spheres of life serve to overlap and reinforce each other with no one sphere having greater or lesser importance. Because ideology works in multiple arenas and institutions with their own specific logics, ideology is multi-causal rather than emanating from any one particular institution, distinct class, or sphere of life. Hall, by showing how social life is inseparable from the ideological categories that constitute the social whole, utilizes Althusser's framework of overdetermination without relying on the 'determination in the last instance by the (economic) mode of production' that Althusser (2005: 111) has certainly retained from Marxism.

FALSE CONSCIOUSNESS

There is no transparent relationship between subject positions and how subjects can come to know and recognize themselves. Although people live their lives through the dominant ideological categories that form the dominant representations and expectations of what they should do, there is no masking of consciousness that prevents them from recognizing the real reality underneath the appearances of everyday life, as if they were cultural dupes or mindless zombies. Social relations formed through ideology are not hiding the real world or preventing people from seeing the world for what it really is. For Hall, false consciousness is a poor diagnostic tool, and here we can see a break with more traditional Marxist thought, which discerned 'false consciousness' in the gap between objectively constituted class relationships and the distorted representations of these relationships in people's understandings of the social order. Instead, we need to get at struggle and conflict that are not determined or imposed from outside or from above. As in Bourdieu's analysis of misrecognition, we need to expose social knowledge that is structured around dominant interests and promotes inequality. But there is never one dominant ideology that is coherent and pervades everything—no single system of dominant ideas into which everything and everyone is absorbed.

THE FUNCTION OF COMMON SENSE

With theories of hegemony and ideology also comes the notion of common sense, the basic agreed-upon and taken-for-granted consensual wisdoms, conventions, and modes of thought that help us make sense of and classify the world. Common sense is antithetical to critical thought because it is spontaneous and appears natural and without question. Common sense is what passes in any particular period as tradition; things fit into already existing schemes of things with an absolute transparency. Common sense is fundamentally aligned with the inability to recognize the historical place of one's own position in relation to the world at any one time. Common sense operates to make the world self-evident, logical, and determined. It turns historical constructions into natural facts or transcendental truths.

INTERPELLATION AND IDEOLOGICAL SUBJECTS

Interpellation means hailing someone—'Hey, you there!' It is a term that is also used in French policing: when a person is stopped by police and asked for identity papers or interrogated, he or she is said to have been 'interpellated'—in other words, hailed and made to account for his or her actions and identity as a subject. Althusser argues that all ideologies rely on interpellation, on inducing the individual to misrecognize himself or herself as a subject: 'all ideology hails or interpellates concrete individuals as concrete subjects' (Althusser 1971b: 173). Christian ideology did so by references to each person's immortal soul, and capitalist ideology by the call for individual responsibility and accountability. These appeals induce people to participate in the social order as subjects. They occur throughout society, in many different kinds of interactions and institutions, from police interrogation to the naming of babies. Here we see Althusser absolutely in accord with Durkheim's view of the scientific analysis of societies and social formations; scientific understanding—as opposed to ideology—cannot be based on an analysis of the subject formed by interpellation, though an analysis of the misrecognition induced by ideologies is certainly a prime topic of study.

Hall uses this term to discuss how individuals are incorporated into the dominant ideologies of society. Individuals are socialized into the discourses, practices, and institutions through which the prevailing norms of consciousness and sense of social relations are generated. The function of these discourses and institutions is to induce people to acquire consciousness of their position and the positions of others in society. For Hall, this process of socialization is key to understanding how ideology works below consciousness so that we speak spontaneously without thinking about the words we use or the categories through which we process the world. In this way, we can say that the ideological categories of thought and the discourses speak us and think us. In the process, ideological subjects are formed through their participation in these practices and discourses. Ideologies produce different forms of social consciousness by working when we are not aware that we formulate ideas and words all underpinned by ideological premises. These discourses become taken for granted and naturalized in common sense. Ideologies work by constructing their subjects in positions of identification and knowledge, so people speak them as if they were their own ideas, mirrored in the positions and discourses through which they formulate and make sense of themselves and social relations. We experience ideology as if it were freely and spontaneously emerging from us. We spontaneously speak, yet we are spoken for in the ideological discourses into which we are socialized and find our place. Ideologies work by constructing for subjects positions of identification and interpretation, and so the subject speaks ideology as if it were truth. Identity is thus the meeting point of the discourses and practices that interpellate us, speak to us, and hail us into place as subjects of a particular discourse; this is the process by which subjectivities are produced and by which the subject is spoken. The concept of interpellation enables us to rethink the subjects of ideology. There is no pre-given, unified ideological subject, but a plurality of selves or identities of which the subject of thought and ideas is composed. Hall emphasizes the collective multifaceted nature of consciousness and the relationship between the self and ideological discourses that compose the cultural terrain of society.

HEGEMONY, IDEOLOGY, AND SOCIETIES STRUCTURED IN DOMINANCE

One of Hall's major contributions is the analysis of the logic of racial domination and the ways in which societies are structured in dominance. The question that Hall raises is, how does racial inequality become reproduced in everyday life? Racially structured formations are the outcome of the economic and the social. Economically, they are formed through development, which includes colonization, imperialism without colonies, underdevelopment based on the exploitive extraction of minerals or mono-crop production (such as rubber, cotton, peanuts, coffee, and so on), and industrialization. These economic features are determining factors of social formations. From a sociological perspective, structures of racial dominance are formed in terms of cultural difference and racial distinctions. Considering race and the meanings that are attached to racial groups, Hall explores how systems of classification function to value different groups differently by ascribing them certain talents and abilities on the basis of the group they belong to. Thus classification is never neutral; classification is a mechanism of power. Power generates meaning and hierarchies, and it structures the social organization based on domination and subordination. Classification is never neutral but a form of power and social control. Once a system of classification is put in place, the maintenance of that order is crucial to keeping society structured in dominance. Thus classification is always a process of struggle. To keep the boundaries in place, to stabilize them, to keep their ranking, to keep the positive and negative attributes in place requires maintenance, effort, and sometimes conflict. However, this exertion is often overlooked because we enter into social relations that are already constructed. Without thinking, we are socialized into them and take them for granted, thereby perpetuating the existing ideologies. The subjective categories and structures in our heads mirror the structure of social relations out there in the world, and therefore the world seems seamless and transparent. Hence our everyday participation in them and complicity in sustaining and reproducing them goes unnoticed.

Economics and race are autonomous, not reducible to one another, yet they are connected through different modes of production at social, political, and ideological levels that are historically specific and socially constructed. For Hall, the project is to map out the relations of linkages between different spheres of society by looking at the mechanisms that connect different features and the correspondences that structure society in terms of domination and subordination. Hall argues that we must explore how modes of exploitation work in different sectors of the labor force. This is not a simple unity but a process of unification founded on alliances between different sectors of social life. For example, in many countries today, there are linkages formed between categories such as 'immigration status,' 'race,' and 'national origin' and conditions such as judicial rights, interpersonal treatment, labor-market opportunities, and access to occupations; these serve to police the boundaries of the distribution of resources in a given society.

Since there is no automatic identity or correspondence between political and ideological practices or their correlation to a particular group, Hall argues that we must pinpoint the culturally specific class formations. Inquiry should focus on the question of how different modes of production get combined within the same social formation, as well as on how these forms have been associated with race or ethnic factors. Racial domination is an historically specific racism not a unitary or trans-historical phenomenon with a universal structure. There is no racial conspiracy from above because racism is one of the dominant modes of ideological representation through which groups link their relations to other groups and to capital and class.

RACE: THE FLOATING SIGNIFIER

Why does race, as physical or physiological differences, matter so much? Hall argues that we need to understand not only the effects of racism but also the logic of it in our cultural imagination—how racial identity is constructed. Therefore, Hall argues, we need to consider not only the ways people look but also the meanings we attach to the ways people look: the stories, values, aesthetics, myths, ideas, and stereotypes that frame the narratives and discourses by which culture teaches us what physical difference means and even which physical differences 'make a difference.'

Hall argues that there is nothing inherent, essential, or permanent to race and racial identity. Race is a floating signifier; it is a constantly changing set of relational differences of meaning taking on different new meanings and values. Race is the product of a system of classifications regarding how people fit into or are made to fit into the world—we classify people by physical characteristics, which then generate meaning. Classification is a system of power associated with a social order in which one group is more positively valued than another— that is how power operates through the process of classification. Hall argues that this happens through the very logic and categories that we deploy to perceive and understand the world, the very systems of classification that form the basis of our thinking. Classification and categories are so important because they are the very boxes through which we think, they define our reality, they divide up the world for us, and our sense making comes through these categories.

How do categories function? Race as a system of classification ascribes characteristics that are attached to a particular group that then become normalized, fixed, naturalized, essentialized, commonsensical, and believed to be true. They become the underlying fundamental assumptions that we make about racial groups in the world. They are the fundamental principles of social organization, and we act on them as if they were natural and could not be otherwise. Since race functions as an underlying principle of social organization, biology and culture become conflated. Stereotypes function to lead us to think what is learned is natural, for example, that black people are good dancers and athletes, that whites are book smart but not street smart, or that Asians are good in math and science. These assumptions and stereotypes are not only negative; they can have positive elements, and, indeed, the label of 'race' can function as a guarantee that a culture is good and authentic.

The idea behind understanding the nature of classification and power is that we cannot simply switch the characteristics of one group (the bad ones) for good ones and everything will be all right. What we need to do is understand how racial essentialism and categorization operate.

Hall argues that race works like a language. Race takes on meaning within the field of relations. Race only has meaning within the structure of social relations—the structure of the system of differences. This does not mean that it is the same everywhere and for all times. The meaning of race changes with context that is subject to social processes that are historically contingent. Shifting relationships shift meanings and create instability in racial classifications and assumptions; hence Hall uses the term 'floating signifier.'

Race works like a language. The body is a text from which we read a series of meanings based on our categories in any given historical period. We think we are making sense of difference by appearance because it is something we believe is fixed and transcendental. Because we do look different we must be different. This essentialism limits who we are and what we can be. Race always works within discourses. These discourses are not, however, only ideas; discourses originate from a point of view situated in society, are associated with particular strategies and investments, and have real socio-economic and material consequences.

Ultimately, for Hall, this understanding of race and discourse undermines all racial essentialism, undercutting both the essentially good and bad racialized subject. For Hall, this means that we must abandon a politics of both racism and anti-racism because both essentialize race in the same mode, albeit with opposite signs (either as inherently bad or inherently good). The implication is that political struggle to eradicate racism must proceed without essentialist, naturalistic, or pseudo-scientific claims to foundations. The task of thinking through the logic of race must no longer have a foundation but rather a continuous, contingent, unguaranteed political argument and debate, which Hall terms 'a politics of criticism.'

MEDIA: THE POLITICS OF REPRESENTATION

Media have an established fundamental hegemonic role in the cultural sphere, whereby the production, circulation, and consumption of social knowledge in societies depends upon modern forms of mass communication. People live their social relations, and these are then reflected back to them through the mass media, which provide images, ideas, meanings, values, practices, and representations of groups. In this way, the media provide the images and representations through which the social totality, even though fragmented and disjointed, can be conceptually grasped as a whole. Hall argues that the machineries and regimes of representation play an active and constitutive role in culture and are not merely reflexive. This places representation in a formative and not just expressive place in the constitution of social life. Therefore, Hall argues for a 'politics of the image.' The politics of representation is not detached from empirical reality; for Hall, the politics of representation is the struggle over the ability to define the conditions, limits, and modalities of meaning.

Media also bring together and organize what has been fragmented, selectively represented, and selectively classified. There is a simultaneous process of fragmenting social reality and making it integrated and cohesive. An imaginary unity is constructed and organized into an acknowledged stabilized order. One important operation is to present power, domination, and exploitation through a language of neutrality. Consensus and consent work through the interplay of free opinions, freely given and exchanged. Consensus shaping, unification, and consolidation are part of the media's ideological work. At the surface, the outlets of media appear pluralistic, multiple, and contradictory; yet, below this surface, they are structured to produce consensus and legitimacy.

By establishing the parameters of interpretation and representation over what is legitimate and what is not, the field of media serves as an effective means of hegemonic reproduction.

Media also serve to mark and define different types of cultures, styles, and forms of social knowledge that are classified, ranked, ordered, preferred, or marginalized so as to make a map of the social reality through which these forms of knowledge are objectified. Here the social knowledges that are produced and circulated come with normative and value-added classifications; there are preferred meanings and interpretations.

For Hall, this classification of knowledge is neither a top-down hierarchical nor a simple class-based model of media control. Although, in general, the knowledge of the economically dominant class and institutions of the state is privileged over the local knowledge of subaltern groups, the media can also marginalize knowledge by labeling it as 'elitist.' Hall's analysis of authoritarian populism as the ideological mechanism underlying Margaret Thatcher's mass appeal pointed to the 'folksy' and populist representations of her program and the celebration of 'good old English traditions,' with undercurrents of xenophobia. The media emphasize that they are open and diverse so that their ideological functions are not readily apparent.

Hall argues that there are ideological practices at work in privileging or discounting and excluding certain activities, forms of knowledge, and practices. It is here that the struggle over the dominant and dominated or preferred and excluded meanings is contested, as images themselves become ideological signs that are open to a plurality of significations. Signs contend in the arena of hegemonic ideological struggle.

Because of the multi-accentual nature of the image, there are dominant and preferred codes that appear to be natural explanations; these are the most readily acceptable, and they serve as templates to cast events and ideas into the dominant ideology. They are made to appear as the only forms available. These modes of interpretation become taken for granted and thus generate invisible common-sense understandings.

The ways that meaning is both produced and consumed happens through the process of encoding and decoding. Encoding is the process by which the dominant definitions structure and accent events and images in a way that reproduces the ideological structures. The dominant encoding of an image works to win the consent of the audience not through the bias of interpreting events but through the legitimacy and range of limits within which encoding operates, which makes the dominant mores of reading events the point of identification through which the receiver decodes the message. But it is not certain that the audience will decode the images through the preferred encodings, because, as Hall argues, there are spaces within which people and groups situate themselves and incorporate alternative readings or decodings, ones different from the preferred hegemonic decodings.

CRITICAL POLITICS OF CONTESTING IMAGES

For Hall, the politics of the image is always an ongoing struggle. Hall invokes the notion of struggle in order to jostle us loose from the transparency of the images around us, images that we take for granted in our common sense everyday lives. Because images have no fixed meaning, they must always be contested. The dominant ideology attempts to fix meaning or hold meanings of images or naturalize them, whereas, for Hall, the task of the reader of the image is to interrogate the image, to deconstruct the image and understand what sort of ideological context it is operating in and what meanings it is articulating. For Hall, this means contesting stereotypes by taking them apart, going inside them, and getting into the mechanism that keeps them fixed and closed. We must open up the very practice of representation itself, investigate the position of the image, and understand how it tries to pull the reader or viewer of that image into the ideological system in order to win hegemonic consent. There is no guarantee that we can reverse or change the meaning of the image for once and for all. Yet through the interrogation of the image, we can understand how ideology operates, how power circulates in a way that naturalizes the way that the world is and closes off alternative meanings and new dimensions. This knowledge, in turn, opens up new possibilities for identities.

CULTURE AS THE ARENA OF STRUGGLE

Popular culture plays a central role in Hall's analysis of society. For Hall, popular culture is not inherently meaningful, but it provides an outstanding vehicle through which society as a whole can be analyzed. Popular culture is the site where everyday struggles between the dominant and the subordinate are fought out at any historical moment. Here we can see how Hall is a cultural Marxist in that he views culture as just as important an arena to analyze as the economic sphere, without reducing one to the other.

Turning to the study of popular culture is not about reversing the hierarchies or elevating it to new status; rather, the purpose is to unsettle the traditional binary approach of analyzing culture in terms of it being highbrow or lowbrow. However, the popular has no class position. It is a contradictory and contentious space because the contents of what is considered popular are always changing, always defined by their specific historical context, and always defined by a shifting set of values and meanings. Cultural forms then take on their specific meanings through the practices they articulate and the groups they are made to resonate with. Hall argues that there are no pure or unadulterated cultural forms; cultural practices are, in effect, the products of synchronizations, engagements across cultural boundaries, the confluence of cultural traditions, the negotiations of dominant and subordinate positions, recoding and transposing, and signification and signifying. Popular culture is always impure, mixed, contradictory, and hybrid.

Hall sees the arena of popular culture as one of both containment and resistance. For Hall, there exists a false distinction between considering popular culture as completely autonomous or as completely encapsulating. Popular culture is always being utilized for subversive or expressive purposes by the subordinate; and yet it is also utilized to control, enclose, and confine representations within the dominant meanings of society that serve to homogenize, commodify, and reify culture. There is no authentic 'outside' of relations of power and domination; Hall sees this flux as a continual state of struggle in power dynamics both within cultural forms and over the issue of culture. Culture is the arena in which the configurations and dispositions of power are revealed; popular culture is where this struggle for and against the powerful is engaged. Popular culture is the stake to be won or lost; it is where hegemony arises, is secured, and contested. There is never pure domination or resistance; it is never a zero-sum game; there is only the shifting balance of power in relations of culture.

For Hall, the question is, how do popular cultural forms stand in relation to ways working people live and their relations to one another within the constraints and the institutions of the dominant cultural production? Popular culture does not function as a new 'opium of the masses' or delude them into false consciousness; people are not cultural dopes or dupes. Rather, popular culture is popular because the people knowingly consume and enjoy it.

Popular culture is different from both folk culture (traditional forms with pre-capitalist origins, now self-consciously revived or preserved) and from commercial mass culture (commodities produced and circulated through corporate media). An example of folk culture would be the traditional acoustical banjo and fiddle music of Appalachia or the nineteenth-century African American spiritual; an example of entirely commercial mass culture would be an advertising jingle. Popular culture partakes of both worlds in a way that is ambiguous and playful. Its creators use, celebrate, and mock the aura of traditional authenticity as well as the modern capitalist commodity form. A popular culture product is always at risk of being turned into a commodity; in fact, its creators often hope that it will become a successful one at the same time that they use it to express resistance (Frank 1997). Jazz, blues, punk, and hip hop are examples of modern and contemporary musical forms of popular culture. In Argentina, cumbia is a particularly striking example of a widely enjoyed and commercially successful type of music and dance that expresses distance from the tastes of the Eurocentric national elite and middle class; it has largely replaced tango as the music of resistance to hegemonic culture. (See also Willis et al. [1990] for a discussion of common culture as a closely related concept and Williams [2002] for analysis of popular culture in contemporary Latin America.)

For Hall, the category 'popular' has strategic importance; the role of the 'popular' in popular culture is to fix the authenticity of popular forms, rooting them in the expressiveness, memories, and traditions of subaltern communities from which they can be used as a resource to draw strength, identity, meaning, and expressions of a social life that resists being treated as vulgar, base, or crude. Popular culture, according to Hall, serves as the theater of popular desire and fantasy where people discover and play with identifications of themselves, where people can exercise creativity and imagination. It gives them an opportunity to define and represent themselves to audiences and to themselves. Therefore, Hall sees popular culture as an arena where positions can be won and where there is a possibility of social resistance as the people articulate their voices through it. For Hall, popular culture matters because it is the site of power struggles and a place where spaces for popular democratic forces might be constituted.

IDENTITY

For Hall, identity is now necessarily a concept under erasure. Erasure is a key term borrowed from Derrida's project of deconstruction, and it means that the task of intellectual thought is to break out of the old language because it does not say what we want it to. Yet we are still trapped inside that old language in our attempt to forge something new and move beyond the previous limitations. Because we must work within this language, we cannot ask questions without it; language still gives us the categories through which we think—so we must think at the limits by pushing the concepts until a new vocabulary emerges by which to capture the irreducibility of identity.

The common sense assumptions about identity and the stable subject imply that there is something we call identity that stays still despite the shifting conditions of the world. Identity provides us with the notion that there is a fixed point of selfhood, an ultimate guarantee that there is a true self or an authentic experience of who one is. Instead, Hall argues for a decentered and destabilized notion of identity. Identity is constructed through history and not under conditions of our own making. It emerges from the dialectic between self and other. Hall argues that the construction of identity is a process. Identity is constructed through representation and in relation to difference without fixity, in an endless play of difference. Identity, for Hall, is a process of formation and identification of self and other.

Because there is no essence to any group or self, nothing is stabilized by nature or by any essential guarantee; everything is only historically and culturally produced. History, culture, and language come into play in the construction of subjectivity and identity. And identity can be placed within a wide range of discourses. For instance, an individual's identity can be placed in discourses of citizenship (who is a Canadian or US citizen?), ethno-racial politics, regional loyalties, religious affiliation, class consciousness, or authentic selfhood. Within any one of these discourses, multiple options exist as well; for example, to state that one has a Buddhist, Christian, Hindu, Jewish, or Muslim identity (in other words, to select an identity within the discourse of faith) still leaves open many possibilities of belief, practice, and more specific religious identity. These different discursive contexts and the multiple options within each discursive context can lead to emphasis of one or another of the individual's many possible identities because identity is never natural but rather an arbitrary act, as ideology intervenes in language itself. Despite the multiple options identity may take, identity is not completely free floating; in the end, there is always an arbitrary act of closure for identity to cohere and stabilize. Hall argues that the result is to problematize the very notion of ever establishing any authority or authenticity around what identity is.

Identity here is always relational, always incomplete, dependent on difference, unstable, temporary, located within processes of defining self and other, multiple, contradictory, hybrid, situational, and contextually bound. Identities are bound up in both how they are produced and how they are represented — in the practices of constitution and representation. Hybridity is a term that emphasizes the multiple forms of identity, identification, affiliations, ways of belonging, links to spatial location, the role of historical social movements, and historical and spatial identifications that can be highly fluid. The subject is now repositioned in this multiple, hybrid, and contradictory process. This placing and positioning of subject happens historically and contemporaneously with the discourses circulating in society. Although capitalism is the dominant economic form and perhaps, in the final instance, the mode of production is the determining element of the whole social formation, the process of identity formation cannot be reduced to class position or to a single isolated category of any type. Instead, we must see all identities as cultural hybrids within a system of globalization that reconfigures how identities are located and represented.

Hall is adamantly against identity politics and strategic essentialism. What identity politics and strategic essentialism do is to reverse the discourse of identity by simply assigning a plus sign instead of a minus sign to the black side of the black-white racial dichotomy (or the woman's side of the gender hierarchy, and so on)—instead of questioning the binary classifications altogether. Furthermore, we cannot solidify identity by a simple return to the past, whether it is a fictive 'Africa,' a mythical 'Merry Olde England,' or the various imagined communities of the Middle East. These utopias of the past cannot be restored, and many of them never existed in the first place (1990). Heritage is an imagined and constructed part of a system of representation, created through narrative and fiction but with real political, economic, and social consequences. Roots are always an imagined relationship, which is always rediscovered, retold, and reinvented.

The essentialism of identity politics erased multi-ethnic dimensions and distinctions and isolated many of the people it wanted to embrace. Identities are now policed along their boundaries as much from inside as from outside, yet the policing remains an essentializing move; it naturalizes and dehistoricizes difference and mistakes the cultural for something natural and biological. Instead of fixing identities and policing the boundaries, Hall argues we need new identities that are constructed with more awareness of their construction, fluid, in transition, cutting across boundaries, and able to let go of the fantasy of a unified whole. Significations constantly defer to each other, but this does not mean that identities are free floating. They are 'minimal selves' defined by self-reflection, contingency, difference, and a politics of articulation that links together individuals to form new alliances around new commonalities (Hall 1987).

THE MOVE TO ETHNICITY

According to Hall, the new mode of theorizing identity is to theorize new forms of ethnicity, so identity is forged around social, cultural, and historical experiences. This rethinking of ethnicity and its multiplicity of identities and experiences is ultimately a political project for Hall. The meanings of being Canadian, Jamaican, British, Iraqi, Israeli, Russian, or French provide examples of the play of ethnicities and nation and the formation of identities in a series of historical shifts. Hall argues that the relation of any of these identities to the past and to its 'origins' (a contested term) is very complex; identities and representations are neither simple nor unmediated, but rather they are complexly mediated by and transformed by memory, fantasy, and desire, as well as by other cultural 'texts' that shaped their interpretation and reinterpretation. For Hall, there is never a simple return or recovery of the ancestral past that is not re-experienced through the categories, technologies, and identities of the present.

Hall is drawn to the concept of ethnicity because the traditional Western notion of an identity of race cannot account for the displacement, migration, hybridity, and decentering social forces that undermine the certainty of race and racial identity. Once we have decentered racial essentialism, we then need to rethink the association between identity and practice, which allows us to create new forms of theorizing identity and new forms of belonging. For Hall, this marks the end of the essential racial subject. The end of the essential racial subject warrants that race be rethought in terms of how race is articulated historically in formation and in relation with other categories of class, gender, ethnicity, and nation, which overlap and crisscross in a myriad of patterns and connections. The focus then of this new ethnicity is to acknowledge and forefront the place of history, language, and culture in the construction of subjectivity and identity; this construction must be understood as historically specific and contextually bound to position and situatedness, which define it in time and space.

THINKING ABOUT MULTICULTURALISM

In order to discuss multiculturalism in today's society, we need, Hall believes, strategies to deal with cultural diversity and heterogeneity. Multiculturalism is always a war of position in which the central issues of race always appear historically within any social formation in articulation with other categories. We cannot rely on multiculturalism as a universal identity or citizenship emphasizing individual autonomy, or as the customs of the majority, or as a segmented yet cosmopolitan social order. All of these modes of theorizing multiculturalism are fixed, monolithic, and essentialized ways of dealing with the issue of diversity, as if it could be defined through one approach. Instead, we must turn the question of multiculturalism into the questions of multiculturalism(s) to explore the multiplicity of differences and envision a future that encompasses multiple diverse backgrounds, cultures, contexts, and experiences. We must take seriously the play of difference that is constantly in flux. There can no longer be one horizon, one notion of identity; rather, we must abandon the search for a ground or a foundation of authenticity. We need to keep in mind 'the question of difference,' a question that is itself constantly in flux, a question that unsettles all universal values, self-sufficient totalities, and certainties. We need to see the heterogeneity of all communities as diverse, divided, contradictory, and pluralistic—without a fixed point of reference.

INTELLECTUAL LABOR AND POLITICS OF RESISTANCE

For Hall, all intellectual labor is in the service of social change. Hall advocates for a cultural politics of difference in which new ethical and democratic frameworks can emerge to account for diversity and equality. Hall's intellectual work of interrogating racial identities, cultural images, discourses through which ideologies circulate, and the processes by which hegemony is won all speak to his multi-sided intervention into the workings of everyday life. For Hall, it is in the everyday, in popular culture, in our everyday existence that we must struggle against the limitations of the dominant ideologies that constrain and confine the possibilities of who and what we can become. Hall builds resistance into his mode of theorizing the world as he seeks to undermine the structures and relations of domination through critically calling into question any policing of identity and thereby moving beyond identity politics to a politics of the identity of difference, reflexivity, and contingency, in which there are no necessary or essential correspondences of anything with anything. We have to take up the difficult intellectual and analytical labor of breaking from our current system of classifications, which is based on stifling binaries, and of understanding how these historical constructions were formed, normalized, and stabilized—in order to undo them. Hall believes we must struggle constantly and strategically position and reposition ourselves. This is politics without a guarantee.

CONCLUSION

To summarize Hall's contributions, we can point to the combination of conceptual innovations and engagement with contemporary changes in society. These contributions include

- Application of Marxist theories of culture and ideology to the contemporary context;
- An enormous strengthening of theories of ethno-racial differentiation and dominance, a previously under-theorized area of the Marxist paradigm;

- Foundational concepts for analysis of the contemporary media;
- Elaboration of the concept of hybridity to understand past as well as contemporary cultures.
- An alternative to Foucault's way of looking at power, one that shares in many of Foucault's innovations while offering a more head-on recognition of the capitalist state and going less far in the direction of power dispersion (at least, compared to Foucault's work before he theorized about governmentality [Hall 1980d]);
- Examination of the relationship among media, ideology, and the establishment of neoliberal state policies.
- New ways of thinking about the multicultural societies that are emerging in Europe and North America as well as in post-colonial regions.

KEY TERMS

- articulation
- critical politics of contesting images
- critique of false consciousness
- culture as the arena of struggle
- function of common sense
- hegemony/ideology
- hybridity
- identity
- intellectual labor and a politics of resistance
- interpellation and ideological subjects
- media: the politics of representation
- move to ethnicity
- overdetermination
- race: the floating signifier
- societies structured in dominance
- thinking about multiculturalism

Conclusion

In these pages, we return to sociology as a field and look at the overall patterns of change. Instead of treating the transition to contemporary theories as the work of a few individuals—the transitional giants—we will look at the changes more impersonally, as response and resistance in the field. We draw attention to the uneven impact of theories on subfields of sociology and identify facilitators and barriers to the adoption of new theories. We emphasize that new paradigms in sociology often involve the reinterpretation of the theoretical legacies of the field. The ideas of the 'ancestors' are reinterpreted, and their writing is read in light of contemporary issues. We end the book by suggesting that the cycle of paradigm change that began in the last decades of the twentieth century may now itself be drawing to a close.

THE UNEVEN IMPACT OF CONTEMPORARY THEORY ON SOCIOLOGY

At this point, readers may be wondering whether sociology in all of its variety was transformed by new theories, and the answer has to be 'no.' Whole subfields and large areas of research remain relatively untouched by contemporary theories and the ideas of the transitional giants while other areas have been deeply affected. Thomas Kuhn recognized that, in some areas of science, paradigm shifts mean a complete transformation—the sun-centered model of the solar system swept away the earth-centered one. In other areas, the grand ideas of the new paradigm coexist with the useful though now limited applications of previous paradigms: although Einstein's theory of general relativity replaced Newtonian physics in our understanding of the universe, Newton's laws are still perfectly valid for a large range of phenomena, and the more down to earth the situation, the more likely it can be understood in Newton's framework. A partial paradigm shift of this type has taken place in sociology.

Contemporary theory has affected subfields and areas of sociology unevenly. Some fields have been transformed or even newly created by contemporary theories, while others resist these theories or veer away from theory altogether. We suggest reasons that paradigms do or don't shift within areas and subfields of a discipline, which are typically defined by research journals, sections at the professional association meetings, and rubrics in comprehensive and review journals of the larger discipline.

In some fields, we can discern a deep impact when the field was transformed or even newly created in conjunction with contemporary theories. One example of a deep impact occurred within the sociology of the self, which underwent paradigm shifts from the central concepts of personality and social influence to entire new formulations influenced by Goffman, Foucault, and deconstruction theorists, who centered on the self as narrative and performance and on the self as an increasingly protean response to flexible capitalism. Even psychoanalytic approaches shifted from sexual to textual as the unconscious was reconceptualized as a narrative that preserves a fantastic and distorted version of each individual's 'forced march' from infancy and a state of 'mamiferous larvae' into human childhood and adulthood (Althusser 1971a: 206).

Another area in which paradigm shifts are decisive is the analysis of the construction of difference and dominance in gender and race or ethnicity, which was utterly purged of the ascriptive and naturalistic assumptions that were still in evidence at mid-twentieth century. Two other areas emerged with historical 'external' changes (those happening outside academia) and therefore evolved with contemporary theories: the study of the globalization of cultures and the study of the media.

In other areas and subfields, we can see 'paradigms in play'—situations in which older paradigms and contemporary theories coexist, sometimes in contestation and sometimes with a peaceful division of the terrain. Examples of these mixed situations can be detected in political sociology, the study of inequalities, spatial analysis and urban sociology, and the subfield formerly known as criminology and the sociology of deviance.

For example, urban sociology persists, but a lively new area—the analysis of space—has emerged alongside. In the analysis of economic inequality, Marxist-influenced paradigms contend against postmodern ones that reinterpret the legacies of Weber and Durkheim. Political sociology has been strongly affected by Bourdieu's concepts of political field, and the sociology of collective action has incorporated new insights on states, civil society, and identities and culture in social movements. The areas of criminology and the study of deviance responded to Foucault's theoretical assault, but they still include older individual and community-based theories as well as new links to public-health research and criminal-justice perspectives. Many of these areas can be described as churning in that new critical perspectives compete with existing ones, which, in turn, may be linked to policy issues. There is no single dominant paradigm; no 'mainstream' has clearly emerged.

In yet other fields, new theories had only a limited impact. The effect of contemporary theories is muted. Some subfields have been resistant to new theories or have quarantined them in special topics within the subfield. For example, sociology of the family has maintained many of the paradigms developed in the second half of the twentieth century, with the influence of Foucault and Butler isolated from mainstream work in this area. Some fields that were once extensively theorized have turned away from theory toward policy-related analysis. Sociology of health, illness, and medical practice is a particularly fascinating case, as it moved from structural-functional theory to conflict theory to a growingly atheoretical discourse, even as researchers dissect contentious and potentially theoretical areas such as the effects of inequality on population health.

CONTEMPORARY THEORIES: BARRIERS AND FACILITATORS

Several forces affected theorizing in the subfields and the extent to which new theories had an impact: Some of these forces are facilitators that encourage sociologists to adopt new theories, and others are barriers.

Facilitators: Forces That Led to the Adoption of New Theories

1. CHANGE IN THE EXTERNAL OR 'REAL' WORLD
Changes such as urbanization, transnational migration, freer transnational markets and neoliberal policies, the growth of enormous transnational corporations, the explosion of new media and information technologies, and the formation of multicultural societies forced sociologists to revise their ideas about social reality. For example, the field of medical sociology had to encompass the rise of HMOs and the entry of profit-making organizations into health care. Urban sociology had to address the fact that half of the globe's population is now urban and that previously agrarian developing nations contain many of the world's poorest and fastest-growing cities. The

sociology of crime and deviance had to include an analysis of the soaring rates of incarceration in the United States.

2. *INTELLECTUAL TRENDS*
The subfields are affected by the shifts in the larger or grander theories and fashions in social thought. These theories are incorporated into middle-range theory in the subfields. For example, the emergence of postmodern theories in a wide range of areas including cultural studies, communication and media studies, philosophy, and many social sciences influenced sociological theories. In areas such as the sociology of the media and urban sociology, theories began to encompass insights and perspectives from postmodern theorists. Deconstruction in philosophy was appropriated by the social sciences and incorporated into social constructionist theories that emphasized the creation through discourse of categories such as race, sex and gender, and deviance and normality.

3. *INTERNAL DYNAMICS OF THE FIELD*
In many of the subfields, we can discern an historical shift over the last half of the twentieth century. Immediately after World War II, the subfields shared with sociology as a whole the view that 'we are all structural-functionalists.' Structural-functionalist theories dominated analysis of the family, education, media, and many other subfields. The emphasis was on shared values, societal cohesion, social roles, institutional functions, and patterns of behavior that became apparent by quantitative analysis. But the dominion of the structural-functionalist paradigm was short lived. By the 1960s, interactionist and conflict theories had become popular, and, in the following decade, it was particularly conflict theories that seemed to be at the exciting new frontiers of sociology. Variants of Marxism and feminism defined the cutting edge of areas such as urban sociology, the sociology of the media, and the sociology of medicine. For instance, Marxist theories guided the analysis of the urban growth machine (developers and their political allies) and grassroots urban activism. Conflict theories in medical sociology criticized professional dominance and the power of physicians. Research on the media was guided by theories of corporate monopolies and hegemonic processes of news construction. By the 1980s and 1990s, conflict theories were increasingly blended with discourse analysis, attention to micro-level interactions, and the influence of postmodernism. The overall movement of sociological theory was an impetus for change and innovation in the subfields.

Barriers to New Theories: Three Conditions That Reduce Theory Impact

1. PARTNERSHIPS WITH APPLIED AND POLICY FIELDS

Researchers in applied and policy-oriented fields are often wary of theories, and when partnerships are formed with these fields, theory may be de-emphasized. For example, the sociology of health is partnered with public health, urban sociology with urban planning, the sociology of deviance and crime with criminal justice and corrections, and the sociology of families with family and child policy. Public policy makers are not thrilled by theories with a negative-critical spin, such as Marxism and feminism. From their perspective, theory gets in the way of looking at empirical data and obscures facts that could be used to develop effective policies. Theories are not congenial to governments and private-sector organizations, where they are considered at best airy and abstract and, at worst, rancorous. When a sociological subfield such as the sociology of health develops partnerships with an applied field such as public health, theory may get in the way of communication and collaboration. From the perspective of practitioners in the more applied field, theories introduce unnecessary abstruseness, abstractness, and critical observations. Too much critical analysis of institutions and policies ultimately seems pointless to practitioners dealing with everyday problems and needs in the 'real' world. These perceptions discourage extensive theoretical discussions in collaborative work, in publications destined to be read by scholars in both fields, and in technical reports or policy papers. For example, in the striking case of the sociology of health, inequalities in population health and access to medical care have been studied empirically but not connected to larger theoretical frameworks, especially those with a Marxist bent. (See Navarro and Muntaner 2004, for further discussion.) In order to create a common discourse about the subject with colleagues in related fields, sociologists in these areas have come to avoid critical theoretical concepts or to use softer, less contentious terms. A very telling sign of this avoidance is the substitution of the word 'disparities' for the harsher and more theoretical term 'inequalities.'

2. MULTIVARIATE ANALYSIS IS THE THEORY

Quantitative analysis has a complicated relationship to theories; on the one hand, ever since Comte and Durkheim, sociologists have based theories on the premise that societies have discernible stable patterns and that careful empirical data collection and quantitative analysis enable us to recognize the patterns. This position was initially most clearly articulated in Durkheim's *Suicide*, in which Durkheim showed that suicide is not a random phenomenon, not simply an individual act, and certainly not a result of racial traits but a highly patterned occurrence whose statistical regularity reveals underlying forces of normative regulation and social integration ([1897] 1991). The power of Durkheim's reasoning continues to guide sociological inquiry. It survived disenchantment with 1950s functionalism, and new information technologies have given it an enormous boost. The combination of very sophisticated survey methodology, the amassing of large data sets of social-indicator and public-records data, and multivariate statistical analysis makes it possible to access, handle, quantify, and interpret huge amounts of social data. Multivariate statistics, the development of highly refined, intricate, and multi-level linear and logistic regression models, has revolutionized the process not only of discerning patterns but also of identifying causal chains. For some sociologists, theory now lies in identifying significant predictor variables for outcomes in complex multi-level models. If we can identify these variables while we control for possible confounding variables, we have established an explanatory and causal model. Complex models are a satisfactory substitute for theoretical paradigms because they demonstrate that we understand causal pathways. When these types of data are available in a field, as they are for epidemiological studies of population health and illness, educational attainment and academic achievement, patterns of crime, and many other areas, there is a strong incentive to develop quantitative models rather than theoretical constructs. Although there is no fundamental reason that theorists and quantitative researchers should be opposed to each other's work—indeed the spirit of Durkheim would want us to recognize these as mutually supportive projects—areas that are highly quantified tend to be resistant to the new paradigms discussed in this book.

3. PARADIGM PERSISTENCE

A third reason that some subfields and areas have resisted contemporary theories is that the pre-existing paradigms seem perfectly serviceable—the same reason that, in applications of physics, we don't need Einstein's theory of general relativity to launch weather satellites. Often paradigm persistence appears in fields where the phenomena themselves seem not to have changed all that much. It seems evident that there has been an explosion of media and information technologies in recent decades. Globalization—however we label the phenomenon—has had a major impact on cultures and economies. With over half of the planet's population living in urban areas, cities and spatial distributions and uses have changed dramatically. These are examples of areas where theories have to address new external conditions. But in other areas—some would argue that the sociology of the family is one of them—although the empirical phenomena have changed, there are also many continuities. People continue to live in families and family-based households, even if these have changed in structure, in the roles and functions of their members, and in the family policy of governments. The existing paradigms seem able to stretch to explain the new behaviors and conditions.

LEGACIES, REINTERPRETATIONS, AND NEW PARADIGMS

Throughout this book, we have focused on the creation of new theories, but a powerful element of theoretical change is the reinterpretation of theoretical legacies. Sociological theory was changed not only by new theories but also by the rereading and transformation of classical and twentieth-century theories. The new readings became part of the new paradigms, as we noted in Goffman's reformulation of Durkheim's ideas and Hall's use of concepts inherited from Marx, Engels, and Gramsci, which Hall applied to and recontextualized in new external circumstances. In this section, we will sketch the ways legacies were reinterpreted to make them vital parts of new theories.

LEGACIES

The Legacy of Durkheim

Durkheim is the most protean of the classical theorists, and his work encourages constant rereading and reinterpretation. Here are a few of the ways in which his legacy is being incorporated into contemporary theory.

NORMATIVE REGULATION AND THE 'EMPTY SELF'
Contemporary sociological theory focuses on regulation through discourses, frames, scripted performances, and rules governing interaction. This Durkheimian legacy marks the work of Goffman and feminist theories. Foucault's analysis of regulatory regimes has an affinity with these aspects of Durkheim's legacy. The postmodern self as a protean persona is an extension of Durkheim's conception of the 'empty self' formed by social regulation.

FOCUS ON PUNISHMENT, CRIME, AND SOCIAL CONTROL
A second key element of Durkheim's legacy is the contemporary emphasis on punishment, definitions of crime, the social construction of deviance, and social control as central topics of sociology. The nature of a society is revealed in its punitive practices. Deviance and crime are products of normative regulation not

of individual dispositions and experiences. This perspective overlaps the focus on normative regulation; both are revisited by Foucault and his interpreters.

THE COMPLEX INTEGRATION OF CAPITALIST SOCIETY

Postmodernists are returning to Durkheim's argument that capitalist society enjoys extremely powerful, non-coercive mechanisms of social cohesion and integration. Its organic composition holds it together through the interlacing of myriads of economic groupings that in turn cross-cut the mechanical solidarities based on religion and ethno-racial identities. Far from splitting into two polarized groups along class lines, capitalist society is held together by these multiple cross-cutting cleavages. Durkheim's ideas connect to Foucault's concept of governmentality, theories of civil society, and postmodernist views such as Baudrillard's contention that 'modes of repression and integration of the simulation order are, in this regard, more comprehensive, more complete, and the prospects for liberation less optimistic' (Koch and Elmore 2006: 572; see also Alexander 2006; Pakulski in Wright 2006).

STATISTICAL REASONING AND QUANTITATIVE ANALYSIS OF SOCIAL PATTERNS

Durkheim's insistence that the force of society becomes visible in social facts, consistent and stable patterns of behavior discernible in rates and variable relationships, underlies contemporary quantitative analysis. As multivariate statistical methods and collection of very large amounts of data become ever more feasible, these patterns can be identified with precision, though always in probabilistic terms. Although, for some researchers, the multivariate analysis is the explanation—the theory in a limited sense—quantitative analysis can also be a gateway to theory construction in a broader sense.

The Legacy of Marx and Engels, Weber, and Simmel

These classical theorists are linked by their attention to capitalism and their understandings of the historical context of human action. Here are five ways in which their ideas influence contemporary theories.

THE HISTORICAL CONTEXT OF HUMAN ACTION

All four theorists insisted that human action is historically situated and that theorists must give attention to the changing social context, which now includes new forms of capitalism, neoliberal state policies, globalization, transnational migration, new media and information technologies, and new patterns of urbanization and collective action.

ANALYSIS OF CAPITALISM AND THE MONEY ECONOMY

All four focused on capitalism, and the neoliberal shift with its global and weakly regulated markets demands the attention of sociologists. We can see this focus in the work of Bourdieu and Hall, as well as in the new theories of inequality. The analysis of capitalism remains a major theme in many areas of sociological inquiry, such as the study of global cities, the examination of media impact, and the attention to inequalities in health care.

CONTINUING ANALYSIS OF INEQUALITIES

Marx and Engels as well as Weber examined the key dimensions of social inequality and the conditions under which these categories of disadvantage turn into social identities and the basis of collective action. Weber and the Marxists had different views of these matters, and their contending positions continue to inform the discussion of global inequalities, classes in contemporary capitalism, and the continued force of status identities such as religion, national origin, citizenship rights, gender, and race or ethnicity.

THE ROLE OF THE STATE

Weber and Marx and Engels focused attention on the state, and contemporary theorists remain committed to understanding the role of the state in the political field, in regimes of social control and punishment, and in the construction of categories of difference and domination. Even though the neoliberal state has withdrawn from economic regulation and social services, it has expanded social control functions and developed new relationships with civil society. 'Bringing the state back in' means rereading the classical theorists.

THE CONFLICT PERSPECTIVE

Weber and the Marxists originated the conflict perspective in sociology, and, although it is unwise to lump all conflict theorists together, there are common themes in their work that challenge the concept of a unified society with shared values. Conflict theories have been revised to include a pervasive play of power and resistance, often defined locally and occurring in the micro- or capillary level of social interactions.

The Legacy of Interwar Marxism, Cultural Analysis, and Critical Theory

Theorists working in a Marxist vein in the early and middle parts of the twentieth century influence contemporary theories in areas such as the construction of gender inequality, the production of 'whiteness' and racial dominance, the production of deviance by criminal codes, the symbolic environment formed by the media, and the creation of identity narratives. Although these topics of theory are quite new, the overall method of analyzing texts, discourses, and narratives has roots in the Marxist analysis of culture proposed by Walter Benjamin and Antonio Gramsci and elaborated in post-World War II critical theory.

The Legacy of Conflict and Micro-Theories

These two streams of theories—originally countercurrents against structural-functionalism in the 1970s and 1980s—provided the basis of contemporary theories. The trajectories of almost every area of sociology passed through a period of conflict theories and micro-theories, such as feminist approaches to family life, the theory of physician dominance in health care, the critical analysis of ownership patterns and the effects of professional routines in the media, and labeling theory in the sociology of deviance. These critical approaches persist even though they have been modified by the contributions of the transitional giants and revised to fit new social contexts; in many cases, the conflict theories have been disaggregated so that Marxist, Weberian, and feminist theories are not casually lumped together; but, on the other hand, macro- and micro-approaches are better integrated with each other.

NEW PARADIGMS, OLD THEMES

Another way of thinking about the persistent legacies of sociological theory is to examine the themes of social thought that contemporary theories still address. These questions and themes cut across the subfields and areas. Among these persistent themes and questions are

> *The relationship between self and society*: How does 'society' get into the self? What is the self, and how is it organized?

> *Difference, inequalities, identities, and collective action*: What are the major inequalities of our times? How are they constructed and reproduced? What is the role of the state in these processes? What is

the relationship between economic inequality and status stratification? Under what conditions are inequalities transformed into identities, and when do these identities become the basis of collective action?

The relationship of culture and society: What is the relationship between ideas and behaviors, between social arrangements and the way people represent these arrangements? How is culture produced and disseminated? What is the explanation for consistent misrecognitions? What roles do culture and the media have in the construction and reproduction of inequalities?

The problem of social order and social control: What is the basis of social order? What forces keep people interacting with each other in relatively stable and consistent ways? What prevents a 'war of each against all,' and when do these arrangements break down? What is the role of the state and of micro-processes in maintaining social order? How is social control related to inequalities? How is order imposed by regimes of regulation and punishment, and how is it inscribed on the body?

To answer these questions, theorists are inventing new concepts (such as habitus, field, the construction of difference and dominance, the microphysics of power, frame analysis, and so on). New circumstances such as new media, globalization and neoliberalism, immigration and urbanization, new organizations of civil society and their relationships to states, and new types of inequalities in the global economy all lead to new answers to these thematic questions. But the questions and themes remain central to the field.

BEYOND LEGACIES: WHAT'S NEW?

At this point, the reader may be wondering if anything in contemporary theory is really new—or is new theory just a recycling of ideas found in classical and twentieth-century theories, suitably cleaned and molded into new shapes—like recycled plastic?

One thing is undoubtedly new: the circumstances—the material conditions and historical moment of our lives. We are thrown into the world here and now, and we have to make sense out of circumstances that we did not choose.

Theory is always related to the conditions in which it is thought. The reworking of old theories and concepts must address puzzles that arise with new conditions, historical events, social processes, and the mechanisms of domination and stratification. When Hall used Gramsci and Althusser to explain the new power bloc that emerged in the Thatcher-Reagan neoliberal regimes, he did not simply apply the existing concepts but transformed the theories to make sense of the new world. Theories must serve the living, and they do that not only through adaptation but also through discussion and contestation. Our theoretical ancestors inspire us, but it is their spirit, not the letter of their work, that guides us. Ultimately, theories must be addressed to citizens, not just to other theoreticians.

WHAT WILL HAPPEN NEXT?

We argue that, after forty years in the wilderness of postmodernism and post-conflict theory, it may be time for a new synthesis. This synthesis could involve a more systematic and explicit linkage between the micro-level (capillaries, the microphysics of power, discourses and interactions, regulation by scripted performance, and so on) and the macro-level with its analysis of neoliberalism, flexible capitalism, global flows of media and products, and enormous inequalities within and among societies. To change the world, we needed to identify objective conditions of inequality at the macro level, but making this identification is not sufficient. However, a slow trickle of change at the micro-, local, and capillary levels, by itself, cannot perceptibly alter the global conditions of wrenching poverty and rapid environmental deterioration either. By clarifying our understanding of the macro-micro linkages, theorists can contribute to changing rather than merely interpreting the world; the changes must happen quickly if they are to halt and (one hopes) reverse environmental disasters and mass misery.

All four transitional giants point in the direction of critical macro-micro analysis: Goffman with his pioneering concept of media framing, Foucault with governmentality, and Bourdieu and Hall throughout their writing. But there is room for more of these syntheses and greater efforts for the 'micro' and the 'macro' to talk to each other. Many theorists are indeed working on these linkages, developing theory as they examine topics such as gender construction in the global economy (Cheng 2006), inequality in global cities and the formation of global civil society (Sassen 2000, 2001), character in the age of flexible capitalism (Sennett 1998), power and resistance in the modern metropolis (Burawoy 1991), and the effects of racial segregation and exclusion (Wacquant 2004, 2007, 2008a).

But beyond a new synthesis, beyond sharpening and refining contemporary paradigms, a more radical break may once again be in the making. It seems entirely possible that dramatic 'external' changes will occur in the next decades, such as a turning away from neoliberalism, and that these shifts will precipitate a new round of paradigm shifts. We may be approaching neither the end of the world nor the end of theory—but a new theoretical turn that we cannot yet envision.

References and Suggestions for Further Reading

NOTE TO READERS

The references and suggestions for further reading are divided into three main sections: general references and suggestions; references for primary materials and selected secondary sources related to the four transitional giants; and two specialized area bibliographies covering theoretical change in the sociology of the family and the sociology of health.

Contributors to the reference section are José Soltero, Tait Runnfeldt Medina, Julie Artis, Grace Budrys, and Greg Scott.

GENERAL THEORETICAL REFERENCES

Abu-Lughod, Janet. 2000. "Can Chicago Make It as a Global City?" A Great Cities Institute Working Paper, College of Urban Planning and Public Affairs, University of Illinois at Chicago, Chicago, IL.

Adorno, Theodor. 2001. *The Culture Industry*. New York: Routledge.

Adorno, Theodor, Else Frenkel-Brunswik, and Daniel Levinson. 1993. *The Authoritarian Personality*. New York: W.W. Norton.

Alexander, Jeffrey. 2006. *The Civil Sphere*. Oxford: Oxford University Press.

Allen, Theodore. 1997. *The Invention of the White Race*. London: Verso.

Althusser, Louis. 1971a. "Freud and Lacan." Pp. 189–220 in *Lenin and Philosophy*. New York: Monthly Review Press.

Althusser, Louis. 1971b. "Ideology and the State." Pp. 127–186 in *Lenin and Philosophy*. New York: Monthly Review Press.

Anderson, Benedict. 1983. *Imagined Communities*. London: Verso.

Ang, Ien. 1996. *Living Room Wars*. New York: Routledge.

Appadurai, Arjun. 1993. "Disjunction and Difference in the Global Cultural Economy." Pp. 295–310 in *Global Culture: Nationalism, Globalization and Modernity*, edited by Mike Featherstone. London: Sage.

Australia Department of the Parliamentary Library. 1995. "The Disappearing Middle: Australia's Increasing Wage Dispersion." *Research Note* 9, August 28, pp. 1–2.

Bagdikian, Ben. 1983. *The Media Monopoly.* Boston: Beacon Press.

Baudrillard, Jean. [1969] 2000. "The Ideological Genesis of Needs." Pp. 57–80 in *The Consumer Society Reader*, edited by J.B. Schor and D.B. Holt. New York: The New Press.

Baudrillard, Jean. 1970. *The Consumer Society.* Translated by Chris Turner. London: Sage Publications.

Bay, Mia. 2000. *The White Image in the Black Mind: African-American Ideas about White People, 1830–1925.* Oxford: Oxford University Press.

Becker, Gary with Kevin M. Murphy. 2000. *Social Economics.* Cambridge, MA: Harvard University Press.

Becker, Howard. 1963. *Outsiders: Studies in the Sociology of Deviance.* New York: Free Press.

Bell, Daniel. 1973. *The Coming of Post-Industrial Society.* New York: Basic Books.

Benjamin, Walter. 1968. "The Work of Art in the Age of Mechanical Reproduction." Pp. 219–253 in *Illuminations*, edited by Hannah Arendt and translated by Harry Zohn. Orlando: Harcourt Brace and Co.

Benjamin, Walter. 2002. *The Arcades Project.* Edited by Rolf Tiedemann. Translated by Howard Eiland and Kevin McLaughlin. Cambridge, MA: Belknap Press.

Bennett, M. 2006. "The Rebirth of Bronzeville." Pp. 213–220 in *The New Chicago*, edited by J.P. Koval. Philadelphia: Temple University Press.

Bernstein, Jared and Larry Mishel. 2007. "Education and the Inequality Debate." (Economic Policy Institute Issue Brief No. 232, February 8, 2007) Retrieved November 11, 2008 (http://www.epi.org/content.cfm/ib232).

Best, Steven and Douglas Kellner. 1991. *Postmodern Theory.* New York: Guilford Press.

Birch, Eugenie. 2005. *Who Lives Downtown.* Washington: Brookings Institution.

Blauner, Robert. 1972. *Racial Oppression in America.* New York: Harper and Row.

Boddy, Janice. 1990. *Wombs and Alien Spirits: Women, Men, and the Zar Cult in Northern Sudan.* Madison, WI: University of Wisconsin Press.

Bonilla-Silva, Eduardo and Karen Glover. 2004. "We are all Americans: The Latin Americanization of Race Relations in the U.S." Pp. 149–183 in *The Changing Face of Race and Ethnicity*, edited by Maria Krysan and Amanda Lewis. New York: Russell Sage.

Boorstein, Daniel. 1964. *The Image: A Guide to Pseudo-events in America.* New York: Harper & Row.

Breed, Warren. 1954. "Social Control in the Newsroom: A Functional Analysis." *Social Forces* 33: 326–355.

Bridge, Gary and Sophie Watson. 2000. *A Companion to the City.* Malden, MA: Blackwell.

Brookings Institution. 2003. *Chicago in Focus: A Profile from Census 2000.* Washington: Brookings Institution.

Buck-Morss, Susan. 1989. *The Dialectics of Seeing: Walter Benjamin and the Arcades Project.* Cambridge, MA: MIT Press.

Burawoy, Michael. 1991. *Ethnography Unbound: Power and Resistance in the Modern Metropolis.* Berkeley: University of California Press.

Burchell, Graham, Colin Gordon, and Peter Miller. 1991. *The Foucault Effect: Studies in Governmentality.* Chicago: University of Chicago Press.

Butler, Judith. 1990. *Gender Trouble: Feminism and the Subversion of Identity.* New York: Routledge.

Butler, Judith. 1993. *Bodies That Matter.* New York: Routledge.

Butler, Judith. 2004. *Undoing Gender.* New York: Routledge.

Cainkar, Louise. 2006. "Immigrants from the Arab World." Pp.182–196 in *The New Chicago,* edited by J.P. Koval. Philadelphia: Temple University Press.

Castells, Manuel. 1996. *The Rise of the Network Society.* Vol. 1. Malden, MA: Blackwell.

Caute, David. 1990. *The Year of the Barricades: A Journey through 1968.* New York: HarperCollins.

Chambliss, William T. 1973. "The Roughnecks and the Saints." *Society.* November/December, pp. 24–31.

Cheng, Shu-Ju Ada. 2006. *Serving the Household and the Nation: Filipina Domestics and the Politics of Identity in Taiwan.* Lanham, MD: Rowman and Littlefield.

Cheng, Shu-Ju Ada. 2007. "Service, Servitude, and Identities: Subaltern Subjectivities in Transnational Care." Pp. 503–519 in *Social Theory,* 2nd ed., edited by Roberta Garner. Peterborough, ON: Broadview Press.

Chodorow, Nancy. 1989. *Feminism and Psychoanalytic Theory.* New Haven, CT: Yale University Press.

Chua, Amy. 2002. *World on Fire: How Exporting Free Market Democracy Breeds Ethnic Hatred and Global Instability.* New York: Doubleday.

Clark, Terry Nichols. 2004. *The City as Entertainment Machine.* Amsterdam: Elsevier.

Cloward, Richard and Lloyd Ohlin. 1961. *Delinquency and Opportunity: A Theory of Delinquent Gangs.* Glencoe, IL: Free Press.

Cohn, Theodore. 2002. *Global Political Economy: Theory and Practice.* New York: Addison, Wesley.

Collins, Patricia Hill. 2000. *Black Feminist Thought.* Rev. ed. New York: Routledge.

Collins, Randall. 1994. *Four Sociological Traditions.* New York: Oxford University Press.

Crapanzano, Vincent. 2004. "Hermes' dilemma: The masking of subversion in ethnographic description." Pp. 593–608 in *Anthropological Theory: An Introductory History,* 3rd ed., edited by Jon R. McGee and Richard L. Warms. New York: McGraw-Hill.

D'Emilio, John. 1983. "Capitalism and Gay Identity." Pp. 100–113 in *Powers of Desire: The Politics of Sexuality,* edited by Ann Snitow, Christine Stansell, and Sharon Thompson. New York: Monthly Review Press.

Davis, Angela. [1984] 1990. *Women, Culture, and Politics.* New York: Random House/Vintage.

Davis, Kingsley. 1959. "The Myth of Functional Analysis as a Special Method in Sociology and Anthropology." *American Sociological Review* 24(6): 757–772.

Davis, Kingsley and Wilbert E. Moore. 1945. "Some Principles of Stratification." *American Sociological Review* 10 (April): 242–249.

Davis, Mike. 1992. *City of Quartz.* New York: Vintage Books.

Davis, Mike. 2004. "Planet of the Slums." *New Left Review* 26 (March-April): 5–34.

Debord, Guy. [1967] 1995. *The Society of the Spectacle*. New York: Zone Books.

Debray, Regis. 1979. "A Modest Contribution to the Rite and Ceremonies of the Tenth Anniversary." *New Left Review* 115: 45–65.

Delaney, Tim. 2005. *Contemporary Social Theory: Investigation and Application*. Upper Saddle River, NJ: Pearson Prentice Hall.

Deleuze, Gilles. 1986. *Foucault*. Minneapolis: University of Minnesota

Denzin, Norman. 1993. *The Alcoholic Society: Addiction and Recovery of the Self*. Edison, NJ: Transaction Books.

Derrida, Jacques. 1994. "Spectres of Marx." *New Left Review* 205: 31–59.

Desai, Manisha. 2002. "Multiple Mediations: The State and Women's Movements in India." Pp. 66–84 in *Social Movements: Identity, Culture, and the State*, edited by David S. Meyer, Nancy Whittier, and Belinda Robnett. New York: Oxford University Press.

Dubois, W.E.B. [1910] 1970. "Souls of White Folk." In *The Selected Writings of W.E.B. Dubois*, edited by Walter Wilson. New York: Penguin Putnam.

Durkheim, Émile. [1893] 1964. *The Division of Labor in Society*. New York: Free Press.

Durkheim, Émile. [1897] 1951. *Suicide*. New York: Free Press.

Durkheim, Émile. [1912] 1965. *The Elementary Forms of Religious Life*. New York: Free Press.

Engels, F. [1845] 1968. *The Condition of the Working Class in England*. Translated and edited by W.O. Henderson and W.H. Chaloner. Stanford, CA: Stanford University Press.

Engels, F. [1884] 1970. *The Origins of the Family, Private Property, and the State*. New York: International Publishers.

Ewen, Stuart and Elizabeth Ewen. 1982. *Channels of Desire*. New York: McGraw-Hill.

Fainstein, Susan. 1999. *The Tourist City*. New Haven, CT: Yale University Press.

Fainstein, Susan. 2001. *The City Builders: Property Development in New York and London*. Lawrence: University Press of Kansas.

Fanon, Frantz. 1965. *The Wretched of the Earth*. New York: Grove Press.

Feyerabend, P. 1975. *Against Method*. London: New Left Books.

Fields, Barbara Jeanne. 1990. "Slavery, Race, and Ideology in the United States of America." *New Left Review* 181: 95–118.

Foner, Eric. 1999. *The Story of American Freedom*. New York: W.W. Norton.

Ford, Kenneth W. 2005. *The Quantum World*. Cambridge, MA: Harvard University Press.

Fox, Kathryn. 2001. "Change and Resistance in Prison." Pp. 176–92 in *Institutional Selves: Troubled Identities in a Postmodern World*, edited by J. Gubrium and J. Holstein. New York: Oxford University Press.

Frank, Andre Gunder. 1971. *Capitalism and Underdevelopment in Latin America*. London: Penguin Books.

Frank, Andrew. 2005. *Creeks and Southerners: Biculturalism on the Early American Frontier*. Lincoln: University of Nebraska Press.

Frank, Thomas. 1997. *The Conquest of Cool: Business Culture, Counterculture, and the Rise of Hip Consumerism*. Chicago: University of Chicago Press.

Frank, Thomas. 2004. *What's the Matter with Kansas? How Conservatives Won the Heart of America*. New York: Henry Holt and Company.

Freeman, Jo. 1982. *Social Movements of the Sixties and Seventies*. Harlow, UK: Longman.

Freud, Sigmund. 1958. *Civilization and its Discontents*. New York: Doubleday Anchor.

Freud, Sigmund. 1960. *The Ego and the Id*. New York: W.W. Norton.

Frey, William. 2005. *Metropolitan America in the New Century: Metropolitan and Central City Demographic Shifts Since 2000*. Washington: Brookings Institution.

Friedman, John. 2002. *The Prospect of Cities*. Minneapolis: University of Minnesota Press.

Gans, Herbert. 2005. *Deciding What's News*. Evanston, IL: Northwestern University Press.

Garcia-Canclini, Nestor. 2003. *Culturas hibridas: Estrategias para entrar y salir de la modernidad*. Mexico: Editorial Grijalbo.

Garner, Roberta. 2001. *Social Theory, Continuity and Confrontation*. Peterborough, ON: Broadview Press.

Garner, Roberta. 2006. "Learning from Chicago." Pp. 305–318 in *The New Chicago*, edited by J.P. Koval. Philadelphia: Temple University Press.

Garner, Roberta, Black Hawk Hancock, and Kiljoong Kim. 2007. "Segregation in Chicago." *The Tocqueville Review* 28(1): 41–74.

Genovese, Eugene. 1976. *Roll, Jordan, Roll*. New York: Vintage Books.

Georgakis, Dan. 1998. *Detroit: I Do Mind Dying: A Study in Urban Revolution*. Boston: South End Press.

Gerbner, George. 2002. *Against the Mainstream: The Selected Works of George Gerbner*. Peter Lang Publishers.

Gergen, Kenneth. 1991. *The Saturated Self*. New York: Harper Collins.

Gerth, Hans and C. Wright Mills. 1953. *Character and Social Structure*. Boston: Beacon Press.

Gilmore, David. 1991. *Manhood in the Making: Cultural Concepts of Masculinity*. New Haven, CT: Yale University Press.

Gilroy, Paul. 1993. *The Black Atlantic and Double Consciousness*. Cambridge, MA: Harvard University Press.

Gilroy, Paul. 1994. *Small Acts: Thoughts on the Politics of Black Cultures*. London: Serpent's Tail.

Gitlin, Todd. 1983. *Inside Prime Time*. New York: Pantheon Books.

Gitlin, Todd. 2003. *The Whole World is Watching*. Berkeley, CA: University of California Press.

Goodman, Paul. 1962. *Growing Up Absurd*. New York: Vintage.

Goodwin, Jeff and Theda Skocpol. 1989. "Explaining Revolutions in the Third World." *Politics and Society* 174: 489-509.

Gramsci, Antonio. 1971. *The Prison Notebooks of Antonio Gramsci*. Edited and translated by Quentin Hoare and Geoffrey Nowell Smith. New York: International Publishers.

Hacking, Ian. 2002. *Mad Travelers: Reflections on the Reality of Transient Mental Illnesses*. Cambridge, MA: Harvard University Press.

Hacking, Ian. 2003. *Rewriting the Soul: Multiple Personality and the Sciences of Memory*. Princeton: Princeton University Press.

Hannerz, Ulf. 1992. *Cultural Complexity: Studies in the Social Organization of Meaning*. New York: Columbia University Press.

Hartigan, John, Jr. 1999. *Racial Situations*. Princeton, NJ: Princeton University Press.

Hartmann, Heidi. 1979. "The Unhappy Marriage of Marxism and Feminism: Towards a More Progressive Union." *Capital and Class* 8: 1–33.

Harvey, David. 1990. *The Condition of Postmodernity*. Cambridge: Blackwell Publishers.

Harvey, David. 2005. *A Brief History of Neo-Liberalism*. Oxford: Oxford University Press.

Hebdige, Dick. 1981. *Subculture: The Meaning of Style*. London: Routledge.

Herdt, Gilbert. 1987. *The Sambia: Ritual and Gender in New Guinea*. Orlando: Holt, Rinehart and Winston.

Herman, Edward S. and Noam Chomsky. 1988. *Manufacturing Consent*. New York: Pantheon Books.

Hertsgaard, Mark. 1989. *On Bended Knee: The Press and the Reagan Presidency*. New York: Schocken Books.

Hobsbawm, Eric. 1987. *The Age of Empire, 1875–1914*. New York: Random House.

Hobsbawm, Eric. 1994. *The Age of Extremes: A History of the World, 1914–1991*. New York: Random House.

Homans, George. 1961. *Social Behavior: Its Elementary Forms*. New York: Harcourt, Brace, and World.

hooks, bell. 1990. *Yearning: Race, Gender, and Cultural Politics*. Boston: South End Press.

Hunter, William T. 2004. "Russia's Experiment with the 'Invisible Hand.'" Pp. 409–423 in *The Invisible Hand and the Common Good*, edited by Bernard Hodgson. Berlin: Springer.

Iceland, John and Rima Wilkes. 2006. "Does Socioeconomic Status Matter? Race, Class, and Residential Segregation." *Social Problems* 53(2): 248–273.

Ignatiev, Noel. 1996. *How the Irish Became White*. New York: Routledge.

Irvine, Leslie. 2000. "Even Better Than the Real Thing: Narratives of Self in Codependency." *Qualitative Sociology* 23: 9–28.

Jacoby, Russell. 1986. *The Repression of Psychoanalysis: Otto Fenichel and the Freudians*. Chicago, IL: University of Chicago Press.

Jameson, Fredric. [1990] 1996. *Late Marxism*. London: Verso.

Jameson, Fredric. 1991. *Postmodernism or the Cultural Logic of Late Capitalism*. Durham, NC: Duke University Press.

Jargowsky, Paul and Isabel Sawhill. 2006. *The Decline of the Underclass*. Washington: Brookings Institution.

Jaskot, Paul. 2000. *The Architecture of Oppression*. New York: Routledge.

Jay, Martin. 1996. *The Dialectical Imagination: A History of the Frankfurt School and the Institute of Social Research, 1923–1950*. Berkeley: University of California Press.

Kardiner, Abram. 1972. *The Mark of Oppression*. New York: World Publishing.

Katz, Elihu. 1957. "The Two-Step Flow of Communication: An Up to Date Report on a Hypothesis." *Public Opinion Quarterly* 21: 67–78.

Katz, Elihu and Paul Lazarsfeldt. 2005. *Personal Influence: The Part Played by People in the Flow of Mass Communication*. Edison, NJ: Transaction Books.

Katznelson, Ira. 1982. *City Trenches: Urban Politics and the Patterning of Class in America*. Chicago, IL: University of Chicago Press.

Katznelson. Ira. 2006. *When Affirmative Action was White: An Untold History of Racial Inequality in America*. New York: W.W. Norton.

Kelling, George and James Q. Wilson. 1982. "Broken Windows: The Police and Neighborhood Safety." *Atlantic Monthly* 248(3): 29–38.

Kerr, Peter. 2001. *Postwar British Politics: From Conflict to Consensus*. London: Taylor and Francis/Routledge.

Khurana, Rakesh. 2002. *Searching for a Corporate Savior: The Irrational Quest for Charismatic CEOs*. Princeton, NJ: Princeton University Press.

Kim, Chang Hwan and Arthur Sakamoto. 2008. "The Rise of Inter-Occupational Wage Inequality in the U.S. 1983–2002." *American Sociological Review* 73: 129–157.

King, Deborah. 1988. "Multiple Jeopardy, Multiple Consciousness: The Context of a Black Feminist Ideology." *Signs* 14(1): 42–72.

Klinenberg, Eric. 2002. *Heat Wave*. Chicago: University of Chicago Press.

Koch, Andrew and Rick Elmore. 2006. "Simulation and Symbolic Exchange: Jean Baudrillard's Augmentation of Marx's Theory of Value." *Politics and Policy* 34(3): 556–575.

Koval, John, ed. 2006. *The New Chicago*. Philadelphia: Temple University Press.

Kuhn, Thomas. 1962. *The Structure of Scientific Revolutions*. Chicago: University of Chicago Press.

Lagrange, Hugues and Marco Oberti. 2006. *Émeutes Urbaines et Protestations*. Paris: Presse de Sciences Po.

Laing, R.D. 1970. *The Divided Self*. New York: Pantheon.

Laumann, Edward, Stephen Ellingson, Jenna Mahay, Anthony Paik, and Yoosik Youm. 2004. *The Sexual Organization of the City*. Chicago: University of Chicago Press. (See in particular Chapter One, "The Theory of Sex Markets," pp. 3–38.)

Leggett, John. 1968. *Class, Race, and Labor: Working Class Consciousness in Detroit*. Oxford: Oxford University Press.

Lerner, Daniel. 1958. *The Passing of Traditional Society: Modernizing the Middle East*. New York: Macmillan.

Light, Donald. 2001. "Cost Containment and the Backdraft of Competition Politics." Pp. 173–200 in *Political and Economic Determinants of Population Health and Well-Being: Controversies and Developments*, edited by Vincente Navarro and Cales Muntaner. Amityville, NY: Baywood Publishing.

Lindesmith, Alfred and Anselm Strauss. 1956. *Social Psychology*. 2nd ed. New York: Henry Holt.

Lipman, Pauline. 2006. "Chicago School Reform: Advancing the Global City Agenda." Pp. 248–258 in *The New Chicago*, edited by J.P. Koval. Philadelphia: Temple University Press.

Lipset, Seymour Martin. 1981. *Political Man: The Social Bases of Politics*. Expanded ed. Baltimore, MD: Johns Hopkins University Press.

Logan, Michael D. and Stephen Ousley. 2001. "Hypergamy, Quantum, and Reproductive Success: The Lost Indian Ancestor Reconsidered." Pp. 184–202 in *Anthropologists and Indians in the New South*, edited by Rachel Bonney and J. Anthony Paredes. Tuscaloosa: The University of Alabama Press.

Lorde, Audre. 2004. *Conversations with Audre Lorde*. Oxford, MS: University of Mississippi Press.

Loseke, Donileen. 1992. *The Battered Woman and Shelter: The Social Construction of Wife Abuse*. Albany, NY: SUNY Press.

Lowenthal, Leo. 1984. *Literature and Mass Culture*. Edison, NJ: Transaction Books.

Lübker, Malte. 2004. "Globalization and Perceptions of Social Inequality." *International Labor Review* 143: 91–128.

Lübker, Malte. 2006. "Inequality and the demand for redistribution: Are the assumptions of the new growth theory valid?" *Socio-Economic Review* 5(1), 117–148.

Mandel, Ernest. 1975. *Late Capitalism*. Translated by J. De Bres. London: New Left Books.

Mandel, Ernest. 1978. *Late Capitalism*. London: Verso.

Mansbridge, Jane and Aldon Morris, eds. 2001. *Oppositional Consciousness: The Subjective Roots of Social Protest*. Chicago: University of Chicago Press.

Marcuse, Herbert. 1955. *Eros and Civilization*. Boston: Beacon Press.

Marty, Martin and Scott Appleby. 1992. *The Glory and the Power: The Fundamentalist Challenge to the Modern World*. Boston: Beacon Press.

Marx, Karl and Friedrich Engels. [1848] 2002. *The Communist Manifesto*. Edited by Gareth Stedman Jones. New York: Penguin Classics.

Marx, Karl and Friedrich Engels. 1960. *The German Ideology*. New York: International Publishers.

Mason-Schrock, Douglas. 1996. "'Transsexuals' Narrative Construction of the 'True Self.'" *Social Psychology Quarterly* 59(3): 176–192.

Massey, Douglas and Mary Denton. 1993. *American Apartheid: Segregation and the Making of the Underclass*. Cambridge, MA: Harvard University Press.

Massey, Douglas and Deborah Hirst. 1998. "From Escalator to Hourglass: Changes in the U.S. Occupational Wage Structure 1949-1989." *Social Science Research* 27: 51–71.

Matza, David. 1961. "Subterranean Traditions of Youth." *Annals of the American Academy of Political and Social Science* 338(1): 102–118.

McLuhan, Marshall. 1964. *Understanding Media: The Extensions of Man*. New York: McGraw-Hill.

Mead, George Herbert. 1932. *Mind, Self, and Society*. Chicago: University of Chicago Press.

Merton, Robert. 1938. "Social Structure and Anomie." *American Sociological Review* 3(1): 672–682.

Messerschmidt, James. 1993. *Masculinities and Crime*. New York: Rowman and Littlefield.

Meyer, David S., Nancy Whittier, and Belinda Robnett. 2002. *Social Movements: Identity, Culture, and the State*. New York: Oxford University Press.

Michael, Robert, John Gagnon, Edward Laumann, and Gina Kolata. 1994. *Sex in America: A Definitive Survey*. Boston: Little, Brown, and Company.

Milanovic, Branko. 2005. *Worlds Apart: Measuring International and Global Inequality*. Princeton, NJ: Princeton University Press.

Milanovic, Branko. 2006. "Global Income Inequality: What It Is and Why It Matters." Policy Research Working Paper No. WPS 3865. The World Bank, Washington, DC.

Milanovic, Branko. 2007. "Where In the World Are You? Assessing the Importance of Circumstances and Effort in a World of Different Mean Country Incomes and (Almost) No Migration." Policy Research Working Paper No. 12321, The World Bank, Washington, DC.

Milkman, Ruth. 2008. "Filling the Bottom of the Hourglass." Presented at the DePaul University and McCormick Tribune Foundation Conference, "Economic Inequality and the Hourglass Economy." Egan Urban Center, DePaul University, April 2–3, Chicago, IL.

Miller, James. 1994. *The Passion of Michel Foucault*. New York: Anchor.

Mills, C. Wright. 1940. "Situated Actions and Vocabularies of Motives." *American Sociological Review* 5: 904–913.

Mills, C. Wright. [1954] 1963. "Mass Society and Liberal Education." Pp. 353–373 in *Power, Politics and People*, edited by Irving L. Horowitz. New York: Ballantine Books.

Mills, C. Wright. [1959] 2000. *The Sociological Imagination*. New York: Oxford University Press.

Mishell, Larry. 2008. "Work Inequality and Stagnation: Skill or Power Shortage?" Presented at the DePaul University and McCormick Tribune Foundation Conference, "Economic Inequality and the Hourglass Economy." Egan Urban Center, DePaul University, April 2–3, Chicago, IL.

Mitchell, Juliet. 1975. *Psychoanalysis and Feminism: Freud, Reich, Laing and Women*. New York: Vintage Books.

Mollenkopf, John. 1983. *The Contested City*. Princeton, NJ: Princeton University Press.

Molotch, Harvey and Marilyn Lester. 1974. "Accidents, Scandals, and Routines: Resources for Insurgent Methodology." Pp. 53–65 in *The TV Establishment*, edited by Gaye Tuchman. Englewood Cliffs, NJ: Prentice-Hall.

Moynihan, Daniel Patrick. 1965. *The Negro Family: The Case for National Action*. Washington, DC: U.S. Department of Labor.

Navarro, Vicente and Carles Muntaner. 2004. *Political and Economic Determinants of Population Health and Well-Being: Controversies and Developments*. Amityville, NY: Baywood Publishing.

Nehamas, Alexander. 1998. *The Art of Living: Socratic Reflections from Plato to Foucault*. Berkeley, CA: University of California Press.

Oberti, Marco. 2005. "School Choice in Paris." Presented at the Conference of Comparative Perspectives on Urban Segregation: Paris, Rio, and Chicago, DePaul University, June 3–4, Chicago, IL.

Oberti, Marco. 2007. "Reforming the *Carte Scolaire*." *Compte Rendu* of the Centre de Recherches Politicques de Sciences-Po, November 11.

O'Leary, Timothy. 2002. *Foucault and the Art of Ethics*. London: Continuum.

Omi, Michael and Howard Winant. 1994. *Racial Formation in the United States from the 1960s to the 1980s*. New York: Routledge.

Pakulski, Jan. 2005. "Foundations of a Post-Class Analysis." Pp. 152–179 in *Approaches to Class Analysis*, edited by Erik Olin Wright. New York: Cambridge University Press.

Parenti, Michael. 1986. *Inventing Reality: The Politics of the Mass Media.* New York: St. Martin's Press.

Park, Robert and Ernest Burgess. 1925. *The City.* Chicago, IL: University of Chicago Press.

Parsons, Talcott. [1937] 1961. *The Structure of Social Action.* Glencoe, IL: Free Press.

Parsons, Talcott. [1951] 1968. *The Social System.* Glencoe, IL: Free Press.

Pattillo. Mary. 1999. *Black Picket Fences.* Chicago: University of Chicago Press.

Pattillo, Mary. 2008. *Black on the Block.* Chicago: University of Chicago Press.

Perdue, Theda. 2003. *'Mixed Blood' Indians: Racial Construction in the Early South.* Athens, GA: University of Georgia Press.

Perrow, Charles. 1999. *Normal Accidents.* Princeton, NJ: Princeton University Press.

Perrucci, Robert and Earl Wysong. 1999. *The New Class Society.* Lanham, MD: Rowman and Littlefield.

Piketty, Thomas and Emmanuel Saez. 2003. "Income Inequality in the United States 1913–1998." *Quarterly Journal of Economics* 118(1): 1–39.

Pitts, Victoria. 2003. *In the Flesh: The Cultural Politics of Body Modification.* New York: Palgrave Macmillan.

Powdermaker, Hortense. 1950. *Hollywood: The Dream Factory.* Boston: Little Brown.

Przeworski, Adam. 1991. *Democracy and the Market.* Cambridge: Cambridge University Press.

Puentes, Robert and David Warren. 2006. *One-Fifth of America: A Comprehensive Guide to America's First Suburbs.* Washington: Brookings Institution.

Putnam, Robert. 2001. *Bowling Alone: The Collapse and Revival of American Community.* New York: Simon and Schuster.

Quinney, Richard. 1974. *Critique of Legal Order: Crime Control in Capitalist Society.* Boston: Little Brown.

Rangaswamy, Padma. 2006a. "Asian Indians in Chicago." Pp. 128–140 in *The New Chicago,* edited by J.P. Koval. Philadelphia: Temple University Press.

Rangaswamy, Padma. 2006b. "Devon Avenue: A World Market." Pp. 221–230 in *The New Chicago,* edited by J.P. Koval. Philadelphia: Temple University Press.

Reich, Robert. 1991. *The Work of Nations.* New York: Alfred A. Knopf.

Riesebrodt, Martin. [1993] 1998. *Pious Passion: The Emergence of Modern Fundamentalism in the United States and Iran.* Berkeley, CA: University of California Press.

Riesman, David, Nathan Glazer, and Reuel Denney. 1961. *The Lonely Crowd.* New Haven, CT: Yale University Press.

Ritzer, George. 1996a. *Sociological Theory.* New York: McGraw-Hill.

Ritzer, George. 1996b. *The McDonaldization of Society.* Thousand Oaks, CA: Pine Forge Press.

Roberts, Kenneth. 1999. *Deepening Democracy: The Modern Left and Social Movements in Chile and Peru.* Stanford, CA: Stanford University Press.

Roediger, David. 1999. *The Wages of Whiteness: Race and the Making of the American Working Class.* Rev. ed. London: Verso.

Rorty, R. 1979. *Philosophy and the Mirror of Nature.* Princeton, NJ: Princeton University Press.

Rosaldo, Renato. 2004. "Grief and a Headhunter's Rage." Pp. 579–593 in *Anthropological Theory: An Introductory History*, 3rd ed., edited by Jon R. McGee and Richard L. Warms. New York: McGraw-Hill.

Said, Edward. 1979. *Orientalism*. New York: Vintage.

Sassen, Saskia. 2000. "The Global City: Strategic Site/New Frontier." *American Studies* 41(2/3): 79–95.

Sassen, Saskia. 2001. *The Global City*. Princeton: Princeton University Press.

Schlesinger, Traci. 2009. "The Failure of Race-Neutral Policies: How Mandatory Terms and Sentence Enhancements Increased Racial Disparities in Prison Admission Rates." *Crime and Delinquency*.

Schor, Juliet. 1998. *The Overspent American*. New York: Harper-Collins.

Schor, Juliet and Douglas B. Holt. 2000. *The Consumer Society Reader*. New York: The New Press.

Schudson, Michael. 1981. *Discovering the News. A Social History of American Newspapers*. New York: Basic Books.

Schudson, Michael. 1986. *Advertising: The Uneasy Persuasion*. New York: Basic Books.

Scott, James. 1987. *Weapons of the Weak: Everyday Forms of Peasant Resistance*. New Haven, CT: Yale University Press.

Sennett, Richard. 1998. *The Corrosion of Character: The Personal Consequences of Work in the New Capitalism*. New York: W.W. Norton.

Simmel, Georg. [1950] 1978. "The. Metropolis and Mental Life." Pp. 409–426 in *The Sociology of Georg Simmel*, translated and edited by Kurt H. Wolff. New York: Simon and Schuster.

Skocpol, Theda. 1979. *States and Social Revolutions: A Comparative Analysis of France, Russia, and China*. Cambridge: Cambridge University Press.

Skocpol, Theda. 2002. "Will 9/11 and the War on Terror Revitalize American Civic Democracy." *PS: Political Science & Politics* 35: 537–540.

Skocpol, Theda. 2005. "David Brooks, Champion of the People?" *Salon Online*, February 8.

Smith, Dorothy E. 1990. *The Conceptual Practices of Power: A Feminist Sociology of Knowledge*. Lebanon, NH: University Press of New England.

Smith, Neil. 1996. *The New Urban Frontier: Gentrification and the Revanchist City*. New York: Routledge.

Snow, David and Leon Anderson. 1993. *Down on Their Luck: A Study of Homeless Street People*. Berkeley, CA: University of California Press.

Soja, Edward. 1996. "Los Angeles 1965–1992: The Six Geographies of Urban Restructuring." Pp. 426–462 in *The City: Los Angeles and Urban Theory at the End of the Twentieth Century*, edited by A.J. Scott and E.W. Soja. Berkeley: University of California Press.

Spirou, Costas and Larry Bennett. 2003. *It's Hardly Sporting: Stadiums, Neighborhoods, and the New Chicago*. DeKalb, IL: Northern Illinois University Press.

Strauss, Anselm. 1959. *Mirrors and Masks: The Search for Identity*. Glencoe, IL: Free Press.

Sutherland, Edwin. 1949. *White Collar Crime*. New York: Dryden Press.

Szelenyi, Ivan and Janos Ladanyi. 2006. *Patterns of Exclusion: Constructing Gypsy Ethnicity and the Making of an Underclass in Transitional Societies of Europe*. Boulder, CO: East European Monographs.

Takaki, Ronald. 1994. *A Different Mirror: A History of Multicultural America*. Boston: Back Bay Books.

Tarrow, Sidney. 1998. *Power in Movement*. Cambridge: Cambridge University Press.

Taussig, Michael. 1985. *The Devil and Commodity Fetishism in South America*. Chapel Hill: The University of North Carolina Press.

Thomas, William I. and Florian Znaniecki. [1958] 1996. *The Polish Peasant*. Urbana, IL: University of Illinois Press.

Thompson, E.P. 1966. *The Making of the English Working Class*. New York: Vintage.

Thorne, Barrie. 1993. *Gender Play: Girls and Boys in School*. New Brunswick, NJ: Rutgers University Press.

Tuchman, Gaye. 1980. *Making News: A Study in the Construction of Reality*. New York: Free Press.

Turkle, Sherry. 1997. *Identity in the Age of the Internet*. New York: Simon and Schuster.

Turner, Jonathan H. 2003. *The Structure of Sociological Theory*. 7th ed. California: Thomson Wadsworth.

Vaughan, Diane. 1990. *Uncoupling: Turning Points in Intimate Relationships*. New York: Vintage.

Vaughan, Diane. 1996. *The Challenger Launch Decision: Risky Technology, Culture, and Deviance at NASA*. Chicago, IL: University of Chicago Press.

Venkatesh, Sudhir. 2002. *American Project: The Rise and Fall of a Modern Ghetto*. Cambridge, MA: Harvard University Press.

Venkatesh, Sudhir. 2006. *Off the Books: The Underground Economy of the Urban Poor*. Cambridge, MA: Harvard University Press.

Wacquant, Loïc. [1993] 2005. "Urban Outcasts: Stigma and Division in the Black American Ghetto and the French Urban Periphery." Pp. 144–151 in *The Urban Sociology Reader*, edited by Jan Lin and Christopher Mele. London: Routledge.

Wacquant, Loïc. 2002. "Scrutinizing the Street: Poverty, Morality, and the Pitfalls of Urban Ethnography." *The American Journal of Sociology* 107(6): 1468–1532.

Wacquant, Loïc. 2004. *Body and Soul*. New York: Oxford University Press.

Wacquant, Loïc. [2004] 2008. *Punishing the Poor: The New Government of Social Insecurity*. Durham, NC: Duke University Press.

Wacquant, Loïc. 2007. *Urban Outcasts: A Comparative Sociology of Advanced Marginality*. Cambridge, MA: Polity Press.

Wacquant, Loïc. 2008a. *Deadly Symbiosis: Race and the Rise of the Penal State*. Cambridge, MA: Polity Press.

Wacquant, Loïc. 2008b. "The Body, the Ghetto, and the Penal State [Interview]." *Qualitative Sociology Online*, 17 September.

Wallerstein, Immanuel. 1974. *The Modern World System*. New York: Academic Press.

Warner, Bijan. 2006. "Measuring Income Mobility Among Nations from 1950 to 2000: An Inquiry into Nation-State Stratification." DePaul University, Chicago, IL. Unpublished manuscript.

Weber, Max. [1946] 1958. "Class, Status, and Party." Pp. 180–195 in *From Max Weber: Essays in Sociology*, edited by Hans H. Gerth and C.W. Mills. Oxford: Oxford University Press.

Weber, Max. [1958] 2003. *Protestant Ethic and the Spirit of Capitalism*. Translated by Talcott Parsons. Mineola, NY: Dover Publications.

Weinstein, Deena and Michael Weinstein. 1993. *Postmodern(ized) Simmel*. New York: Routledge.

Western, Bruce. 2006. *Imprisonment and Inequality in America*. New York: Russell Sage Foundation.

Williams, Gareth. 2002. *The Other Side of the Popular: Neo-liberalism and Subalternity in Latin America*. Durham, NC: Duke University Press.

Williams, Rhys. 2002. "From the 'Beloved Community' to 'Family Values' Religious Language, Symbolic Repertoire and Democratic Culture." Pp. 247–265 in *Social Movements: Identity, Culture, and the State,* edited by David S. Meyer, Nancy Whittier, and Belinda Robnett. New York: Oxford University Press.

Willis, Paul, Simon Jones, Joyce Canaan, and Geoff Hurd. 1990. *Common Culture: Symbolic Work at Play in the Everyday Cultures of the Young*. Maidenhead, Berkshire, UK: Open University Press.

Wilson, Elizabeth. 1992. "The Invisible Flaneur." *New Left Review* 191: 90–110.

Wilson, William Julius. 1996. *When Work Disappears*. New York: Random House.

Winant, Howard. 2004. *The New Politics of Race: Globalization Difference Justice*. Minneapolis, MN: University of Minnesota Press.

Wolf, Eric R. 1982. *Europe and the People Without History*. Berkeley, CA: The University of California Press.

Wolf, Eric R. 1999. *Peasant Wars of the Twentieth Century*. Norman, OK: The University of Oklahoma Press.

Wright, Erik Olin. 2006. "Foundations of a Neo-Marxist Class Analysis." Pp. 4–30 in *Approaches to Class Analysis*. New York and Cambridge: Cambridge University Press.

Yanow, Dvora. 2003. *Constructing 'Race' and 'Ethnicity' in America: Category-Making in Public Policy and Administration*. Armonk, NY: M.E. Sharpe.

Zerubavel, Eviatar. 1999. *Social Mindscapes: An Invitation to Cognitive Sociology*. Cambridge, MA: Harvard University Press.

Zinn, Maxine Baca and Bonnie Thornton Dill. 1990. *'Difference and Domination' in Women of Color in U.S. Society*. Philadelphia: Temple University Press.

Zukin, Sharon. 1991. *Landscapes of Power: From Detroit to Disneyland*. Berkeley, CA: University of California Press.

REFERENCES AND READING SUGGESTIONS FOR THE TRANSITIONAL GIANTS

This section follows the organization of the chapters, presenting works by and about Erving Goffman, Michel Foucault, Pierre Bourdieu, and Stuart Hall. Citations within the bibliography for each transitional giant are arranged so that works by the individual come first, followed by works about that scholar.

ERVING GOFFMAN

Primary Materials

Goffman, Erving. 1959. *The Presentation of Self in Everyday Life*. Garden City, NY: Anchor Books.

Goffman, Erving. 1961a. *Asylums: Essays on the Social Situation of Mental Patients and Other Inmates*. Garden City, NY: Anchor Books

Goffman, Erving. 1961b. *Encounters: Two Studies in the Sociology of Interaction*. Indianapolis, IN: Bobbs-Merrill.

Goffman, Erving. 1963a. *Behavior in Public Places: Notes on the Social Organization of Gatherings*. New York: Free Press.

Goffman, Erving. 1963b. *Stigma: Notes on the Management of Spoiled Identity*. Englewood Cliffs, NJ: Prentice-Hall.

Goffman, Erving. 1967. *Interaction Ritual: Essays on Face-to-Face Behavior*. Garden City, NY: Anchor.

Goffman, Erving. 1971. *Relations in Public: Microstudies of the Public Order*. New York: Basic Books.

Goffman, Erving. 1974. *Frame Analysis: an Essay on the Organization of Experience*. New York: Harper & Row.

Goffman, Erving. [1979] 1988. *Gender Advertisements*. Rev. ed. New York: Harper Collins.

Goffman, Erving. 1981. *Forms of Talk*. Philadelphia: University of Pennsylvania Press.

Secondary Sources and Works Cited

Fine, Gary Alan and Gregory W.H. Smith, eds. 2000. *Erving Goffman: Sage Masters of Modern Social Thought*. 4 volumes. London: Sage.

Ditton, Jason, ed. 1980. *The View from Goffman*. New York: St. Martin's Press.

Drew, Paul and Anthony Wooton, eds. 1988. *Erving Goffman: Exploring the Interaction Order*. Cambridge: Polity Press.

Gamson, William A. 1985. "Goffman's Legacy to Political Sociology." *Theory and Society* 14: 605-622.

Manning, Philip. 1992. *Erving Goffman and Modern Sociology*. New York: Polity Press.

Marx, Gary T. 1984. "Role Models and Role Distance: A Remembrance of Erving Goffman." *Theory and Society* 13: 649–662.

Riggins, Stephen Harold. 1990. *Beyond Goffman: Studies on Communication, Institutions, and Social Interaction*. New York: Walter de Gruyter.

Smith, Greg, ed. 1999. *Goffman and Social Organization: Studies in a Sociological Legacy*. New York: Routledge.

MICHEL FOUCAULT

Primary Materials

Bouchard, Donald F., ed. 1977. *Michel Foucault: Language, Counter-Memory, Practice: Selected Essays and Interviews*. Ithaca, NY: Cornell University Press.

Foucault, Michel. 1965. *Madness and Civilization: A History of Insanity in the Age of Reason*. New York: Vintage.

Foucault, Michel. 1966. *The Order of Things: An Archaeology of the Human Sciences*. New York: Vintage.

Foucault, Michel. 1969. *The Archaeology of Knowledge and the Discourse of Language*. New York: Harper Collophon Books.

Foucault, Michel. 1975. *The Birth of the Clinic: An Archaeology of Medical Perception*. New York: Vintage.

Foucault, Michel. 1979. *Discipline and Punish: The Birth of the Prison*. New York: Vintage.

Foucault, Michel. 1980. *The History of Sexuality*. Vol. 1, *An Introduction*. New York: Vintage.

Foucault, Michel. 1980. *Power/Knowledge: Selected Interviews and Other Writings, 1972-1977*. Edited by C. Gordon. New York: Pantheon.

Foucault, Michel. 1985. *The History of Sexuality*. Vol. 2, *The Use of Pleasure*. New York: Random House.

Foucault, Michel. 1986. *The History of Sexuality*. Vol. 3, *The Care of the Self*. New York: Random House.

Foucault, Michel. 1990. *Politics, Philosophy, Culture: Interviews and Other Writings*. New York: Routledge.

Foucault, Michel. 1997. *Essential Works of Foucault, 1945-1984*. Vol. 1, *Ethics: Subjectivity and Truth*. Edited by P. Rabinow. New York: The New Press.

Foucault, Michel. 1997. *Essential Works of Foucault, 1945-1984*. Vol. 2, *Aesthetics, Method, and Epistemology*. Edited by J.D. Faubion and P. Rabinow (Series Editor). New York: The New Press.

Foucault, Michel. 1999. *Essential Works of Foucault, 1945-1984*. Vol. 3, *Power*. Edited by C. Gordon and P. Rabinow (Series Editor). New York: The New Press.

Secondary Sources and Works Cited

Burchell, Graham, Colin Gordon, and Peter Miller. 1991. *The Foucault Effect: Studies in Governmentality*. Chicago: University of Chicago Press.

Butler, Judith. 1990. *Gender Trouble: Feminism and the Subversion of Identity*. New York: Routledge.

Butler, Judith. 1993. *Bodies That Matter*. New York. Routledge.

Butler, Judith. 2004. *Undoing Gender*. New York: Routledge.

Davidson, Arnold. 1994. Ethics as Aesthetics: Foucault, The History of Ideas and Ancient Thought." Pp. 115–140 in *The Cambridge Companion to Foucault*, edited by Gary Gutting. Cambridge: Cambridge University Press.

Deleuze, Gilles. 1986. *Foucault*. Minneapolis: University of Minnesota Press.

D'Emilio. John. 1983. "Capitalism and Gay Identity." Pp. 100–113 in *Powers of Desire: The Politics of Sexuality*, edited by Ann Snitow, Christine Stansell, and Sharon Thompson. New York: Monthly Review Press.

Dreyfus, Hubert and Paul Rabinow. 1982. *Michel Foucault: Beyond Structuralism and Hermeneutics*. Chicago: University of Chicago Press.

Gutting, Gary. 1994. *The Cambridge Companion to Foucault*. Cambridge: Cambridge University Press.

Herdt, Gilbert. 1987. *The Sambia: Ritual and Gender in New Guinea*. Orlando: Holt, Rinehart and Winston.

Light, Donald. 2001. "Cost Containment and the Backdraft of Competition Politics." Pp. 173–200 in *Political and Economic Determinants of Population Health and Well-Being: Controversies and Developments*, edited by Vincente Navarro and Cales Muntaner. Amityville, NY: Baywood Publishing.

Macey, David. 1993. *The Lives of Michel Foucault*. New York: Random House.

Maloutas, Thomas. 2007. "Segregation, Social Polarization and Immigration in Athens during the 1990s." *International Journal of Urban and Regional Research* 31: 733–758.

Miller, James. 1994. *The Passion of Michel Foucault*. New York: Anchor Books.

Nehamas, Alexander. 1998. *The Art of Living*. Berkeley, CA: University of California Press.

Nietzsche, Friedrich. [1887] 2001. *The Gay Science*. Cambridge: Cambridge University Press.

Oberti, Marco. 2005. "School Choice in Paris." Presented at the Conference of Comparative Perspectives on Urban Segregation: Paris, Rio, and Chicago, DePaul University, June 3–4, Chicago, IL.

O'Leary, Timothy. 2002. *Foucault and the Art of Ethics*. London: Continuum.

Paras, Eric. 2006. *Foucault 2.0*. New York: Other Press.

Pasquino, Pasquale. 1991. "Theatrum politicum: The genealogy of capital—police and the state of prosperity." Pp. 105–119 in *The Foucault Effect*, edited by G. Burchell, M. Foucault, C. Gordon, and P. Miller. Chicago: University of Chicago Press.

Rabinow, Paul. *The Foucault Reader*. New York: Pantheon.

Scott, James. 1987. *Weapons of the Weak: Everyday Forms of Peasant Resistance*. New Haven, CT: Yale University Press.

Simmel, Georg. [1911] 1949. "The Sociology of Sociability." *American Journal of Sociology* 55(3): 254–261.

Smart, Barry. 1985. *Michel Foucault*. London: Tavistock Publications.

Tucker, Robert C., ed. 1999. *The Marx-Engels Reader*. New York: Norton.

Visker, Rudi. 1995. *Michel Foucault: Genealogy as Critique*. New York: Verso.

White Hayden. 1979. "Michel Foucault." Pp. 81–115 in *Structuralism and Since: From Levi-Strauss to Derrida*, edited by John Sturrock. New York: Oxford University Press.

PIERRE BOURDIEU

Primary Materials

Bourdieu, Pierre. 1958. *Sociologie de L'Algérie*. Paris: Presses Universitaires de France.

Bourdieu, Pierre. 1977a. "Cultural reproduction and social reproduction. " Pp. 487–511 in *Power and Ideology in Education*, edited by Jerome Karabel and A.H. Halsey. New York: Oxford University Press.

Bourdieu, Pierre. 1977b. *Outline of a Theory of Practice*. Translated by Richard Nice. Cambridge: Cambridge University Press.

Bourdieu, Pierre. 1984. *Distinction: A Social Critique of the Judgment of Taste*. Translated by R. Nice. Cambridge, MA: Harvard University Press.

Bourdieu, Pierre. 1986. "The Form of Capital." Pp. 241–258 in *Handbook of Theory and Research for the Sociology of Education*, edited by J. Richardson. New York: Greenwood Press.

Bourdieu, Pierre. 1988. *Homo Academicus*. Translated by P. Collier. Stanford, CA: Stanford University Press.

Bourdieu, Pierre. 1989a. *La Noblesse d'État: Grands Écoles et Esprit de Corps*. Paris: Editions de Minuit.

Bourdieu, Pierre. 1989b. "The Corporatism of the Universal: The Role of Intellectuals in the Modern World." Translated by C. Betensky. *Telos* 81: 99–110.

Bourdieu, Pierre. 1990a. "Critique of theoretical reason." Pp. 23–143 in *The Logic of Practice*, edited and translated by Richard Nice. Palo Alto, CA: Stanford University Press.

Bourdieu, Pierre. 1990b. *In Other Words: Essays Towards a Reflexive Sociology*. Translated by M. Adamson. Stanford, CA: Stanford University Press.

Bourdieu, Pierre. 1990c. *The Logic of Practice*. Translated by R. Nice. Palo Alto, CA: Stanford University Press.

Bourdieu, Pierre. 1991. *Language and Symbolic Power*. Edited by J.B. Thompson and translated by G. Raymond and M. Adamson. Cambridge, MA: Harvard University Press.

Bourdieu, Pierre. 1993a. *Sociology in Question*. Translated by R. Nice. Thousand Oaks, CA: Sage.

Bourdieu, Pierre. 1993b. "Concluding Remarks: For a Sociogenetic Understanding of Intellectual Works." Pp. 263–275 in *Bourdieu: Critical Perspectives*, edited by C. Calhoun, E. LiPuma, and M. Postone. Chicago, IL: University of Chicago Press.

Bourdieu, Pierre. 1993c. *The Field of Cultural Production*. Edited by R. Johnson. New York: Columbia University Press.

Bourdieu, Pierre. 1996a. *The State of Nobility: Elite Schools in the Field of Power*. Translated by L.C. Clough. Palo Alto, CA: Stanford University Press.

Bourdieu, Pierre. 1996b. *The Rules of Art: Genesis and Structure of the Literary Field*. Translated by S. Emanuel. Palo Alto, CA: Stanford University Press.

Bourdieu, Pierre. 1998a. *Practical Reason*. Translated by G. Sapiro, B. McHale, and R. Johnson. Palo Alto, CA: Stanford University Press.

Bourdieu, Pierre. 1998b. *On Television*. Translated by P.P. Ferguson. New York: New Press.

Bourdieu, Pierre. 1998c. *Acts of Resistance: Against the Tyranny of the Market*. Translated by R. Nice. New York: New Press.

Bourdieu, Pierre. 1998d. "A Reasoned Utopia and Economic Fatalism." Translated by J. Howe. *New Left Review* 227: 125–30.

Bourdieu, Pierre. 1998e. "Utopia of Endless Exploitation: The Essence of Neoliberalism." *Le Monde Diplomatique*, December 1998, 18 paragraphs. Retrieved October 30, 2008 (http://www.mondediplo.com/1998/12/08).

Bourdieu, Pierre. 1998f. "At the Heart of Any Political Battle: On Male Domination." Translated by E. Emery. *Le Monde Diplomatique*, October 1998, 14 paragraphs. Retrieved June 26, 2003 (http://www.mondediplo.com/1998/10/10).

Bourdieu, Pierre. 1999a. "On the Cunning of Imperialist Reason." *Theory, Culture & Society* 16(1): 41–58.

Bourdieu, Pierre, ed. 1999b. *The Weight of the World*. Translated by P.P. Ferguson (translation editor), S. Emanuel, J. Johnson, and S.T. Waryn. Palo Alto, CA: Stanford University Press.

Bourdieu, Pierre. 2000a. *Pascalian Meditations*. Translated by R. Nice. Palo Alto, CA: Stanford University Press.

Bourdieu, Pierre. 2000b. "Participant Objectivation." Given in receipt of the Aldous Huxley Medal for Anthropology, November 12, University of London, London, UK.

Bourdieu, Pierre. 2001. *Masculine Domination*. Translated by R. Nice. Palo Alto, CA: Stanford University Press.

Bourdieu, Pierre. 2002a. "Against the Policy of Depoliticization." *Studies in Political Economy* 69: 31–41.

Bourdieu, Pierre. 2002b. "The Politics of Globalisation." *Open Democracy Web Site*, February 20. Retrieved October 30, 2008 (http://www.opendemocracy.net/globalization-vision_reflections/article_283.jsp).

Bourdieu, Pierre. 2003. *Firing Back: Against the Tyranny of the Market 2*. Translated by L. Wacquant. New York: New Press.

Bourdieu, Pierre, Jean-Claude Chamboredon, and Jean-Claude Passeron. 1991. *The Craft of Sociology*. Translated by R. Nice. Berlin, Germany: Walter de Gruyter.

Bourdieu, Pierre and Loïc Wacquant. 1992. *An Invitation to Reflexive Sociology*. Chicago, IL: University of Chicago Press.

Bourdieu, Pierre and Loïc Wacquant. 2001. "New Liberal Speak: Notes on the New Planetary Vulgate." *Radical Philosophy* 105: 2–5.

Bourdieu, Pierre, Loïc Wacquant, and Samar Farage. 1994. "Rethinking the State: Genesis and Structure of the Bureaucratic Field." *Sociological Theory* 12: 1–19.

Secondary Sources and Works Cited

Carles, Pierre. 2001. *Sociology is a Martial Art*. Documentary film. New York: First Run/
Icarus Films.

Debray, Regis. 1979. "A Modest Contribution to the Rite and Ceremonies of the Tenth
Anniversary." *New Left Review* 115: 45–65.

Derrida, Jacques. 1994. "Spectres of Marx." *New Left Review* 205: 31–59.

Khurana, Rakesh. 2002. *Searching for a Corporate Savior: The Irrational Quest for Charismatic
CEOs*. Princeton, NJ: Princeton University Press.

Macey, D. 1993. *The Lives of Michel Foucault*. London: Hutchinson.

Mishell, Larry. 2008. "Work Inequality and Stagnation: Skill or Power Shortage?" Presented at the
DePaul University and McCormick Tribune Foundation Conference, "Economic Inequality
and the Hourglass Economy." Egan Urban Center, DePaul University, April 2–3, Chicago, IL.

Putnam, Robert. 2001. *Bowling Alone: The Collapse and Revival of American Community*.
New York: Simon and Schuster.

Swartz, David. 1997. *Culture and Power: The Sociology of Pierre Bourdieu*. Chicago: The
University of Chicago Press.

Tarrow, Sidney. 1998. *Power in Movement*. Cambridge: Cambridge University Press.

Venkatesh, Sudhir. 2002. *American Project: The Rise and Fall of a Modern Ghetto*. Cambridge,
MA: Harvard University Press.

Venkatesh, Sudhir. 2006. *Off the Books: The Underground Economy of the Urban Poor*.
Cambridge, MA: Harvard University Press.

Wacquant, Loïc. [1993] 2005. "Urban Outcasts: Stigma and Division in the Black American
Ghetto and the French Urban Periphery." Pp. 144–151 in *The Urban Sociology Reader*,
edited by Jan Lin and Christopher Mele. London: Routledge.

Wacquant, Loïc. 2004. "Critical Thought as Solvent of Doxa." *Constellations* 11: 97–101.

Wacquant, Loïc, ed. 2005. *Pierre Bourdieu and Democratic Politics*. Malden, MA: Polity Press.

Wacquant, Loïc. 2008a. *Deadly Symbiosis : Race and the Rise of the Penal State*. Cambridge,
MA: Polity Press.

STUART HALL

Primary Materials

Hall, Stuart. 1977. "Culture, the Media and the Ideological Effect." Pp. 315–348 in *Mass Communication and Society*, edited by J. Curran, M. Gurevitch, and J. Wollacott. London:
Edward Arnold.

Hall, Stuart. 1980a. "Cultural Studies: Two Paradigms." *Media, Culture and Society*
2: 57–72.

Hall, Stuart. 1980b. "Cultural Studies and the Centre: Some Problematics and Problems." Pp. 15–47 in *Culture, Media, Language*. London: Hutchinson.

Hall, Stuart. 1980c. "Encoding/Decoding" Pp. 128–38 in *Culture, Media, Language*. London: Hutchinson.

Hall, Stuart. 1980d "Nikos Poulantzas: State, Power, Socialism." *New Left Review* 119: 60–69.

Hall, Stuart. 1980e. "Race, Articulation and Societies Structured in Dominance." Pp. 305–45 in *Sociological Theories: Race and Colonialism*. Paris: UNESCO.

Hall, Stuart. 1981a. "The Whites of Their Eyes: Racist Ideologies and the Media." Pp. 28–52 in *Silver Linings: Some Strategies for the Eighties*, edited by G. Bridges and R. Brunt. London: Lawrence & Wishart.

Hall, Stuart. 1981b. "Notes on Deconstructing 'The Popular.'" Pp. 227–240 in *People's History and Socialist Theory*, edited by R. Samuel. London: Routledge.

Hall, Stuart. 1982. "The Rediscovery of 'Ideology': Return of the Repressed in Media Studies." Pp. 56–90 in *Culture, Society and the Media*, edited by M. Gurevitch, T. Bennett, J. Curran, and J. Woollacott. London: Methuen.

Hall, Stuart. 1985. "Signification, Representation, Ideology: Althusser and the Post-Structuralist Debates." *Critical Theories of Mass Communication* 2: 91–114.

Hall, Stuart. [1986] 1996. "The Problem of Ideology: Marxism without Guarantees." Pp. 25–46 in *Stuart Hall: Critical Dialogues in Cultural Studies*, edited by D. Morley and K. Chen. London: Routledge.

Hall, Stuart. 1987. "Minimal Selves." Pp. 44–46 in *Identity: The Real Me*. ICA Documents 6. London: Institute of Contemporary Art.

Hall, Stuart. [1988a] 1996. "New Ethnicities." Pp. 441–449 in *Stuart Hall: Critical Dialogues in Cultural Studies*, edited by D. Morley and K. Chen. London: Routledge.

Hall, Stuart. 1988b. *The Hard Road to Renewal: Thatcherism and the Crisis of the Left*. London: Verso.

Hall, Stuart. 1988c. "The Toad in the Garden: Thatcherism Amongst the Theorists." Pp. 35–73 in *Marxism and the Interpretation of Culture*, edited by C. Nelson and L. Grossberg. Urbana: University of Illinois Press.

Hall, Stuart. 1989a. "Cultural Identity and Cinematic Representation." *Framework* 36: 68–82.

Hall, Stuart. 1990. "Cultural Identity and Diaspora." In *Identity Community, Culture, Difference*, ed. Jonathan Rutherford. London: Lawrence & Wishart.

Hall, Stuart. 1991a. "The Local and the Global: Globalization and Ethnicity." Pp. 19–39 in *Culture, Globalization and the World-System: Contemporary Conditions for the Representation of Identity*, edited by A. King. Basingstoke: Macmillan.

Hall, Stuart. 1991b. "Old and New Identities, Old and New Ethnicities." Pp. 41–68 in *Culture, Globalization and the World-System: Contemporary Conditions for the Representation of Identity*, edited by A. King. Basingstoke: Macmillan.

Hall, Stuart. 1991c. "Brave New World." *Socialist Review* 21: 57–64.

Hall, Stuart. 1992a. "What is this 'Black' in Black Popular Culture?" Pp. 21–33 in *Black Popular Culture*, edited by Gina Dent. Seattle: Bay Press.

Hall, Stuart. 1992b. "Cultural Studies and its Theoretical Legacies." Pp. 277–294 in *Cultural Studies*, edited by L. Grossberg, C. Nelson, and P. Treichler. New York: Routledge.

Hall, Stuart. 1992c. "The Question of Cultural Identity." Pp. 274–316 in *Modernity and its Future*, edited by S. Hall, D. Held, and T. McGrew. Cambridge: Polity Press.

Hall, Stuart. 1993a. "Cultural Identity and Diaspora." Pp. 392–401 in *Colonial Discourse and Post-Colonial Theory*, edited by P. Williams and L. Chrisman. London: Harvester Wheatsheaf.

Hall, Stuart. 1993b. "Reflections upon the Encoding/Decoding Model: An Interview with Stuart Hall." Pp. 253–274 in *Viewing, Reading, Listening: Audiences and Cultural Reception*, edited by J. Cruz and J. Lewis. Boulder, CO: Westview.

Hall, Stuart. 1995a. "Authoritarian Populism: A Reply to Jessop et al." *New Left Review* 151: 115–124.

Hall, Stuart. 1995b. "Negotiating Caribbean Identities." *New Left Review* 209: 3–14.

Hall, Stuart. 1996a. "Introduction: Who Needs 'Identity'?" Pp. 1–17 in *Questions of Cultural Identity*, edited by S. Hall and P. Du Gay. London: Sage.

Hall, Stuart. 1996b. "When was 'The Post-Colonial'? Thinking at the Limit." Pp. 242–260 in *The Post-Colonial Question: Common Skies, Divided Horizons*, edited by I. Chambers and L. Curti. London: Routledge.

Hall, Stuart. 1996c. "For Allon White: Metaphors of Transformation." Pp. 287–305 in *Stuart Hall: Critical Dialogues in Cultural Studies*, edited by D. Morley and K. Chen. London: Routledge.

Hall, Stuart. 1996d. "The Formation of a Diasporic Intellectual: An Interview with Stuart Hall by Kuan-Hsing Chen." Pp. 484–503 in *Stuart Hall: Critical Dialogues in Cultural Studies*, edited by D. Morley and K. Chen. London: Routledge.

Hall, Stuart, ed. 1997a. *Representation: Cultural Representations and Signifying Practices*. London: Sage Publications.

Hall, Stuart. 1997b. "Subjects in History: Making Diasporic Identities." Pp. 289–99 in *The House that Race Built*, edited by W. Lubiano. New York: Pantheon Books.

Hall, Stuart. 1997c. "The Centrality of Culture: Notes on the Cultural Revolutions of Our Time." Pp. 208–238 in *Media and Cultural Regulation*, edited by K. Thompson. London: Sage.

Hall, Stuart. 2000. "The Multicultural Question." Pp. 209–241 in *Un/settled Multiculturalisms*, edited by B. Hesse. London: Zed Books.

Hall, Stuart, C. Critcher, T. Jefferson, J. Clarke, and B. Roberts. 1978. *Policing the Crisis*. London: Macmillan.

Hall, Stuart, D. Hobson, A. Lowe, and P. Willis. 1980. *Culture, Media, Language: Working Papers in Cultural Studies*. London: Hutchinson.

Hall, Stuart and Martin Jacques, eds. 1989. *New Times: The Changing Face of Politics in the 1990's*. London: Lawrence & Wishart.

Hall, Stuart and T. Jefferson, eds. 1976. *Resistance through Rituals: Youth Subcultures in Post-War Britain*. London: Hutchinson.

Hall, Stuart and Paddy Whannel. 1964. *The Popular Arts*. London: Hutchinson.

Secondary Sources and Works Cited

Althusser, Louis. 1971a. "Freud and Lacan." Pp. 189–220 in *Lenin and Philosophy*. New York: Monthly Review Press.

Althusser, Louis. 1971b. "Ideology and the State." Pp. 127–186 in *Lenin and Philosophy*. New York: Monthly Review Press.

Althusser, Louis. 2005. *For Marx*. Translated by Ben Brewster. New York: Verso.

Davis, Helen. 2004. *Understanding Stuart Hall*. London: Sage.

Fiske, John. 1993. *Power Plays Power Works*. London: Verso.

Gilroy, Paul, L. Grossberg, and A. McRobbie, eds. 2000. *Without Guarantees: In Honour of Stuart Hall*. London: Verso.

Morley, Dave and Kuan-Hsing Chen, eds. 1996. *Stuart Hall: Critical Dialogues in Cultural Studies*. London: Routledge.

Rojek, Chris. 2003. *Stuart Hall*. Cambridge: Polity Press.

Williams, Gareth. 2002. *The Other Side of the Popular: Neo-liberalism and Subalternity in Latin America*. Durham, NC: Duke University Press.

Willis, Paul, Simon Jones, Joyce Canaan, and Geoff Hurd. 1990. *Common Culture: Symbolic Work at Play in the Everyday Cultures of the Young*. Maidenhead, Berkshire, UK: Open University Press.

TWO SPECIALIZED AREAS: REFERENCES AND READING SUGGESTIONS

THEORETICAL DEVELOPMENT IN THE SOCIOLOGY OF FAMILIES (PREPARED BY TAIT RUNNFELDT MEDINA AND JULIE ARTIS)

Adler, Marina A. 2002. "German Unification as a Turning Point in East German Women's Life Course: Biographical Changes in Work and Family Roles." *Sex Roles* 47: 83–98.

Baca Zinn, Maxine and Bonnie Thornton Dill. 1996. "Theorizing Difference from Multiracial Feminism." *Feminist Studies* 22: 321–331.

Becker, Gary Stanley. 1991. *A Treatise on the Family*. Enlarged ed. Cambridge, MA: Harvard University Press.

Bengston, Vern L., Alan C. Acock, Katherine R. Allen, Peggye Dilworth-Anderson, and David M. Klein, eds. 2004. *Sourcebook of Family Theory & Research*. Thousand Oaks, CA: Sage.

Bianchi, S.M., M.A. Milkie, L.C. Sayer, and J.P. Robinson. 2000. "Is Anyone Doing the House-work? Trends in the Gender Division of Household Labor." *Social Forces* 79: 191–228.

Bittman, Michael, Paula England, Nancy Folbre, Liana Sayer, and George Matheson. 2003. "When Does Gender Trump Money? Bargaining and Time in Household Work." *American Journal of Sociology* 109: 186–214.

Blau, Peter. 1964. *Exchange and Power in Social Life*. New York: Wiley.

Blood, Robert and Donald Wolfe. 1965. *Husbands and Wives: The Dynamics of Married Living*. New York: Free Press.

Booth, A., K. Carver, and D.A. Granger. 2000. "Biosocial Perspectives on the Family." *Journal of Marriage and the Family* 62: 1018–1034.

Brines, Julie. 1994. "Economic Dependency, Gender, and the Division-of-Labor at Home." *American Journal of Sociology* 100: 652–688.

Burgess, E.W. 1926. "The Family as a Unity of Interacting Personalities." *Family* 7: 3–9.

Catlett, Beth Skilken and Julie E. Artis. 2004. "Critiquing the Case for Marriage Promotion: How the Promarriage Movement Misrepresents Domestic Violence Research." *Violence Against Women* 10: 1226–1244.

Cohany, Sharon R. and Emy Sok. 2007. "Trends in Labor Force Participation of Married Mothers of Infants." *Monthly Labor Review* (February): 9–16.

Cook, Karen, ed. 1987. *Social Exchange Theory*. Newbury Park, CA: Sage.

Daly, Martin and Margo Wilson. 1999. *The Truth About Cinderella: A Darwinian View of Parental Love*. New Haven, CT: Yale University Press.

Daly, Mary, and Jane Lewis. 2000. "The Concept of Social Care and the Analysis of Contemporary Welfare States." *British Journal of Sociology* 51: 281–298.

Downey, Douglas B., James W. Ainsworth-Darnell, and Mikaela J. Dufur. 1998. "Sex of Parent and Children's Well-Being in Single-Parent Households." *Journal of Marriage and the Family* 60: 878–893.

Downey, Douglas B. and Brian Powell. 1993. "Do Children in Single-Parent Households Fare Better Living with Same-Sex Parents?" *Journal of Marriage and the Family* 55: 55–71.

Ehrenreich, Barbara and Arlie Russell Hochschild. 2003. *Global Woman: Nannies, Maids, and Sex Workers in the New Economy*. New York: Metropolitan Books.

Elder, Glen. 1974. *Children of the Great Depression*. Chicago: University of Chicago Press.

Esping-Andersen, Gøsta. 1990. *The Three Worlds of Welfare Capitalism*. Princeton, NJ: Princeton University Press.

Freese, J., J.C.A. Li, and L.D. Wade. 2003. "The Potential Relevances of Biology to Social Inquiry." *Annual Review of Sociology* 29: 233–256.

Gelles, Richard J. *The Violent Home: A Study of Physical Aggression Between Husbands and Wives*. Beverly Hills, CA: Sage.

Goldthorpe, J.E. 1987. *Family Life in Western Societies: A Historical Sociology of Family Relationships in Britain and North America*. New York: Cambridge University Press.

Hamilton, L., S. Cheng, and B. Powell. 2007. "Adoptive Parents, Adaptive Parents: Evaluating the Importance of Biological Ties for Parental Investment." *American Sociological Review* 72: 95–116.

Hochschild, Arlie Russell. 2002. "Love and Gold." Pp. 15–30 in *Global Woman: Nannies, Maids, and Sex Workers in the New Economy*, edited by Barbara Ehrenreich and Arlie Russell Hochschild. New York: Metropolitan Books.

Hochschild, Arlie and Ann Machung. 1989. *The Second Shift: Working Parents and the Revolution at Home*. New York: Viking.

LaRossa, Ralph. 1988. "Fatherhood and Social Change." *Family Relations* 37: 451–457.

LaRossa. Ralph. 1997. *The Modernization of Fatherhood: A Social and Political History*. Chicago: University of Chicago Press.

Marshall, Katherine. 2006. "Converging Gender Roles." *Perspectives on Labor and Income* 7(7): 5–17.

Molm, Linda and Karen Cook. 1995. "Social Exchange and Exchange Networks." Pp. 209–235 in *Sociological Perspectives on Social Psychology*, edited by Karen Cook, Gary Fine, and James House. Needham Heights, MA: Allyn and Bacon.

O'Connor, Julia S., Ann Shola Orloff, and Sheila Shaver. 1999. *States, Markets, Families: Gender, Liberalism and Social Policy in Australia, Canada, Great Britain and the United States*. Cambridge: Cambridge University Press.

Orloff, A.S. 1993. "Gender and the Social Rights of Citizenship: The Comparative Analysis of Gender Relations and Welfare States." *American Sociological Review* 58: 303–328.

Parrenas, Rhacel Salazar. 2002. "The Care Crisis in the Philippines: Children and Transnational Families in the New Global Economy." Pp. 39–54 in *Global Woman: Nannies, Maids, and Sex Workers in the New Economy*, edited by B. Ehrenreich and A.R. Hochschild. New York: Metropolitan Books.

Parrenas, Rhacel Salazar. 2005. "Long Distance Intimacy: Class, Gender and Intergenerational Relations Between Mothers and Children in Filipino Transnational Families." *Global Networks* 5: 317–336.

Parsons, Talcott and Robert F. Bales. 1955. *Family Socialization and the Interaction Process*. New York: Free Press.

Pleck, Joseph H. 1987. "American Fathering in Historical Perspective." Pp. 83–97 in *Changing Men: New Directions in Research on Men and Masculinity*, edited by M.S. Kimmel. Beverly Hills, CA: Sage.

Popenoe, David. 1993. "American Family Decline, 1960–1990: A Review and Appraisal." *Journal of Marriage and the Family* 55: 527–542.

Powell, Brian and Douglas B. Downey. 1997. "Living in Single-Parent Households: An Investigation of the Same-Sex Hypothesis." *American Sociological Review* 62: 521–539.

Risman, Barbara J. 1987. "Intimate Relationships from a Microstructural Perspective: Men Who Mother." *Gender and Society* 1: 6–32.

Sainsbury, Diane. 1996. *Gender, Equality, and Welfare States*. Cambridge: Cambridge University Press.

Sarkisian, Natalia, Mariana Gerena, and Naomi Gerstel. 2007. "Extended Family Integration Among Euro and Mexican Americans: Ethnicity, Gender, and Class." *Journal of Marriage and Family* 69: 40–54.

Schmalzbauer, Leah. 2004. "Searching for Wages and Mothering from Afar: The Case of Honduran Transnational Families." *Journal of Marriage and Family* 66: 1317–1331.

Smock, Pamela J. 2000. "Cohabitation in the United States: An Appraisal of Research Themes, Findings, and Implications." *Annual Review of Sociology* 26: 1–20.

Statistics Norway. 2006. "Fewer children live with both parents." *Statistics Norway Web Site*, June 20. Retrieved October 30, 2008 (http://www.ssb.no/english/subjects/02/01/20/barn_en/arkiv/art-2007-01-26-01-en.html).

Sullivan, Maureen. 1996. "Rozzie and Harriet? Gender and Family Patterns of Lesbian Coparents." *Gender and Society* 10: 747–767.

West, Candace and Don H. Zimmerman. 1987. "Doing Gender." *Gender & Society* 1: 125–151.

SOCIOLOGY OF HEALTH (PREPARED BY GRACE BUDRYS)

Aday, LuAnn and Ronald Andersen. 1975. *Development of Indices of Access to Medical Care.* Ann Arbor, MI: Health Administration Press.

Albrecht, Gary. 1992. *The Disability Business: Rehabilitation in the United States.* Newbury Park, CA: Sage.

Anderson, Odin. 1972. *Health Care Can There Be Equity? The United States, Sweden and England.* New York: Wiley and Sons.

Anspach, Renee. 1993. *Deciding Who Lives: Fateful Choices in the Intensive-Care Nursery.* Berkeley: University of California Press.

Banks, James, Michael Marmot, Zoe Oldfield, and James P. Smith. 2006. "Disease and Disadvantage in the United States and in England." *Journal of the American Medical Association* 295: 2037–2045.

Becker, Howard, Blanche Geer, and Everett C. Hughes. 1961. *Boys in White.* Chicago: University of Chicago Press.

Bell, Susan. 2000. "Experiencing Illness In/And Narrative," Pp. 184–199 in *Handbook of Medical Sociology,* edited by Chloe Bird, Peter Conrad, and Allen Fremont. Upper Saddle River, NJ: Prentice-Hall.

Blakely, Tony, Bruce Kennedy, and Ichiro Kawachi. 2001. "Socioeconomic Inequality in Voting Participation and Self-Rated Health." *American Journal of Public Health* 91: 99–104.

Blendon, Robert, Robert Leitman, Ian Morrison, and Karen Donelan. 1990. "Satisfaction with Health Systems in Ten Nations." *Health Affairs* (Summer): 185–192.

Bloom, Samuel. 2002. *The Word as Scalpel.* New York: Oxford University Press.

Bosk, Charles. 1979. *Forgive and Remember: Managing Medical Failure.* Chicago: University of Chicago Press.

Brown, Phil. 1995. "Naming and Framing: The Social Construction of Diagnosis and Illness." *Journal of Health and Social Behavior* 33: 267–281.

Bucher, Rue and Anselm Strauss. 1961. "Professions in Process." *American Journal of Sociology* 46: 325–344.

Budrys, Grace. 1997. *When Doctors Join Unions*. Ithaca, NY: Cornell University Press.

Budrys, Grace. 2005. *Our Unsystematic Health Care System*. Lanham, MD: Rowman and Littlefield.

Buroway, Michael. 2005. "For Public Sociology." *American Sociological Review* 70: 4–28.

Bury, Michael. 1991. "The Sociology of Chronic Illness: A Review of Research and Prospects." *Sociology of Health and Illness* 13: 451–467.

Carr-Saunders, A.M. 1933. *The Professions*. Oxford: Clarendon Press.

Charmaz, Kathy. 1991. *Good Days, Bad Days: The Self in Chronic Illness and Time*. New Brunswick, NJ: Rutgers University Press.

Coburn, David. 2000. "Income Inequality, Social Cohesion and Health Status of Populations: The Role of Neoliberalism." *Social Science and Medicine* 51: 139–150.

Cockerham, William. 1999. *Health and Social Change in Russia and Eastern Europe*. New York: Routledge.

Conrad, Peter. 1996. "Medicalization and Social Control." Pp. 137–162 in *Perspectives in Medical Sociology*, edited by Phil Brown. Prospect Heights, IL: Waveland Press.

Conrad, Peter and Joseph Schneider. 1992. *Deviance and Medicalization: From Badness to Sickness*. Philadelphia: Temple University Press.

Davey-Smith, G.M., J. Shipley, and G. Rose. 1990. "Magnitude and Causes of Socioeconomic Differentials in Mortality: Further Evidence from the Whitehall Studies." *Journal of Epidemiology and Community Health* 44: 265–270.

Diez-Roux, Ana, Mary Northridge, Alfredo Morabia, Mary Bassett, and Steven Shea. 1999. "Prevalence and Social Correlations of Cardiovascular Disease Risk Factors in Harlem." *American Journal of Public Health* 89: 302–307.

Esty, Daniel et al. 1998. *State Failure Task Force Report: Phase II Findings*. McLean, VA: Science Applications International Corporation.

Etzioni, Amitai. 1969. *The Semi-Professions and Their Organization*. New York: Free Press.

Evans, Robert. 1994. "Introduction." Pp. 3–26 in *Why Some People are Healthy and Others Are Not?* edited by Robert Evans, Morris Barer, and Theodore Marmor. New York: Aldine.

Foucault, Michel. 1973. *The Birth of the Clinic*. New York: Tavistock Press.

Fox, Renee. 1957. "Training for Uncertainty." Pp. 207–241 in *The Student Physician*, edited by Robert Merton, George Reeder, and Patricia Kendall. Cambridge, MA: Harvard University Press.

Freidson, Eliot. 1961. *Patients' Views of Medical Practice*. New York: Russell Sage Foundation.

Freidson, Eliot. 1970a. *Professional Dominance*. New York: Atherton Press.

Freidson, Eliot. 1970b. *Profession of Medicine*. New York: Dodd, Mead.

Goffman, Erving. 1961. *Asylums*. New York: Anchor.

Goode, William. 1957. "Community Within a Community: The Professions." *American Sociological Review* 25: 483–496.

Gramlin, Edward, Richard Kasten, and Frank Sammartino. 1993. "Growing Inequality in the 1980s: The Role of Federal Taxes and Cash Transfers." Pp. 225–249 in *Uneven Tides: Rising Inequality in America*, edited by Sheldon Danziger and Peter Gottschalk. New York: Russell Sage Foundation.

Gray, Bradford. 1983. *The New Health Care for Profit*. Washington, DC: National Academy Press.

Gray, Bradford. 1991. *The Profit Motive and Patient Care*. Cambridge, MA: Harvard University Press.

Greenwood, Ernest. 1957. "Attributes of a Profession." *Social Work* 2: 44–45.

Hafferty, Frederic. 1991. *Into the Valley of Death*. New Haven, CT: Yale University Press.

Hafferty, Frederic and John McKinlay. 1993. *The Changing Medical Profession: An International Perspective*. New York: Oxford University Press.

Kaplan, George and John Lynch. 1997. "Editorial: Whither Studies on the Socioeconomic Foundations of Population Health?" *American Journal of Public Health* 87: 409–1411.

Kawachi, Ichiro and Bruce Kennedy. 1997. "Health and Social Cohesion: Why Care About Income Inequality?" *British Medical Journal* 314: 1037-1040.

Kawachi, Ichiro, Bruce Kennedy, and Richard Wilkinson. 1999. *The Society and Population Health Reader*. Vol. 1. New York: The New Press.

Kreiger, Nancy. 2001. "Theories for Social Epidemiology in the 21st Century: An Ecosocial Perspective." *International Journal of Epidemiology* 30: 668–677.

Kunst, Anton and Johan Machenback. "The Size of Mortality Differences Associated with Educational Level in Nine Industrialized Countries." *American Journal of Public Health* 84: 932–937.

Light, Donald. 1992. "The Practice and Ethics of Risk-rated Health Insurance." *Journal of Health and Social Behavior* 29: 307–322.

Light, Donald and Sol Levine. 1988. "The Changing Character of the Medical Profession: A Theoretical Overview." *The Milbank Quarterly* 66: 10–32.

Link, Bruce and Jo Phelan. 1995. "Social Conditions As Fundamental Causes of Disease." *Journal of Health and Social Behavior* (extra issue): 90–94.

Lorber, Judith. 1997. *Gender and the Social Construction of Illness*. Thousand Oaks, CA: Sage.

Lynch, John. 2000. "Income Inequality and Health: Expanding the Debate." *Social Science and Medicine* 51: 1001–1005.

Marmot, Michael. 2004. *The Status Syndrome*. New York: Henry Holt and Company.

McKeown, Thomas. 1976. *The Role of Medicine*. London: The Nuffield Provincial Hospitals Trust.

McKinlay, John. 1974. "The Case for Refocusing Upstream: The Political Economy of Illness." *Applying Behavioral Science to Cardiovascular Risk*. Washington, DC: American Heart Association.

McKinlay, John and John Stoeckle. 1988. "Corporatization and the Social Transformation of Doctoring." *International Journal of Health Services* 18: 191–205.

Mechanic, David. 1972. *Public Expectations and Health Care*. New York: Wiley-Interscience.

Mechanic, David. 1978. *Medical Sociology*. New York: Free Press.

Mechanic, David. 2006. *The Truth About Health Care*. Piscataway, NJ: Rutgers University Press.

Merton, Robert, George Reeder, and Patricia Kendall. 1952. *The Student Physician*. Cambridge, MA: Harvard University Press.

Navarro, Vincente. 1976. *Medicine Under Capitalism*. New York: Prodist.

Navarro, Vincente. 1986. *Crisis, Health and Medicine: A Social Critique*. New York: Tavistock.

Parsons, Talcott. 1951. *The Social System*. New York: Free Press.

Pearlin, Leonard, Elizabeth G. Menaghan, Morton A. Lieberman, and Joseph T. Mullan. 1981. "The Stress Process." *Journal of Health and Social Behavior* 22: 337–356.

Perrow, Charles. 1963. "Goals and Power Structures: A Historical Case Study." Pp. 112–146 in *The Hospital in Modern Society*, edited by Eliot Freidson. New York: Free Press.

Pescosolido, Bernice, Jane McLeod, and Margarita Alegria. 2000. "Confronting the Second Social Contract: The Place of Medical Sociology in Research and Policy for the Twenty-First Century." Pp. 411–426 in *Handbook of Medical Sociology*, edited by Chloe Bird, Peter Conrad, and Allen Fremont. Upper Saddle River, NJ: Prentice-Hall.

Quadagno, Jill. 2006. *One Nation, Uninsured*. New York: Oxford.

Roth, Julius. 1973. *Timetables*. Indianapolis, IN: Bobbs-Merrill.

Ruzek, Sheryl. 1979. *The Women's Health Movement*. New York: Praeger.

Sapolsky, Robert. 1998. *Why Zebras Don't Get Ulcers*. New York: W.H. Freeman.

Scheff, Thomas. 1974. "The Labeling Theory of Mental Illness." *American Sociological Review* 39: 444–452.

Sen, Amartya. 1992. *Inequality Reexamined*. Cambridge, MA: Harvard University Press.

Smith, Harry. 1955. "Two Lines of Authority Are One Too Many." *Modern Hospital* 84: 59–64.

Starr, Paul. 1982. *The Social Transformation of Medicine*. New York: Basic Books.

Strauss, Robert. 1957. "The Nature and Status of Medical Sociology." *American Sociological Review* 22: 200–204.

Suchman, Edward. 1965. "Social Patterns of Illness and Medical Care." *Journal of Health and Human Behavior* 6: 2–16.

Thoits, Peggy. 1995. "Stress, Cooing, and Social Support Processes: Where Are We? What Next?" *Journal of Health and Social Behavior* (extra issue): 53–79.

Waldman, R.J. 1992. "Income distribution and Infant Mortality." *Quarterly Journal of Economics* 107: 1283–1302.

Wilensky, Harold. 1964. "The Professionalization of Everyone?" *American Journal of Sociology* 70: 137–158.

Wilkinson, Richard. 1996. *Unhealthy Societies, The Afflictions of Inequality*. London: Routledge.

Wolinsky, Frederic. 1980. *The Sociology of Health*. Boston: Little Brown and Company.

Zola, Irving. 1972. "Medicine as an Institution of Social Control." *Sociological Review* 20: 487–504.

Zola, Irving. 1982. *Missing Pieces: A Chronicle of Living With a Disability*. Philadelphia: Temple University Press.

Index

advanced capitalism, 47–48
advertising images, 101, 120
agency
    as myth, 46, 160
    Bourdieu on, 160, 169
    choice and, 43–44
    controlled in institution, 113–15
    Foucault's changing views, 129, 144
    gender-free (Butler), 153–54
    Goffman's view, 104, 111–12, 114
    market choices, 70–71
    Marxist view, 93
    vs structuralism, 47, 63, 101, 160
AIDS epidemic, 33–34, 45
Alexander, Jeffrey, 90
Althusser, Louis, 140, 182, 191–92, 193–94, 195
anomie, 11, 55
applied rationalism (Bourdieu), 162–63
articulation, 192–93
Asylums (Goffman), 110–15, 123, 125

barriers to new theories, 213–15
Behavior in Public Places (Goffman), 118, 123
Benjamin, Walter, 57, 69, 74, 77, 85
bio-power, 123
biotechnology, 30
Boas, Franz, 81
body, 83–84
    Bourdieu, 165, 167–68
    Foucault, 136–37
    Goffman, 83, 126
Bourdieu, Pierre
    capital, 172, 176, 179–80, 182–83

fields, 90, 171–75, 188
    habitus, 165–67, 170, 172, 187
bourgeoisie, 4–5
Bowling Alone (Putnam), 183
Butler, Judith, 79, 122, 147, 151–54

capillaries of power, 138–39
capitalism, 4–5, 55, 56, 57, 74
    transformation in, 19, 20
capitals (Bourdieu), 172, 175, 176, 179–80, 182–83
Care of the Self (Foucault), 139, 143–47
categories, 78, 81–82, 84, 88, 198
changes in theory
    external forces (*see* external forces for change)
    history (*see* history of theory)
    internal forces (*see* internal forces for change)
Chicago School, 5, 57
child workers, 29
civil rights movement, 42, 58, 83
class. *See also* elites; inequalities
    and cultural capital, 179–82
classical theory, 4–5, 55, 56
classification
    Bourdieu, 170–71, 180–82, 187
    Foucault, 132–34, 187
    Goffman, 120–22
    Hall, 196–97, 198
collective action, 44, 45
commodification, 11
common sense (Hall), 194, 195

transitional giants, 7, 8, 99–102
  shared characteristics, 99–101
trends in social thought, 67–73
triad, 7, 20, 59, 60, 64–65, 91

understanding of the world
  limits for interviewees, 164
United States
  inequality, growing, 38, 39
urbanization, 29, 31, 32

Vietnam War, 19, 20, 60
voluntary associations, 183

Wacquant, Loïc, 85, 89, 90, 186
weapons of mass destruction, 35
Weber, Max, 4, 9, 32, 56, 58, 79, 149
  influence on current theories, 216, 217
  theoretical perspective, 10
welfare state. *See* embedded liberalism
women, 39–40. *See also* feminism
  discrimination against, 83
  exploitation at work, 29, 40
women's rights movements, 83
world systems analysis, 37–38
world wars, 5, 41–42